Scratching the Surface: Posties, Privatisation and Strikes in the Royal Mail

Scratching the Surface: Posties, Privatisation and Strikes in the Royal Mail

Phil Chadwick

Winchester, UK
Washington, USA

First published by Zero Books, 2014
Zero Books is an imprint of John Hunt Publishing Ltd., Laurel House, Station Approach,
Alresford, Hants, SO24 9JH, UK
office1@jhpbooks.net
www.johnhuntpublishing.com
www.zero-books.net

For distributor details and how to order please visit the 'Ordering' section on our website.

Text copyright: Phil Chadwick 2013

ISBN: 978 1 78279 524 7

A CIP catalogue record for this book is available from the British Library.

Design: Stuart Davies

Printed and bound by CPI Group (UK) Ltd, Croydon, CR0 4YY

We operate a distinctive and ethical publishing philosophy in all
areas of our business, from our global network of authors to
production and worldwide distribution.

CONTENTS

Acknowledgements

Thanks must first and foremost go to my wife, Mim for her unfailing support in helping me persevere with this project; to a family friend, Ila for her thoughts and suggestions; to Fran and Joy Choules and Kevin Beazer the South West Regional Secretary of the CWU for checking over the book to make sure I had not made any glaring errors in my recollection of events. We all knew however that others may think it's not so much any errors, as glaring omissions that is the issue! The subject is too vast and in giving a potted history some omissions are just unavoidable as our memories fade with the passing of time! Finally, to Luke Mason the Branch Secretary of the CWU Western Counties Branch for kindly allowing me access to the Branch archive, without which the project would not have come to fruition.

Foreword

On October 11th 2013, an Initial Public Offering of Royal Mail shares was floated on the London Stock Exchange. The disservice done to the public became evident when the trading price immediately soared beyond the government's anticipated range. Within a few minutes it was obvious the industry had been sold short by the Coalition Government.

For many CWU members, the sale felt like a physical blow. Campaigning against privatisation had been a regular part of our activity for decades. Postal workers had first organised rallies against privatisation at the start of the 1980's.

Phil Chadwick's book offers insight into the events leading up to the sale. He also outlines the path the CWU took in campaigning for a positive future for the industry and postal workers. He provides a wealth of detail from internal sources, making this book a valuable tool for researchers and historians.

The CWU will not be ejected from Royal Mail by privatisation. Addressing new and difficult problems has been a way of line for the Union – despite smears about our supposed inability to change.

Phil's writing has force because it is the view of a front line participant. It helps to illustrate our future, as much as our past.

Billy Hayes
General Secretary
Communication Workers Union

Introduction

It can't be all bad news, can it?

For at least the last 13 years in one way or another Royal Mail has been a Company receiving more attention than it would ideally wish for. Most of it has not been of a positive nature, but no matter the headlines keep rolling in with the same old lazy narrative of worker/management conflict, a public sector behemoth incapable of change and a general public left understandably wondering whether the best position to adopt was to assume a "plague on both your houses."

Industrial conflict between Royal Mail and the Communication Workers Union (CWU), who represent non-managerial postal staff, has been on-going both above and below the radar for some considerable time. Every couple of years or so for the last decade and a bit, national strikes break out and the TV cameras are out in force to visit local picket lines. At the time of writing (October 2013) the Coalition Government has privatised Royal Mail and a national strike is in the offing.

Thankfully, the natural inclination of the public – conflict or no conflict – is to assume that this much loved national treasure is full of good people (it is, by the way) going about their daily business in ensuring the mail is delivered in time and on time. How many times have we seen on our television screens footage of Posties out in all weathers, braving the elements to ensure the mail gets through?

The many stories of postal staff going the extra mile to help people is something genuinely special and the rapport with customers built up over many years is something that cannot and should not have a price put on it.

And yet, whilst it is possible to write page after page of the good that Royal Mail does thanks to its workforce, something is missing from the narrative that the public get; something that is rarely spoken about but which causes untold anguish and upset year after year after year.

If it is a truism that a workforce is a Company's most precious asset, then one has to wonder just why conflict keeps breaking out as it has done over the last 13 years or so and, more importantly, why the workforce keep engaging in strike action by voting in large numbers to do so and why, on occasions there are unofficial strikes with postal staff simply walking out of their workplaces in response to an action or perceived injustice by Royal Mail. Are these people mad? Are they just being led by a trade Union that simply will not wake up to the reality that employers have a tough time running their establishments and can do without people arguing the toss all the time? Are they simply just living in a bubble unaware of what is happening elsewhere?

Well, from the vantage point of someone who was deeply involved with the Communication Workers Union as a Branch Official it never ceased to amaze me just how conflict ridden Royal Mail was and is. If there is a way to get peoples backs up, Royal Mail are still, arguably, able to manage this with ease.

To those who say, "Well he would say that wouldn't he", take a look at the following scores from the Company's employee engagement survey from 2012. According to Royal Mail 69% of staff responded. If that isn't a good turnout, I don't know what is and the turnout for 2013 was some 6% higher. And a snap shot of some of the results for 2012 which Royal Mail headlined to their staff: 33% felt "valued and recognised", 51% felt "appreciation" for a job well done, 33% felt "involved in decisions that affect me and my work" and 46% said their "ideas and suggestions" were listened to and some 61% felt "proud to work for Royal Mail."

By the same token, it isn't hard to reverse those figures : 67% don't feel valued, 49% shown no appreciation for a job well done, 67% not involved in decisions affecting them, 54% whose ideas were not listened to and 39% who don't feel proud to work for

Royal Mail. Indeed, at the risk of stating the obvious, a response rate (good as it is) of 69% leaves 31% who chose not to express their views. Such employees it can reasonably be guessed at, will have not responded because they feel valued and part of the Company, but from a mixture of apathy and negativity. Suddenly those figures above now seem a little worse than at first sight.

This may appear an unfair way of making a point, but one has to ask how on earth these results are possible? Moya Greene, the current CEO, saw them as proof that "great strides" had been made against a backdrop from the 2010/11 accounts that "for many years our employee engagement scores have been disappointing."[1]

By 2013, the survey revealed that 14% of employees said they had "personally been the recipient of bullying and harassment in the last 12 months while at work." Of those, 35% was from a colleague and 62% from a manager. For the South West the picture was the worst in the UK. 16% bullied and harassed with 31% from colleagues and 64% from managers. As for people "work(ing) together and treat(ing) each other fairly", just 50% said yes.[2]

In point of fact, like many large employers, employee surveys are used quite rightly to gauge opinion and to act on the results where ever possible. This not only gives staff a feeling that they are being listened to, but also ensures that those with responsibility for running these companies keep their feet on the ground and accept that sometimes they have got things wrong and need to change.

Anyone in Royal Mail will tell you that year after year surveys are carried out. Staff can answer a questionnaire and give their views on most things (until recently this was known as Have Your Say (HYS)), including their local management. The concept is genuinely good. The intention was to put the results to good use.

So, I ask that question again. How on earth are such low scores possible after so many years of surveys and mountains of returns to plough through by those in positions of responsibility? What happened to these returns? Goodness me, what scores were being achieved say, five years ago to end up with such paltry results now?

No, something is badly wrong with Royal Mail. A continuing disconnect exemplified by an initiative set in place by Moya Greene in the summer of 2011 where, "... around 150 of our senior managers will be taking part in workplace visits around the country briefing our people."[3] By early 2013 the Company and the CWU were meeting to reiterate that treating the workforce with respect is crucial following a national survey carried out by the Union on the prevalence of bullying and harassment by managers.[4]

Why is all this important? Because it begs the question, is Royal Mail institutionally incapable of valuing its employees? A Company that on the face of it wants to treat its employees well and to hear what they have to say, fails to do so over and over again, year in year out. However, it isn't all bad news. In 2013 in response to the employee survey, they told their workforce that a "corporate action plan" with a "joint Union and employee panel" would be set up. One step forward and no steps backwards perhaps? Let us hope so.

As to this book it is intended for the general reader. The subject of Royal Mail is so vast and the changes that have taken place so complicated that unless you are a "Royal Mail anorak", you'd have little chance of keeping up with it all. Hopefully what is written will be understandable. To the extent that it isn't, the fault clearly is mine. A note of caution is also in order. This book is not a dispassionate, neutral account. It is opinionated and some will disagree strongly. To those who say "I can do better than that. He missed off this issue or that issue and that isn't a fair reflection of what happened", the challenge is to write a book yourself to get your story out.

Context is vitally important if you are going to try and see what is really going on within the Company and so no examination can take place without looking at some of the big picture developments that have taken place such as the continuing effect that the regulatory climate has had since the Postal Services Act 2000 came into being and the long, slow inexorable march of the ideologues to privatise this great British industry.

Following on from that, we will examine more closely how the Company has responded to the strictures placed upon it by Government and Postcomm, the regulator for postal services (and since 2011, Ofcom). What collective agreements have been possible between the Company and the Posties Union and how have the huge industrial relations problems played out. There have been major disputes in 2003, 2007 and 2009. A further one is pending at the time of this book. How on earth can such disputes keep breaking out and is it the Company or the workforce who are demonstrating such apparently suicidal tendencies?

Finally, we will look carefully at the nitty-gritty of life as a postal worker. Just what has been actually happening on the ground as all these huge issues of deregulation, privatisation, pay, terms and conditions, were and are being, argued about. What does it really mean to experience the full force of an employer determined to meet those budgetary and regulatory targets by hook or by crook? Is there really a perennial problem within the Company in relation to bullying and harassment – something that seems to simmer away in the background and then surface with such ferocity whenever a dispute flares up?

At this juncture a point of clarification needs to be made. For the most part, I will be referring to Royal Mail as just that – Royal Mail. It needs to be borne in mind however that this great industry has in the last 20 years changed its name from The Post Office to Consignia in 2001 until 2002 and then to Royal Mail Group from 2002 (which consists of Royal Mail, Parcelforce and

Post Office Limited). Latterly, from 2010 the Coalition Government took a decision to split off Post Office Limited to become a separate Company with a view to it becoming mutualised in the public sector. Royal Mail therefore is a discrete part of the newly privatised Royal Mail Group PLC.

Now, we can let the story commence.

PART 1

Chapter 1

Beginnings

It is now nearly 20 years since the first efforts were made to privatise The Post Office as it was then known. Back in the 1990s the Conservatives were ideologically predisposed to selling off pretty much everything (they still are) so that even that pillar of the Tory Establishment and former Prime Minister Harold MacMillan commented that Mrs Thatcher was "selling off the family silver" – not as far as I can remember, in relation to attempts to sell off the Royal Mail, which came after the said utterance, but the point was sound nevertheless: once sold off the profits and benefits are beholden to commercial interests only.

In any event, the efforts made by the Conservative Government in 1994 were fought off by the then Union of Communication Workers (UCW).[1] Up and down the country local UCW Branches and members were out and about campaigning and pointing out that once privatised, what would happen to the Universal Service Obligation (USO) to deliver to all addresses, 6 days a week at an affordable price? What would happen to rural areas of the UK? Would they still get a delivery? Who knew? Who could actually guarantee the outcome would ensure that the best aspects of the Company could continue.

Of course no one could. The free market would decide and in the end Conservative MPs in rural areas took fright and said this was one privatisation too many. How times have altered. The seeds of change however, were sown. Free marketers were down but not out.

Interestingly, during the 1990s the Royal Mail was profitable, there was relative stability, there were two deliveries each day and the price of a stamp was low by any stretch of the imagination, to the extent that by 2002 the CWU were able to state that had stamp increases merely kept pace with inflation there would have been around £500 million extra in revenue to invest.[2] Even the pension fund was in surplus to the extent that there was a 13 year pension contributions holiday by Royal Mail. Just think about that for a moment. Low prices, profits and a pension fund in surplus – if it ain't broke, don't fix it, as they say.

The following will help to illustrate these points:

Profits between 1981/82 to 1998/99 were £3.365 billion or around £187 million per year. In fact the average profits from 1994/95 to 1998/99 were much higher at £377 million. The end of the 90s however was clearly a high point for profit – in 1998/99 profit was £496 million.

Within 12 months of this high point however, there was a loss of £415 million. This was against the backdrop of increased mail volumes, a Government-imposed external financing limit (more of which later) and a pension contribution holiday by the Company. No Company experiences such loses over a 12 month period without there being a reason other than the performance of the workforce. In fact, a massive amount of that, some £571 million was due to a write-off on a computerised system for Post Office Counters, known as Horizon.[3]

In fact, such a huge loss was to be followed with exceptional losses by 31 March 2002 of some £1.112 billion covering items such as redundancy provision, restructuring costs around Parcelforce, transport and the initial moves to end two deliveries a day. Huge and costly issues, but nothing to do with your average Posties, who would soon find themselves vilified as lazy Union militants. In fact, as with much in life, the reality was different. The then Chairman Allan Leighton was able to state that he had "the support of the Unions who acknowledge the need to drive greater efficiency through the mail's operation." Can anyone really recall any coverage permeating the public consciousness that characterised the CWU as forward thinking and progressive either in the early 2000s or now?[4]

For those in the industry in 2000 and before, in addition to the legitimate demands of employees for improved pay the issue was investment to repair and renovate some of the clapped out workplaces which really hadn't changed for goodness knows how many years and put in place some investment in new equipment. Ominously such investment was already being introduced to postal services on the continent, but no one was looking in that direction and those with responsibility self evidently did not see the necessity to invest when the excess profits made by Royal Mail could be siphoned off to the Treasury via the External Financing Limit or EFL.

In this way between 1981 and 1999 some £2.4 billion of the then Post Office profit was syphoned off. Truly huge sums to which we can add lost revenue due to artificially cheap postage of £500 million, which pretty much left Royal Mail as an operator providing a very cheap, fairly reliable if un-automated postal service that was overwhelmingly labour intensive.[5]

That this needed investment didn't take place between the 1990s and late 2000s can hardly be blamed on the workforce, but nevertheless as we shall see, a blame culture has been part and parcel of any self respecting politician eager to get some cheap applause for their incisive yet deliberately flawed analysis. It is little known that the German and Dutch postal services invested heavily in the 1990s – well in advance of any liberalisation. In Germany's case that sum was in the region of £3 billion during the 1990s. Holland's TNT and Germany's Deutsche Post would come to take chunks out of Royal Mail's market as a consequence of their competitive advantage and unfair regulation, more of which later.

At the same time as money was siphoned off by the Government's EFL, mail volumes were increasing and did so until 2005/06, as was the growth in delivery points – individual addresses to you and me. Today of course the growth of addresses continues even as letter volumes decline, with nearly

30 million addresses today.

In 1997 New Labour were elected and in 2000 introduced the Postal Services Act. On the face of it, this Act enshrined in law a six day service with an obligation to deliver to every address in the UK at a uniform tariff. Although it hardly seems significant to put into law these obligations, it seems that it was the first time it had been done and additionally the Act went further than the 1997 European Union Postal Services Directive, which was to provide a service over five days. It is sometimes forgotten that in fact this Act was to all intents and purposes the UK embodiment of this European Directive. In 1998 a decision was made to allow Royal Mail an element of commercial freedom to borrow to invest and this Postal Services Act re-confirmed that position. In effect, this meant that the Royal Mail could apply to Government for funding subject to commercial rates of interest being applied.

Each EU member state could however implement the Directive in their own way and the UK was no exception.

Still the cornerstone of our national postal service, the Universal Service Obligation (USO) not only refers to a six day service, but includes the necessity of collecting from the UKs post boxes each day, delivering to each letter box of each address (many countries don't require this) at an affordable and uniform price. The reliability of the USO is also required to be monitored within standards set by the regulator.

The Act would establish this regulator, known as Postcomm (the Postal Services Commission) whose remit was not just to protect and regulate the USO, but was at the same time to ensure that other postal operators could enter the market and obtain a licence from Postcomm in order to compete. In other words, to open up the monopoly that Royal Mail enjoyed and which delivered a service to the whole country with profitable urban mail services subsidising unprofitable rural parts of the UK, known as cross subsidisation.

Postcomm's Corporate Plan from 7 April 2000 could not have

been clearer in its assumptions and direction, "monopolies all too often lead to inefficiency and poor service." This would be rectified by introducing competition although they stressed it would be "fair competition" (bear in mind, "fair" did not mean having to abide by the USO) to ensure that the Government's objective of satisfying business and public needs at "affordable prices" was deliverable.[6]

The competition would be introduced in stages. In effect, up until then Royal Mail had a monopoly on handling mail at or below 350g. Postcomm, following the remit given to them and also taking cognizance of the European Directive on Postal Services, would cut this monopoly so that above certain weights and in relation to bulk mail of 4,000 items or more, competition would be allowed. Indeed, in a letter from the then Postcomm Chairman Graham Corbett to the then Minister for Competitiveness Alan Johnson (ironically a former UCW/CWU General Secretary) the reduction was all but secured as it was noted in this letter that a phased reduction down to 150g by 2003 was actually supported by the Post Office. It would subsequently become difficult to fathom such a stance as the opening of the postal market hacked away at the Company's finances.

Another aspect that would become contentious was that it was reiterated in this same letter that Postcomm was authorised to accept applications from overseas postal administrations and others who wish to compete with areas licenced by Postcomm. It would be noted by postal workers, that Royal Mail were not allowed to do the same on the continent.

It's worth noting if only for the record that Corbett stressed in this letter the "importance of safeguarding the universal service at a uniform tariff." Also, it is also worth noting that the vast bulk of Royal Mail's then business was delivering items considerably less than 350g – an average letter is no more than 10 to 30g. Simply allowing competition in this way then would not have made much of a dent. No, the issue was not just competition per se, the issue was how to make the small dent, much bigger and the chosen instrument of choice was a price cap regime and efficiency targets predicated on projected future mail volumes. This gradual opening up of competition would conclude in January 2006 with the complete opening up of the market. A free for all, in other words.[7]

Such a remit provided to Postcomm in the Act – quite specifically and deliberately done – would have a massive and profound impact on the provision of postal services and on the ability of Royal Mail to survive. Indeed, before anyone asks whether competition with Royal Mail is even possible, the answer is that such a question is in fact the wrong question. When Postcomm said "competition" the reality was "cherry picking." Private carriers could pick and choose just the profitable parts leaving the uneconomic social obligations to Royal Mail.

However, the Act seemed fairly innocuous at the time so that even the CWU briefing on the key points did not see it as being anything more than a "balanced package" which while allowing competition also allowed an element of commercial freedom for Royal Mail to invest to help it compete. The iniquity of the EFL whereby Government creamed off a chunk of profits each year also ceased under the Act.[8]

The CWU also noted, no doubt with genuine relief that, "after a decade of debate, it settles the ownership issue in favour of continued public ownership." Such a sentence now looks like the thoughts of a naïve idealist hanging onto the apparent reassurances of those in power. Unsurprisingly, it didn't feel like that at the time though.

However, things soon developed in ways which clearly demonstrated that the genie had been let out of the bottle so far as the future of the industry was concerned.

The fact that things would change rapidly speaks volumes for the ideological standpoint of those in the New Labour

Government. The Act contained clauses which would potentially allow for a sale of shares via joint venture or partnership as long as both Houses of Parliament agreed. It pretty much fired the starting gun and it meant in reality that "continued public ownership" would only continue for as long as the Government said. A statement of the obvious perhaps, but nevertheless the issue was now out in the open. Indeed as part of the changes made by the Government, the business became a public limited Company with all the shares being held by the State.

Of course what this also represented was a decision to dispense with the idea of a public service ethos. In the 1990s when the Conservative Government failed to privatise the Company, many quite rightly held tight to the idea of a great British institution. To sell it off, not only offended some, but to others it was more an abandonment of the great traditional conservative philosophy of conserving the best – continuity and tradition in other words. Whilst many may baulk at this, the Left is similar. The Labour Party stressed (and still just about does today) solidarity, tradition and stability for working people and their families from the ravages of capitalism. At root then, there is that idea that "competition" and "profit" are slightly dirty words which offend our sense of fairness and tradition.

Ironically both political parties found Royal Mail ripe for change in a way that pretty much abandoned any pretence of a public service ethos and ignored public opinion.

To those in these two political parties who fret away at finding the middle ground, a publicly owned Royal Mail was and is, smack in the centre of that centre ground. As for the remit of Postcomm referred to above – that deluded concept of protecting a postal service whilst simultaneously introducing competition, this effectively fell into what some refer to as the New Labour Government policy of "triangulation". A concept borrowed from the US Democratic Party strategists who would split the difference between policy ideas that they and the

Republican Party had. In this way it was believed that this would command most public support as you would not look to alienate your opponent's supporters and you might even attract them to your side.

As with so much else involved with this concept, it inevitably alienated most of the public who found no one party represented their views and led to educated apathy that said, "You're all the same." As we will see with Royal Mail, the policies pretty much alienated both customers and employees in equal measure. The fact that such triangulation was always leading to the privatisation of Royal Mail, proved just how cynical politicians could be.

Indeed, perhaps more to the point for the purposes of trying to get a grip on what subsequently happened to Royal Mail , you might reasonably expect those in authority, those running and setting the regulatory framework to have "recreated" a Company that the country could be proud of. The return (?) to some golden era of excellent service nudged back into place by intelligent and thoughtful regulation from which the country could benefit and which would leave the Company's employees with an enthusiasm for going to work to serve the public, that any employer would be proud to see in its own workforce. We shall see if such a vision came to fruition.

Chapter 2

The Genie's Out of the Bottle

By December 2001 the newly named Consignia in response to the direction of Postcomm, announced 30,000 job losses. The busiest month of the year. Hard working postal staff could feel the warmth and support emanating from the Company at this festive time. Interestingly, advice for local CWU Branches noted amongst other things that the announcement of 30,000 job losses couldn't be confirmed as the Consignia Board had gone straight to their Christmas party.[1]

The trigger, after some years of profits was a sudden six-month half year loss of £281 million. The CWU Deputy General Secretary at the time, John Keggie gave the Company an ultimatum. Withdraw the proposals or face a strike ballot. Consignia CEO John Roberts rowed back and was quoted as saying in a Radio 4 interview that in fact the 30,000 job losses could "well be a lot less." The Department for Trade and Industry said for their part that the projections were "indicative" rather than set in stone.[2]

What was beyond question was the rapid panic inside Consignia to what they thought was coming down the line.

The position of Consignia was best summed up in an Parliamentary Early Day Motion (293 dated 23 October 2001), noting "that Consignia after decades of providing an excellent and profitable range of postal services within the public sector the industry has now slipped into a loss making situation; is deeply concerned that the wholesale redundancies, outsourcing and sell offs being planned ... will jeopardise its ability to fulfil its universal service obligations, destroy the morale of its workforce and have the potential to plunge the country's postal services into chaos; and calls on Her Majesty's Government to urgently communicate these concerns to Consignia."

For postal staff the uncertainty after many years of profit was understandable. There was a complete failure by Consignia to make any effort to engage with their employees. It is now little known – and probably ignored by the media at the time of the announcement – that in making this announcement, the Company had broken job security agreements and had moved into the realms of telling all and sundry that in effect there would be compulsory redundancies.

What is even less known is that the deadline given by the CWU was specific. A response from Consignia on this announcement was required by 1pm on the 13 December 2001. A meeting duly took place at 2pm that day and went on into the night covering job security, an outstanding pay claim and possible joint ventures in relation to cleaners, vehicle services and Parcelforce. In fact, in relation to the upsetting news for staff about their jobs, the Company agreed the following, "Consignia confirms that the number of potential staff surpluses has not yet been established and that earlier announcements relating to 30,000 job losses were calculated on the basis of speculative arithmetical answers to questions raised externally on the 15% cost reduction targetry and are not firm figures."

The foregoing should also provide pause for thought, namely the huge strains that were suddenly upon the workforce and especially their Union. A press release at the time from the CWU in response to an announcement of £1 billion in cuts, stated amongst other things, "blaming efficiency levels and the workforce is just not on ... after all this is the same workforce that made the Post Office a profitable and successful organisation for over two decades ... therefore the Board cannot use the same old excuse about blaming the workforce."[3]

It was disappointing that matters had deteriorated to the extent that the CWU felt they had to state publicly that the Board was blaming the workforce for the state of the business, but arguably this was the start of a strategy that Consignia and subsequently Royal Mail would continue to use. Behind this was the threat centred approach around job losses which in turn came back full circle to whether a postal worker was actually working hard enough. If you were a Postie at that time, the figures told their own story. By 2001 you had seen a rise in the number of items posted go from 16.521 billion to 19.092 billion in just 4 years, you were handling around a third more mail and delivering it to just over 22 million addresses.[4] Your pay was poor – the vast majority working 6 days a week for a take home of around £18,000 and yet you had helped the Company remain profitable for the last 20 years.[5]

By the following February, another Early Day Motion (820, 6 February 2002) would join up the jigsaw by focussing on Postcomm:

> That this House is concerned that Postcomm's recent proposals for postal competition will threaten the provision of a universal postal service ... is further concerned that Postcomm's obsession with an accelerated opening of the postal market to private sector exploitation to a much greater level and to a degree that is far in advance of that called for in the relevant European Directive is driven by ideology regardless of the damage that will result to the universal service; and calls on the Government to reject the Postcomm proposals and support the management and workforce of Consignia in a balanced transition to new working arrangements that will allow Consignia to compete in a market opened up in line with the European Directive whilst maintaining the universal postal service...

Amongst other things, changes subsequently made under the auspices of Postcomm, would see the end of two deliveries a day, Sunday collections going, weekly collections reducing and later daily deliveries introduced. As for outsourcing, cleaning, catering services went as did the Consignia employee health services. As will be seen, there was a good degree of accurate crystal ball gazing encapsulated in these two EDMs.

If nothing else, this flashpoint with the CWU was a powerful backdrop as the new regulatory regime kicked in. It is probably accurate to say that both the Union and the employer knew that things wouldn't be the same again, the question was whether the fear factor and the new regulation would bounce the workforce into accepting whatever was dished out. A pay document presented to the Unions' Branches in October 2001, stated as much, "We are at a crossroads on both industrial and our pay policy ... We must recognise that the industry is changing from a monolithic slow moving integrated organisation to a fast changing commercially driven business and it is for this reason that we must place our own stakes in the ground.... Once the organisation has changed it maybe too late to pursue our objectives we must therefore stake our claim now."[6]

What would transpire over the subsequent decade was an extremely difficult process of putting this document into practise by protecting their members, enhancing their pay, trying to improve their working lives and fighting off an employer determined to get change in by hook or by crook.

The job loss announcement above was proof enough of the Unions' worries and the need to move fast or face becoming irrelevant if Consignia got their stake in first as they clearly had tried to do. A letter to the Unions' members on 5 December 2001 graphically shows how high these stakes were, describing the move by Consignia as to place "the Union and its members in the most serious situation in the history of the Post Office."

Behind the row over whether a postal worker would have a job the next day, was an increasingly bitter set of arguments about pay and productivity. This was then the perfect storm into which Allan Leighton stepped following an approach by the then

New Labour Government to take over as Chairman.

What was also to become beyond question was the lack of sensible debate that would mask what was all along the hoped for end product for New Labour and subsequently the Coalition Government, namely the privatisation of the industry.

By the Spring of 2002, the writing was definitely on the wall. Consignia were being quoted again in the press to the effect that thousands of jobs would go (a job security agreement would subsequently be agreed with the CWU known as the Managing the Surplus Framework or MTSF for short, from 18 March 2002), that the Company wanted to reduce the power of the CWU and, tellingly that one Consignia insider was able to confidently state that he "expected to be knocked over in the rush (for redundancy as) morale is very low."[7]

That this was in response to the new climate created by Postcomm was not in doubt, but a telling quote from the then Director of Corporate Affairs Alan Williams suggested that not everyone could see the future with confidence. He said, "The Government has decided to put us partly in the private sector ... and the jury is still out on whether this model works to be honest."[8]

It is important however at this juncture, to recap that the Company had seen little investment in updating and automating its sorting processes. The investment was perfectly capable of being introduced without a regulator of course and were Postcomm not established in 2000, investment could easily have happened. The idea that it only subsequently happened because of Postcomm is false, but difficult to shift as it formed pretty much the backbone of those wishing to see a privatised, free market model for postal services: Investment and innovation can only happen in a competitive environment was the mantra. Postal workers and their families were beginning to sense the enormity of what was going on. It was not long then, before those fears became manifest and a huge unofficial strike broke out in 2003 over pay, the move to a single delivery and job losses as we shall see later on.

Around this time, the CWU produced a report on Postcomm entitled No Logic. Separately the National Audit Office (NAO) also weighed in that year and said the individuals within Postcomm had virtually no expertise in the field of postal services. The NAO also warned against opening up the postal market too quickly or else risk the Universal Service Obligation. That these individuals were a mixture of career civil servants, management consultants and Directors of companies was disappointing, but at least one could glimpse – quite clearly as it happened – where things were going. Postcomm soon asked the then consultants, Arthur Anderson to compile a report on the impact of liberalisation on the finances of Consignia. Amazingly, they found themselves apparently able to predict the future of this new free market.

Postcomm also involved another firm of consultants, Frontier Economics. Their apparent expertise was in relation to opening up the electricity and gas markets to competition. It was their advice as an American outfit that contributed indirectly to the establishing of the now notorious Enron. It was Arthur Anderson who ended up auditing Enron's accounts.

It was through advice garnered from these two organisations, together with Postcomm's predisposition to introducing competition come what may (which included opening up the UK to full competition some 3 years before any other EU country), that we can see the results of today. Interestingly, the author of this CWU publication, Barckley Sumner then deputy Editor of Tribune, felt able to state in response to Postcomm's view that the introduction of competition will improve things, that "the practise will demonstrate how ill conceived the theory is, but by then it will be too late if the universal obligation and universal tariff are damaged." Sumner also added, "It is possible that Postcomm's plans will lead to some cheaper services for big business.

However, ordinary households can expect to receive their post much later while paying a great deal more for the privilege of sending a letter." The absolute tragedy of course is that no one was listening to Sumner or the CWU who assisted him in his deliberations.[9]

Of course, without wishing to labour the point, if the CWU could see the future then why was such faith put in this experiment by Postcomm and so rigorously supported by New Labour? It only makes sense if you look at the projected end game, which was a privatisation and a postal market that would respond to the big players – organisations who posted literally millions of items each day and who expected to be able to do so at a cheaper price than anyone else. Any disruption and upheaval that might manifest itself as a result of the changes towards opening up the postal market was looked at along the lines of "no pain without gain".

No one can compete with a national postal service of course. That's not the intention. The intention was and is, to allow competitors to "cherry pick" certain areas and customers, with a view to privatising the industry, and no, this did not involve private companies delivering mail to the middle of nowhere. Why on earth would any competitor want to do that with all the costs involved? Driving down a country lane and up the drive of a farmhouse to deliver a letter or packet costs rather more than the price of the stamp stuck to that same letter or packet. No, far cheaper to undercut Royal Mail in the urban areas and with the help of Postcomm lobby for access to the huge network of mail processing centres; lobbying which was entirely successful and which resulted in Royal Mail having to negotiate access to its mail centres at a price of 13p per letter.

And how did this work? Many large organisations post out millions of letters every day by using Royal Mail – banks, insurance companies, utility companies etc. – and they all pay a certain price for the collection, sorting and delivery of their mail.

A price that was far in excess of 13p per item.

With Postcomm allowing access to Royal Mail's processing centres, these large companies would secure the services of private postal carriers such as TNT and Business Post (now UK Mail). They would collect and carry out some preliminary sorting based on information provided by Royal Mail before dropping the mail off at the nearest Royal Mail processing centre. From there, Royal Mail would have to process and deliver to each address in the normal way, but for just 13p per item. Such an innovation was known as Downstream Access (DSA).

The CWU view was that DSA meant the privatisation of one part of the work that Royal Mail would normally undertake, namely collecting and transporting mail to a processing centre. Indeed, that is exactly what it was – private carriers doing the work of Royal Mail. The cost of collecting and transporting mail to a processing centre was of course not as expensive as sorting and delivering that same mail to each address in the UK.

Royal Mail's then CEO Adam Crozier was bullish, and the subsequent public utterances were of the same crystal ball nature that characterised Postcomm. Crozier was able to say amongst other things, "The contract we've signed today (10 February 2004) gives Royal Mail a commercial income stream without undermining our ability to continue providing a one price goes anywhere universal service to the UK's 27 million addresses ... the key test for Royal Mail is that any access deal is a commercial one which does not pose a threat to the universal service."

That "commercial income stream" would soon show however as a negative income steam. The CWU General Secretary Billy Hayes said the news was not welcome and he added that this was "artificial competition which will be dangerous if it prevents Royal Mail from making the investment in services that customers need." It would appear with the benefit of hindsight that Billy Hayes' crystal ball was operating at a higher level of accuracy than some others.[10]

It doesn't take a mathematician to figure out that millions of items posted every day at just 13p each will inevitably result in a loss of revenue which itself runs into hundreds of millions of pounds. In fact, that is just what happened to the tune of around £100m to £120million per year. Indeed, in 2009/10 the amount being lost was £157 million.[12] Royal Mail's loss was of course a gain for the competition, who effectively were being subsidised by that same amount. It was however, a little more complicated than this as we shall see later.

That this "deal" on DSA came after Postcomm's price control regime which Royal Mail had stated in their half yearly accounts some months earlier, "would put any sustainable recovery at risk and the financial viability of the regulated business, and in turn our ability to deliver the USO into question", perhaps showed the shift in the balance of power as Postcomm flexed the muscles it had been given.[11] First restrict its income via a price regime and then force it to deliver millions of items at just 13p each.

Of course restricting prices, allowing cherry picking and access to mail centres drained Royal Mail of funds for investment and given the fickle nature of free markets, meant that they couldn't predict their income with any reasonable degree of certainty. Indeed, the position now is that in around 6 years since that agreement of 13p, around 50% of volumes goes by DSA which means circa 7 billion items per year.

Just two years or so after the downstream access arrangements had been negotiated and agreed by Royal Mail (most postal staff at the time could not understand how a price of 13p was fair), the following appeared in their accounts for the year ending March 2007:

It is clear that competition has developed much more quickly than anyone forecast. When the tough control on our prices was fixed, Postcomm forecast that rivals in 2006-07 would be handling around 1.9 billion letters under access arrangements to Royal Mail Letters' delivery network. In fact, the competition picked up 2.4 billion letters in 2006-07 – one in every eight posted – and we expect from current volumes that rivals will this year be handling around 4 billion letters, around one letter in every five posted. This was a level Postcomm had forecast would not be reached until 2010. At the same time, the average 13p revenue Royal Mail Letters receives for delivering access mail does not cover our costs and this has generated a loss of £44 million in 2006/07.

Clearly the crystal ball gazing was not producing the insights required. Now, for the academic, these are interesting points to examine and dissect. I am not an expert in all the machinations of regulatory control and access arrangements. However, for those working in the industry the impact cannot be overstated. Did those in charge really know what they were doing? As we have seen above, the volumes of mail converted to DSA were to far exceed those stated in the 2007 Accounts.[12]

And if it seems confusing that such arrangements can be welcomed by Royal Mail only to be seen to be damaging later on, how's this from Royal Mail's interim accounts in the half year to 28 September 2003, before the introduction of DSA took place:

In August, we submitted our response to Postcomm on its proposals to allow other mail companies access to Royal Mail's delivery network. Royal Mail is vigorously defending its position that access arrangements should have a broadly neutral impact on our finances instead of under Postcomm's published proposal – a £650m reduction in profitability over a three year period. Unless the Regulator changes its proposals, access on the proposed terms will destroy Royal Mail's ability to continue providing a one-price-goes-anywhere service to the UK's 27 million addresses.[13]

Now, to the uninitiated this could seem like going round in circles. I freely accept that with most of the rest of Royal Mail's employees, I was uninitiated. If nothing else it confirmed as nothing else could, the futility of trying to second guess a competitive market, albeit one that was rigged. Ironically, the fact that it was rigged, meant that what was to happen should have been predictable! Royal Mail would come to note in their 2011 accounts that they were virtually alone in the European Union in having to allow such unfair access to their network.

But this wasn't all. Postcomm also intervened to restrict the pricing of different types of mail. These restrictions were premised on Royal Mail having an unfair advantage over private postal carriers. If anyone wants to plough through the reports and public consultations undertaken by Postcomm they are welcome to do so. Even a cursory glance will take you into a world of profit margins, "head room", business mail, stamped mail, "reserved areas", packets, zonal pricing and price caps to name but a few.

Underneath all this industriousness from Postcomm was that old chestnut, the USO. How on earth could Royal Mail continue to deliver to each address in the UK against such a backdrop? Indeed, more to the point, just how much does it cost to deliver mail to each address anyway? Could we just pause for a moment to work that one out before we move on please? Apparently not.

In fact, the way to calculate the cost of providing the USO has always been problematic. A delivery van carries business mail and social mail. A delivery office sorts all sorts of mail, both profitable mail and mail destined for rural areas. Is it really possible to break all this down and analyse it? If there is a purpose, then it will be lost on the public and is certainly lost on those employees working for the Company. Of course, there is a purpose as nothing involving large amounts of money is generally done by accident. How can Postcomm continue to chip away at Royal Mail if it doesn't understand every last dot and comma of the operation? In 2007/08 Royal Mail's best estimate of the cost was £3.5 billion per year.[14] By 2011, this cost would be in excess of £6 billion per year.[15]

Oh, and before we end up missing the wood for the trees, from 1 January 2006 Postcomm opened up all the postal market to competitors to deliver any size and weight of mail. This was some 3 years in advance of any other country affected by the Postal Services Directive. Such a development is easy to note, but for those working for Royal Mail, this created nothing other than a fear for their jobs and demoralisation premised on whatever they did was never going to be enough to satisfy either the Government or Postcomm. Interestingly, Postcomm also prevented Royal Mail from expanding into Europe to compete, but it did allow European competitors, predominantly DHL and TNT to come to the UK to carry out DSA work for large organisations like the banks and insurance companies.

Chapter 3

Complexity Rules

To those working within Royal Mail – from the CEO down – this meant huge upheaval, crisis management, instability, job losses, industrial disputes, a pension crisis and an inability to generate income to both invest in new machinery and to assist in the reconfiguring of the Company in response to the unequal playing field that they were lumbered with.

To give a flavour of the situation it is worth quoting from the Independent who were reporting on the high profile attempts in 2005 by Allan Leighton, then Chairman, to argue his case with the regulator that proposals to have a formula for prices at RPI-3% was not realistic (in other words, the rate of inflation, less 3%). And one thing that can't be denied, is that he used his profile to argue the case. From the Independent:

> In order to keep prices down, Postcomm has suggested that various categories of business mail, which helps subsidise the cost of a first class stamp, be retained within the basket of regulated products. Royal Mail wants them taken out so that it can meet the competition that is heading its way when the UK postal market is liberalised entirely from next January.
>
> The Posties say that unless they are allowed to raise prices by a reasonable amount (though how a 60% increase over 4 years fits this category is unclear) then they will have to shed 40,000 jobs. The regulator replies that Royal Mail's own strategic plan already envisages 30,000 job cuts between now and 2011. It reckons that a 3% improvement in annual efficiency would save Royal Mail £700 million a year by the end of the price control – more than enough to limit the rise in first class postage to 4p.[1]

That for the uninitiated again, is a fairly simple, yet accurate picture of part of the dilemma that faced Royal Mail since the arrival of Postcomm. The pricing regulations were effectively preventing Royal Mail from increasing the price of its business mail. By taking such mail out of this regulated area, Royal Mail could in theory work out a more commercial rate for business mail and use that income to modernise which in turn would – in theory ! – reduce the price of postage generally.

Interestingly, this debate was taking place at the same time as the newly installed Finance Director Marisa Cassoni was quoted in the Daily Telegraph as saying that due to the pension situation, Royal Mail was "technically insolvent." Of course the big picture was that an insolvent Company would, if a deal could be thrashed out, enable the Postcomm pricing regime to remain and have the Government take over the running of the pension scheme liabilities, which at that time were reckoned to be around £4.5 billion. Such a deal was not done and perhaps if it was, then Allan Leighton would truly have been seen as a visionary leader who sorted out Royal Mail. As it was, his hands were also tied and perhaps – although we'll never know – he always knew it wouldn't happen.[2]

Another argument subsequently re-appearing was the way Postcomm regulated access to Royal Mail operations by DSA – yes Downstream Access again. Postcomm, to use the crystal ball analogy once more, was expecting that the changes it would make to Royal Mail would spur competition even to the extent of having private companies set up in direct competition, known in the jargon as "end to end" competition. In effect another postal service. In fact as was clearly evident by 2008/09 the opposite had happened. In simple terms, DSA was cheap as we have seen (13p per item) and this cheapness was expected to enable economies of scale to set up alternative end to end postal services, i.e., delivery networks.

What happened instead was that Royal Mail lost revenue and

those accessing via DSA just got a cheap service. To compound this problem, Postcomm added what was referred to as "head room" pricing, namely the difference between the access price of 13p and the normal retail price of posting business mail, called the retail price. Postcomm said this head room must be the same or to put in another way, income neutral. In effect if Royal Mail wanted to increase its access price it must reduce the retail price or it would end up making money from the change. To all intents and purposes this meant they were stuck. Royal Mail's view then and now was that this created "artificial competition" which they said was unfair. To which Postcomm replied, "And your point is...?"

The supreme irony of all this complexity was that Postcomm had inadvertently provided a disincentive to what they wanted to see. A low access price would mean that alternative postal operators would be lumbered with providing a service at too low a price as they would have to undercut the 13p Royal Mail charged (and as we have seen, 13p per item was loss making anyway), so why set up your own delivery/processing network when you can piggy back Royal Mail's for 13p?[3]

Now the two examples above (price caps and access) are not meant by any stretch of the imagination, to provide a comprehensive look at what the regulator was doing. Rather, it should put in perspective the fact that if delivering letters was supposed to be a simple business carried out by dedicated postal staff, it wasn't anymore. Indeed, price caps and access was only the half of it. Arguably the sting in the tail was that such arrangements were predicated on projected volumes of mail. Get the projections wrong and the impact in cash terms could be horrendous.

More to the point, it shows if not with complete clarity, then enough, to hopefully see how Postcomm were spending their time tweaking around with Royal Mail on the basis of trying to second guess the market. I stress again, that for your average postal worker, never mind those fronting up the CWU both locally and nationally, this was a complete nightmare. And if staff and Unions were struggling with all this complexity, it was also painfully clear that your average Royal Mail manager had little idea either – and why should they! Thankfully, the CWU had a Research Department who ploughed through the details and made sense of what was going on. As for the public, well who are they anyway? What they don't know about, they won't worry about.

By December 2006 the CWU were giving evidence to the Select Committee on Trade & Industry. They noted that the efforts by Postcomm to tighten the screws had been revisited and the price formula, which was being argued about above, moved from a proposal of RPI-3% to RPI-0.1% which they welcomed.

The statistic behind this however, namely the volume of mail being handled and the increase in DSA would mean any benefits of the price formula concession were in fact negated. How so? If you are losing money anyway and the volume of mail going via DSA is increasing, then unless you can put up the price of mail that is not DSA to cover the shortfall, you are pretty much stumped. A good job then that the RPI-3% didn't actually happen then or there would have been an implosion of Royal Mail.

As for the "Royal Mail is technically insolvent" quote from Marisa Casoni above, the CWU noted in its evidence to the Select Committee that Royal Mail had reached an agreement with the Post Office Pension Trustees to pay off the deficit at the rate of £750 million per year for the next 17 years.[4]

If all this reads like "what on earth is going on!" then you are in good Company. For those working in the industry it was a time when most were bemused at what was coming next. For the CWU however, they expressed concern to the Trade and Industry Select Committee that even if Royal Mail could pay such huge sums to the Pension Fund, it would surely mean the possibility of new entrants being stopped from joining, the end of the final salary scheme and a later retirement date. All of which subsequently came in albeit on the back of some difficult negotiations which followed a huge strike over pay, conditions and new ways of working, more of which later.[5]

A little clarity is perhaps in order at this point. Mail volumes from 2005/06 started to decline. Less mail equals less revenue and less revenue means less profit and less profit means it is harder to deliver to all parts of the UK (rural and urban), invest to modernise and keep the show on the road. If the revenue you do have is being eaten away as more companies use DSA at 13p an item, you begin to see the calamity that some reckoned was just around the corner. This scenario would form the backdrop to the CWU and its members fighting to get things changed before it was too late.

For those inside Royal Mail the picture was unbelievably ropey, never mind complicated and stressful as people simply didn't know if they would have a job or not, never mind a pension. If front line postal workers were in the firing line, then they had up to now, seen nothing yet. The following quote from the Company in 2006 gives a flavour of where things might go in response to the strictures placed upon them by the Regulator: "...improving efficiency in a declining market is much tougher than making productivity gains in a growing one." These few words would manifest themselves in a ruthless drive to cut costs, as we shall see later.[6]

If the future seemed pretty shaky for the workforce, it is worth noting that in 2006 Adam Crozier was able to state that, "I want everyone to enjoy working for the Company and that means ensuring they are motivated, they have the right working environment, the tools for the job and they are treated properly at all times." The question to ask of course is whether these sentiments were sincere and would be embedded into the Company, or whether they were perhaps the sort of lip service that can sometimes be paid in a glossy annual report and accounts?[7]

At the same time as all this was going on, the rise in the

number of delivery points (addresses) kept on going up and has now reached some 29 million whilst since 2006 mail volumes have been dropping in response to electronic communication (emails, etc.) and the increasing price of a stamp – currently 60p for first class and 50p for second class.

More addresses, more mail delivered at 13p per item as a percentage of declining volumes, more price controls and a response from Royal Mail in the months running up to the market opening in January 2006 of what the workforce knew as being a "slash and burn" approach. In other words, cut jobs, cut wages, cut terms, cut the second delivery, cut rural collections, cut the Postbus Service, cut Sunday collections, cut whatever. Of course once all the cutting has been done, then there is a warped argument that says, "We're still standing." Of course another reason to cut was to create surpluses to reinvest to modernise. Sounds fine in theory, but could the Company slash and burn fast enough to get ahead of the downward spiral in mail volumes and the strictures around price formulas?

In addition to this backdrop, the matter of the Pension Scheme was looming large, as mentioned above. From 1990 until 31 March 2003, three years after Postcomm had started their grand plan and six years into the New Labour Government, there was a pension contribution holiday taken by the Company. If anyone thought that such a "holiday" came about only under a Conservative Government, then such thoughts need to be revised.

It goes without saying, but for postal workers and their families, their pensions are hugely important. Without doubt, the pensions holiday is one of the most well known aspects of the whole sorry mess of the last decade or so for Posties. In a debate in the House of Lords on 31 March 2009, Lord Clarke of Hampstead – who was the UCWs Deputy General Secretary (before the UCW merged with the NCU to become the CWU) – noted in debate about his efforts on behalf of postal workers to get the holiday stopped. In reality, postal staff continued to pay 6% of their wages in while the Post Office paid nothing at all. Increased profits of course went back to the Government. The lawyers advised nothing could be done if that is what was decided and so, "it was game set and match to the lawyers. I folded up my tent and went home. I could not do anything about it....."[8]

Such a holiday amounted to around £1.3 billion or revalued as of 2010 around £1.9 billion. If such money was notionally there to invest, it didn't seem to go anywhere and from a surplus of £760 million in 2000, the pension position worsened dramatically in the years that followed in response to the undermining of Royal Mail by Postcomm (this, despite Postcomm making some allowance for the pension position in its 2006-2010 price and quality review), increasing life expectancy and other regulatory changes to pension schemes made by Government.

The actual management of the pension funds' mix of investments against the backdrop of lower equity returns and more stable but less attractive investments such as Government bonds only compounded the problem.

The subsequent financial crash in 2008 added to the gravity of the situation. Indeed, to put this pension issue into cash terms, in 2007 Royal Mail were paying some £830 million into the Pension Scheme, made up of £280 million in relation to the historic deficit (thanks in part to the pension holiday taken for 13 years or so) and around £550 million in regular payments to the Scheme.[9]

Add the pension issue to the picture painted above of less revenue, falling volumes and Postcomm regulation and the crisis begins to take on immense proportions.

The topsy-turvy nature of the pension situation is graphically illustrated as follows. In 2003 there was a deficit of £2.5 billion to be repaid following agreement with the pension Trustees over 40 years at the rate of £150 million per year. In 2006 this had become

£3.4 billion but agreement with the trustees was reached to deal with this deficit over 17 years at some £280 million per year. By the 2009 valuation, the deficit was some £10.3 billion and agreement from the Trustees was given to dealing with it over 38 years at some £282 million per year rising each year with inflation. An updated valuation in 2010 showed a deficit of £8.4 billion. These figures exclude the regular payments Royal Mail had to pay to the Scheme.[10]

Against this backdrop it should be noted that in 2008 postal workers and their families saw the Royal Mail pension Plan closed to new entrants, the final salary scheme gone from April 2008, a career average scheme came in and an increase in the retirement age to 65. These changes, coming as they did as part of a major strike in 2007, were billed as saving the pension scheme – at least that was the message from Royal Mail. Safeguards were negotiated by the CWU and the changes came in just as the financial crash kicked in.

Postcomm and the New Labour Government saw all these issues quite differently of course. Such an inability to invest, modernise and increase productivity simply led to proponents of radical change to state that the Company was over-manned with a low productivity workforce that had been featherbedded for far too long by a management that lacked a "can do" attitude and who took the customer for granted. As for the pension issue, if they modernised and cut pension entitlements for postal workers, all would be well.

In their eyes, any instability and upheaval was absolutely necessary to transform Royal Mail and provide a better service for the public who could choose who delivered their mail. Perhaps the phrase "creative destruction" fits the bill for such ideological purists. From the ashes of Royal Mail, that inefficient public sector, Union ridden behemoth, a new vibrant and reinvigorated Company would arise, ideally in the private sector.

It wasn't that Government or Postcomm couldn't see the

historical position (a dearth of investment caused by Governments creaming off profits for themselves coupled with very low prices in comparison with pretty much any country in the world) it was that to keep repeating a mantra that blamed the organisation and its workforce resonated far more with its intention to make a case to privatise the Company and introduce competition. And believe it or not, that is pretty much the philosophy that New Labour adopted which would be facilitated by a Postcomm stuffed full of free marketers.

Such a philosophy was arguably strengthened due to major industrial confrontations in 2003, 2006/2007 and 2009. It is an arguable point as to whether these confrontations came about as part of a deliberate attempt to assert management's right to manage, but it is undoubtedly the case that those running the Company knew change was required and began to see the CWU as an obstacle in the way of that same change. Collaboration with the workforce and the CWU was presumably not mentioned at Board level with any great gusto. What such people could not, or did not want to see, was the impact their own actions were having on their own employees.

Indeed as if to emphasise the point of ideological change regardless, within one year of Postcomm's "Corporate Plan" in 2000, the Sunday Times[11] ran an article that the New Labour Government had already got a plan to privatise what was then Consignia. A source was quoted as saying that Ministers believed that the Post Office was the "last great state owned commercial public service and in the modern world there is no case for it remaining under the Government umbrella." This article, coming as it did after a large unofficial strike in Royal Mail will presumably only have persuaded those members of the Labour Party who were now Ministers that privatisation was right and that no ideological barrier should be put in the way.

Subsequently the Government would have extended dialogue with the then Chairman Allan Leighton in 2005/2006 in relation to a share scheme whereby the workforce would have a stake in the Company, which it was thought, would help the workforce to change their outlook and tackle the competition with an incentive built in, in the form of shares. The intention was that these shares representing a percentage of the Business could be traded within Royal Mail between workers. This would in effect, build upon Allan Leighton's "Share in Success" scheme which put much store on paying a bonus, but resisted putting that same money into the basic pay of a postal worker. The sums were fairly substantial. In 2005 and 2006, bonuses were paid totalling £418 and £1074 repectively per full time employee. If this was meant to demonstrate how valued employees should feel, it fell short. The fault line was that it was the Company's vision on what "valuing" the workforce actually meant. It was theirs alone. It did not involve the workforce, grateful though they were to get the money.[12]

Such discussions around the Share in Success scheme between Allan Leighton and the Government did not result in a partial sell off due to the huge pressure and campaigning by the CWU and its members, who ceaselessly lobbied the Labour Party and obtained a policy that would inform the Party's subsequent manifesto. Ultimately Leighton had wanted the shares to be sellable on the open market, but had to settle for "Colleague Shares" only which allocated money to the workforce depending on the performance and estimated value of the Company. The huge gap between the aspirations of Royal Mail and their own workforce in particular are best summed up in the evidence from the CWU to the Select Committee on Trade and Industry in December 2006:

14. The CWU clearly favours a greater degree of employee involvement in the running of the business and a permanent share in the success of Royal Mail. But the degree and nature of employee involvement and the form and timing of any reward scheme must be a matter for negotiation and

agreement with the employees' recognised trade Union—not debated through the national media.

15. To date the CWU has seen no proposal from Royal Mail managers on the structure of any share scheme. All we have seen are a series of press reports which refer to Allan Leighton's proposal to release £1 billion of equity to private individuals which he describes as giving a 20% stake to the workforce.

16. The CWU have a number of serious concerns about the principle and practical application of Leighton's proposed share scheme. We believe the option of issuing private shares to individual staff is a particular form of privatisation. It changes Royal Mail's ownership structure and is a clear breach of Labour's election manifesto to keep Royal Mail 100% in public hands. Given Labour's explicit manifesto commitment we believe Leighton is abusing his position as chair of a public corporation to push for a change of ownership. This is for Government not Leighton to determine. Issuing shares represents a sugar-coated pill on the road to future privatisation of the industry. The experience from other privatisations of UK utilities is that the issuing of shares is an opening step which ultimately leads to further share issues and eventual privatisation.

17. Shares will be a costly distraction from the real challenges facing Royal Mail. Issuing shares will do nothing to raise revenues and help tackle the real problems of chronic under-investment, a record pensions deficit and the threat from private competition.

18. The CWU want workers to have a stake in the Company they work for but we don't believe this can only be done

through issuing shares. We reject the suggestion that postal workers do not currently have an interest or "stake" in the business. Employment in the industry, wages and a guaranteed pension represent a massive investment for all employees.

19. There is little support for Leighton's share plan among Royal Mail's workforce. Despite offering "free shares" to staff, extending the balloting deadline and boosting the return by including Royal Mail managers and sub-postmasters, just one in three (37%) of the workforce have actually registered their interest in shares—hardly the ringing endorsement Leighton was seeking. Moreover, our own poll of members found 98.5% in support of the CWU's alternative agenda of higher basic pay, a better work-life balance and fairer workloads, maximising job security and safeguarding pensions.

20. In our submission to the Bain Review the CWU signalled our willingness to enter into a serious debate about employee involvement aimed at improving efficiency and raising the status and financial rewards of postal workers. But there is no clear evidence that share schemes will actually improve productivity. Indeed, postal workers have already delivered record levels of service quality without a 20% stake in the business.

21. Leighton's proposals could actually prove divisive and demotivating as the lowest paid staff sell their shares for an instant financial return. This will create a situation of "haves" and "have nots"—those who sell their shares will have no stake in the business and no prospect of one in the future. There is also a risk that senior managers and executives on higher incomes will look to buy up large tranches of shares over time.

22. Leighton's share proposal would be an impractical and inappropriate model for Royal Mail. This view is also supported by the Job Ownership Ltd (JOL), the voice of employee owned business. In a recent report, the JOL argued that a collective profit share would be a far better model for Royal Mail than imposing an individual share plan which it said was "inappropriate" in the context of a publicly-owned Royal Mail and collective bargaining with a recognised trade Union.

23.The CWU believe that Royal Mail have failed to make the case to support Leighton's share plan. Instead of embarking on a costly, time consuming and potentially damaging debate about issuing shares, it may be better, as the *Financial Times* recently suggested, to adapt and agree the current *Share in Success* scheme—which is a straight profit sharing scheme— and perhaps look to add in quality of service measures and even some form of savings plan.

If this passage tells anyone anything of note it is that the views of postal staff were being ignored by Royal Mail. Paragraph 23 perhaps sums things up well. The CWU were saying that if the Company wanted a scheme to incentivise people then talk to them and something could be agreed. The fact that Royal Mail balloted their employees and tried to get them to sign up to so-called free shares and failed, surely speaks volumes. It was, in retrospect one of the many attempts made by those running Royal Mail to try and ignore the views of its workforce and their Union.

Colleague Shares did however become embedded following the decision of the New Labour Government to allow the Company to allocate 20% of the "value generated through the efforts of everyone in the Business over the next few years in the form of Colleague Shares ... worth up to £5300 depending on performance."[13] Some money was paid out, but the workforce remained alienated. How could such a positive initiative fail? What was going on inside the organisation that had led to this?

Bizarrely, this Colleague Share scheme would end in 2010 when Royal Mail told its own workforce that the shares were worthless and there was no more money to give out. Many would wonder just what the reality and future now was for them. Shares in a valueless Company? That, you couldn't really make up if you tried. The impact on the workforce was entirely predictable and understandable. The inevitable row with the workforce and the Company led to a watered down use of the money the CWU said should be paid out as part of a nationally negotiated 2010 Transformation and Beyond Agreement. In effect, the Company said there was no money and the Union said there was. In point of fact, such was the poor level of trust at that time that the CWU demanded an independent examination of Royal Mail's accounts.

If there was one thing happening within Royal Mail during the 2000s it was the apocalyptic scenario being painted for the workforce. It was claimed the Company was a basket case and was "only three years from being wiped out"[14], that Postcomm were projecting a minimum of 25% of the postal market going private between 2003 and 2010 and that Royal Mail had plans to franchise out delivery offices – the talk was that Posties would become self employed delivering rather like those few milkmen we occasionally see today. Another talking point across the industry was that "one year we are losing a million a day and now we are being thanked as we are making a million a day." Go figure, as they say. Alternatively, plough through those Royal Mail accounts for some answers...

Ultimately, perhaps inevitably given the quality of those managing the Company, the "you must change or else" message cascaded down to staff as Royal Mail struggled with having to change with one hand (and sometimes two) tied behind its back. In that regard, an ominous article appeared in 2005 in the Daily

Telegraph quoting then CEO Adam Crozier as saying that of his 15,000 managers, "5,000 are fantastic, 5,000 are good and 5,000 are not up to the mark." The managers' Union Amicus said the comments were "ill judged and frankly insulting." For your average Postie, the only surprise was that 5,000 were apparently fantastic.[15]

You may of course ask yourself, what exactly was wrong with Royal Mail before 2000 that led to so much upheaval being judged necessary. The phrase, "if it ain't broke don't fix it" probably sums up the organisation by saying that it pretty much did "what it says on the tin." Did that mean Royal Mail was as responsive to the customer as it could be or that industrial relations were on a sound and positive footing? No, not always, but is that a reason to privatise the industry or force massive unsustainable change upon it? No, this was simply about gradually introducing a free market into the postal sector come hell or high water. It was a stick to force the Company to change. If the wish was that this change would come about collaboratively with their staff, then such wishes were based on fantasy, as we shall see further on.

The lack of USO obligations upon the competition was to be the driver to ensure a more efficient and responsive Royal Mail. What a touching faith there was in the operation of free markets. Well, if competition is supposed to bring benefits, shall we state the obvious here for a moment, the price of a stamp that joe public pays for hasn't exactly plummeted. More competition has equalled higher stamp prices for the many and lower prices for the few, i.e., the large companies posting out millions of items per day and effectively calling the tune. In 2009 just 50 companies accounted for 40% of mail volumes.[16]

By 2008 such was the timely and expert touch applied to the postal market by Postcomm and the Government that the British Chambers of Commerce (BCC) were able to say, "Royal Mail has increased costs for businesses and delivered no corresponding improvements in the service they provide." The Federation of Small Businesses in the same year said that 48% of their members said their mail now arrived later and some 31% said the service was now worse since the introduction of a single daily delivery.[17]

How could such warning signs not trigger a change in attitude? Picture it now, you are an employee of the Company and being told that this is the way we have to go, but all around you your experience tells you something is wrong here. For goodness sake, Posties knew their customers. The quote from the BCC was not in reality a surprise for Posties, sad though it is to say it. In fact, that sadness was quite genuine. Before their very eyes the deterioration was plain to see. It would get much worse.

Chapter 4

Wake Up and Smell the Coffee

Any alternatives for the ownership and governance of the Royal Mail during these years were completely ignored to the extent that no detailed response was ever received from the New Labour Government to alternatives put to them by the CWU. Their ideas were doable, comprehensive and researched. The fact that so few know about these alternatives is a damning indictment of the media and lazy journalism and not a lack of effort on the part of the Union to get its message across via press releases and suchlike.

A report from the think tank Compass set out sensible and realistic options around how issues of governance and structure could be looked at which would include the Company, the workforce and, crucially, input from the public. Examples were given of Network Rail (who have access to Government and private funding streams) and the BBC. Not to replicate these models exactly as such, but to show that privatisation was not necessary (unless of course you were ideologically predisposed to such an outcome) and with a pragmatic approach Royal Mail could remain as a great postal service and not beholden to commercial imperatives. In fact Compass noted that to privatise the Company and therefore the profits whilst nationalising the pension liabilities would be to "alienate the British people."[1]

It is possible then to get a broad picture in which to place Royal Mail by the mid 2000s?

A much loved national institution with historically cheap prices (the cheapest in Europe according to Compass) and around £2.5 billion of profits going straight to the Treasury via the EFL between 1991 and 2002 (according to the CWU, a staggering 80 to 90% of pre-tax profits[2]) had meant hardly any money to pay for the upkeep and modernisation required.[3] Such a backdrop was then brought to a critical state, as we have glimpsed above, with the introduction of a deliberately set unfair playing field, price caps and formulas from Postcomm and a pension deficit which whilst stable in 2000 with a surplus of some £760million became a huge millstone around the Company's neck which led to crisis, instability, strikes and so much else including some television documentaries on Channel 4 providing an insight, such as it was, to the machinations of life in Royal Mail. The phrase, "a perfect storm", sums up the scenario pretty well.

Remember those programmes from 2004 and 2005? Postal workers certainly did. Oh how we watched in delight and disgust at the same time, seeing staff employed on god knows what contracts from goodness knows what agency, left with a map and told to get on with it. We also saw apparent theft from Royal Mail, something both Royal Mail and the CWU challenged. Channel 4 would subsequently issue an apology for their error, but the damage was done and everyone forgot that the vast majority of postal staff were honest. We saw arguments between the workforce and managers and disgruntled customers and we wondered how anything actually got delivered. Indeed, one of the programmes actually appeared to show a sorting machine kept going by the use of a rubber band.

There were three Dispatches programmes of the undercover sort which to be frank about it, no one could really take their eyes off, especially if you worked in Royal Mail. A real fly on the wall look at an apparently ailing organisation in the death throes before it is rightfully privatised and becomes a fantastic, customer focussed and friendly organisation. Yeah, right.

The last one was a follow up entitled "Post Office Undercover" which went out on 8 February 2010.[4] The programme generated a huge response from postal workers and the public alike. A visit to the Dispatches pages on the Channel 4 web site records some 336 online responses. It strikes me as rather ominous that the "little people" can have their say without really understanding that their beloved (or hated?) Royal Mail is the subject of a grotesque experiment designed to create the circumstances which will allow it to be criticised and then privatised as being the only "rational" alternative. It's not their fault of course, just another of those annoying situations we all find ourselves in from time to time, shouting out, "it's not like that, you don't understand what's happening!"

Nevertheless the comments mirrored the tragedy which had by then been unfolding for some time. A "hard working postwoman", one of the 336 posted on 9/2/10, wrote, "...the majority of staff including management try their very best to keep up and improve on the service we provide far more than any Company I have ever worked for. I am proud to work for Royal Mail."

Another comment from a postal worker on 14/2/10 said, "...great postmen doing a good job despite all the crap they have to put up with ... and Royal Mail management due to this (sic) heaping more and more workloads on Posties in some cases very unfairly."

As for comments from the public, well it would be a cliché just to say some good and some bad, but that is pretty much what you got; angry and let down customers, others who got a wonderful service and felt the programme was not representative. Postal workers posting comments to say that this was not how it was for them and that Royal Mail in London – the focus of much of the programmes – was a mess and shouldn't be used to tar the rest of the country. And if you were a hard working postal worker in London? Well, let's just say no one believed you. How's that for generating frustration, people actually within Royal Mail saying their area is better than another with all the loaded connotations that such comments bring with them.

If such comments point to the fact that it is our Royal Mail and we all have a right to an opinion, then there is some hope, surely? Strong feelings and yes, exasperation from many at the problems but behind it all is the hopefully reassuring sense that in fact this is a simple industry – collecting, sorting and delivering the mail. Allan Leighton was famous for saying he wanted to make Royal Mail a "great place to work" and that we should keep it simple and not get bogged down in what he said was the "treacle." How can such genuine enthusiasm end up with an undercover Channel 4 journalist pointing out the myriad faults of the Company just a decade later?

Just a year before this final Channel 4 programme went out, an unknown Postie (Roy Mayall) came to the attention of us all. Amongst other things he did your average postal worker a massive favour by actually telling it how it is. His book "Dear Granny Smith – A letter from your Postman" was a genuine hit. But for the purposes of Allan Leighton's treacle, Roy Mayall was commenting in the New Statesman that the number of items Royal Mail was handling was incorrect.[5]

He pointed out that mail came to delivery offices in grey boxes which contain around two hundred letters. Over time it had been possible to accurately estimate the number by weighing the box so a figure of 208 was arrived at. Royal Mail in their wisdom had arbitrarily reduced this from 208 to 150. This was now apparently part of the reason for the workforce being told the mail was dropping.

He was also picked up by the London Review of Books[6] and was able to provide the alternative fly on the wall stuff. How's this to get a snap shot of reality then,

It's the joke at the delivery office. 'Figures are down' we say and laugh as we pile the fifth or sixth bag of mail onto the scales and write down the weight in the log book. It's our daily exercise in fiction writing... 'Figures are down' we say again, but more wearily now as we pile yet more packages into our panniers, before setting off on our rounds.

According to Royal Mail figures published in May 2009, mail volume declined by 5.5% over the preceding 12 months and is predicted to fall by a further 10% this year. Every Postman knows these figures are false. If the figures are down, how come I can't get my round done in under four hours anymore? How come I can work up to five hours at a stretch without time for a sit down or a tea break? How come my knees nearly give way with the weight I have to carry? So who's right? Are the figures down or aren't they? Royal Mail couldn't lie, could it? Well no, maybe not. But it can manipulate the figures. And it can avoid telling the whole truth.

Now, you might be wondering what this has got to do with the public's frustration at their postal service, but if you think about it for a moment, it might well be unfair, but if they can't even accurately count the number of items entering the system, no wonder so many other things are wrong with the Company. Royal Mail had either dispensed with all the treacle as they couldn't count how much mail they were handling or alternatively, they had drowned in the treacle from the conflicting demands of the regulator to the extent they were like a rabbit in the headlights not knowing what to do for the best.

Ominously, this reality gap between Royal Mail's staff and its managers was to become – and in fact, already was – a feature that led to awful and shocking treatment of many staff.

This unfolding mess was of course predicted. The many reports from the CWU together with evidence to various Select Committees over the years set out in detail the consequences of the actions that Postcomm wanted to undertake. Simply put, the process to alter regulation involved a Postcomm report followed by a period of consultation before its recommendations were put into practise. It is fair to say that pretty much what Postcomm said they wanted, they got.

And how do we know this? Can it really be the case that Postcomm regulated the postal market wanting Royal Mail to fail? Well, the quick answer to that is yes. If Royal Mail weren't set up to fail how on earth would any so called competition get a foot in the door?

The public had now endured six years of regulation (it's amazing how suddenly we have to "regulate" whereas before Royal Mail simply delivered the mail!) by Postcomm, which was enthusiastically supported by the then New Labour Government who would give no concession to the CWU or, for that matter, to any argument that said, perhaps things are not going to plan and more pointedly, suggested ways things could be changed.

In fact whilst supporting Postcomm, the Government did, under pressure, agree to a demand from the CWU for a review into the operation of the postal market since the introduction of the Postal Services Act 2000 and in the light of Postcomm's intention to completely open up the postal market to competition from 2006. Facilitated by a motion to the 2004 Labour Party Conference the subsequent discussions between the Labour Government and the CWU led to a manifesto commitment to this review and to keeping Royal Mail "wholly publicly owned."

That such a review was needed, was best illustrated by the fact that in 2005 the Company was struggling with a lack of investment, thousands of unfilled vacancies and around 20,000 casuals such was the desperate need from the Royal Mail Board's perspective, to remain profitable and pay for the USO.[7]

New Labour went on to win the General Election in 2005 and finally appointed Sir George Bain to undertake this review. His report in 2005 was never published, but the CWU did submit evidence, which in clinical detail explained why Royal Mail was stuck where it was. They noted the lack of investment (only £320million in the 3 years to 2005) and the historic issue of some £2.4 billion going back to the Treasury via the EFL which had stymied investment compared to the competition who had already automated. They also said there was an urgent need to re-examine and change the Postcomm pricing formula from an

"RPI minus" approach, which had meant a combination of artificially low stamp and business mail prices which in turn meant a shortage of funds to invest in modernisation. The CWU proposed instead an RPI+Y formula where Y represented an additional percentage to compensate for Royal Mail's historic position of underinvestment, the pension scheme costs and the fixed costs of providing the USO. It is worth stating once more, that the competition had no equivalent USO.

Regarding the intention to move to a full and complete market liberalisation in 2006 some 3 years ahead of anyone else in the EU when the Company was in such a weak state, the Union said would be fool hardy and that issues raised should be sorted before any move to carry out this liberalisation. The CWU additionally noted that once the market had fully opened within 18 months of this the EU Directive meant a review would have to take place to ensure a level playing field in postal services across Europe, so why go it alone now?[8]

Also mentioned was a previous report they had produced in 2002 to show how innovative new services and products could be developed and to which no Royal Mail response had been forthcoming.

The Unions' submission to Bain and the lobbying of MPs by local CWU Branches, the numerous stalls set up in the High Streets of the UK to get the public's support, the meetings with Government officials undertaken by the Union, the meetings with Postcomm , all came to nought as the market was opened up fully in 2006. Clearly such an outrageous demand from a trade Union that the Government should review fully the impact of the regulatory climate before allowing a free for all, could never have been countenanced. "Who is running this country, them or us!?"

Interestingly, during the early to mid 2000s, the CWU and Royal Mail were pretty much on the same side in relation to the regulatory climate and the need to review what was happening.

Allan Leighton's hope, not unreasonable of course, was that the CWU would cosy up to New Labour and things would be sorted. This did not happen.

Chapter 5

A Grotesque Experiment Comes of Age

Subsequently New Labour – again under pressure from the CWU – asked Sir Richard Hooper to undertake another review of postal liberalisation in December 2007. He would go on to produce an interim report in May 2008 and a final one in December 2008.

The CWU again submitted detailed evidence to the Hooper review reiterating points already made which had been ignored and also others around the imbalance between UK and overseas postal competitors who had been protected and had investment the like of which Royal Mail had not; the fact that comparable EU countries like Germany, France and Holland had not opened up their postal markets, the continual "cherry picking" and the pricing formulas that starved the Company (Postcomm's view was that the competition would create efficiencies which in turn would generate revenue for investment – to which some would add as an after thought, "LOL").

The CWU also picked up the glaring weakness in Postcomm's approach. They had projected mail volume growth inaccurately – yes, some more crystal ball gazing again. They stated that volumes would from 2006 rise by between 1 and 2% per annum. In fact, volumes had fallen. Such trends were mirrored elsewhere in Europe. The issue was that if Postcomm reckoned on 24.7 billion items being posted but only 21.9 billion had actually been posted, that is a significant loss of revenue. Postcomm had also under estimated the loss of revenue due to downstream access. The CWU also noticed that due to the lack of investment and also Postcomm's price caps regime, only 50% of letters were sorted via automation. The competition, thanks to proper investment programmes to prepare them for competition as per the EU

Directives were automatically sorting – in the case of TNT 90 to 95% and Deutsche Post were managing 95%.[1]

The interim report from May 2008 stated that the public and small and medium sized enterprises had not seen any improvement and that only the larger organisations via DSA had done so. The exact quote is, "There have been no significant benefits from liberalisation for smaller businesses and domestic consumers."

Can we just re-read that sentence again.... After all this time and all this upheaval and trauma, we find that Postcomm and New Labour's regulatory framework had not delivered improvements to the many, only the few. It gets better though. Other quotes from Hooper's report begin to show the enormity of the grotesque experiment undertaken by Postcomm and the New Labour Government:

> They (the 50 largest mail users) and other large businesses, have seen clear benefits from liberalisation: choice, lower prices and more assurance about the quality of the mail service.
>
> The abolition of Sunday collections and two deliveries per day are "perceived as a reduction in service, particularly for small businesses who want earlier and more predictable delivery times.
>
> In 2003 Royal Mail aimed to complete the first delivery by 9.30am. The Company now aims to deliver mail by 2pm for most customers and 3pm in outlying areas of the country.

The final Hooper report would quote small businesses as being unhappy with the timing and lateness of deliveries. What Hooper and no one else made clear, was that this was a direct result of DSA. DSA customers (i.e., big mail posters) wanted to post as late the previous evening as they could. All this meant was that millions of items were subsequently arriving the following morning at delivery offices, later on rather than the traditional "crack of dawn". Another triumph for Postcomm. Another unintended consequence?

In its accounts for 2006/07 Royal Mail estimated that it was 40% less efficient than its rivals for two main reasons: because competitors had already invested in technology to modernise their operations and because competitors operating in the UK provided 25% less in pay and benefits....

It is worth pausing here for a moment. The wage then paid to the average postal worker was some 20% below the average for a UK worker. As for the efficiency issue it is clear this is down to a lack of investment which itself had been stymied by Postcomm with some 91% of Royal Mail revenues subject to price controls or price caps which in turn had exacerbated the ongoing issue over the pension scheme costs.

The incumbent (i.e., Royal Mail), its competitors and the regulator (i.e., Postcomm) have fundamentally different expectations of the regulatory regime.

There is now a substantial threat to Royal Mail's financial stability and therefore the universal service. We have come to the conclusion, based on evidence submitted so far, that the status quo is not tenable.

Now clearly the above quotes don't paint the full picture, but nevertheless they are significant. In other words a review of Royal Mail hasn't concluded that all is well after some eight years of regulation by highly skilled and expert officials from Postcomm. No, we find the opposite is the case. How could such a situation have come about? Was it really sheer incompetence that enabled staff and customers to go through year after year of upheaval and change, and for what exactly? Are we really to say that if Postcomm and New Labour hadn't rigorously pursued their agenda, that things would have been worse?

Ominously, although the CWU broadly welcomed the interim report from Hooper, it was paragraph 59 that would be the beginning of yet another attempt to sell off the industry. Hooper stated that although given commercial freedom, in order to access capital Royal Mail would be competing with other demands "on the public purse" and any monies loaned would be subject to European State Aid procedures. This would be reinterpreted to mean that only a sell off would suffice.[2]

To those within the industry and to the CWU who had spent the intervening years trying to get the policy makers to listen, this interim report was indeed confirmation of the position taken a few years previously that competition would not deliver for people. Perhaps it was also confirmation as well, if such were needed, that the representations made by a trade Union are invariably given scant regard. Talk to those who represent those actually doing the work, well why on earth would anyone want to do that? The CWU was clearly seen as an entity with its own agenda and therefore not worthy of being taken seriously.

Of course such a viewpoint could be completely wrong. Employees were being listened to during those years and the Government welcomed the interim Hooper report by expressing its thanks to the CWU for having so much of its concerns verified. The Government added that it wished "to apologise to the workforce, their Union and the great British public for not listening to their concerns earlier as we can now see clearly that the experiment to reinvent the wheel has not been a stunning success." And pigs might fly.

From May 2008 onwards the sense that the future of Royal Mail would be finally decided was palpable. As for the CWU they not only worked the corridors of power they also targeted that years' Labour Party Conference (September 2008) to get the assurances they needed. The slogan, "It's Time To Deliver" was apt and the Union had thought that they had got what they needed which was to honour the manifesto commitment to keep the Company wholly publicly owned. The then Minister responsible, John Hutton had apparently said as much.

Interestingly, the final Hooper report noted that tensions between a regulator and the body being regulated are not unusual, but that in this he was

> struck by the depth and range of disagreements between Royal Mail and Postcomm. Even the most basic facts are disputed. The definition of the postal market, the Company's performance against efficiency targets and the size and distribution of ... costs, are notable examples. The systems and necessary data needed to build constructive and professional regulatory relationships are not yet in place.

Given that Postcomm would be abolished by the incoming Coalition Government, this quote perhaps demonstrates as nothing else could, the "we know best" approach that Postcomm deployed; and that their approach had failed – unless judged by the yardstick of how far can we push it until the Company breaks – shows just how disastrous their tenure had been up until then.

It is useful at this point to backtrack, albeit briefly to quote from Postcomm some six years previous to Hooper. A row between Postcomm and the then Consignia Board was made public and the Daily Telegraph, who quoted Postcomm's Martin Stanley. He said, in response to accusations that their intentions to open up yet more of the market (this time bulk items of 4,000 or more) was not half the postal market but only 30% of it, "You seek to justify your action by suggesting that Postcomm is proceeding with reckless haste and has a flawed understanding of the postal market. Both these claims are untrue." [3]

Looking back now and in the light of the Hooper conclusions, it is perhaps a quote that is best amended by deleting the word "untrue" and inserting the word, "true."

To return from our brief diversion, Hooper quoted from a Postcomm report in relation to Royal Mail's overall financial stability. Postcomm said, "...without extensive change, the Royal Mail's business model will become unsustainable." And why would that be then? This from a regulator that has the power – which it used to the full – to directly control prices and so much else. One could easily get the impression that in fact Postcomm direct things and those managing Royal Mail simply carry out instructions as best they can. If that sounds a little far fetched, then the following quote from Royal Mail's accounts for 2007/08 leaves little room for doubt:

> Postcomm regulates the prices of nearly 90% of Royal Mail's letters business, controls the terms and conditions for nearly all its services, sets the quality of service targets and determines compensation arrangements.[4]

Just prior to Hooper commencing his work, the depth of the denial from the New Labour Government was apparent in that the then Minister responsible for postal matters, Pat MacFadden stated in a letter dated 15 November 2007, that "Postcomm has given the commitment that liberalisation will not undermine a universal service in the UK (and that the Postal Services Act 2000) will help ensure that postal services in the UK are more responsive to the needs of customers."[5] The view of Government should be set against the reality on the ground. Is there any wonder that all the research documents from the CWU and others, had been ignored when all along their view was that Postcomm had it all under control? If only.

Quite rightly, Hooper also stated the obvious, namely that not everyone was posting letters anymore. In addition to "downtrading" where customers would use second and not first class, he also noted that email and social networks had changed the landscape and it would be ridiculous to argue otherwise. By 2008 just 11% of mail was what we would describe as between individual members of the public. Moreover he noted that just 50p per week was now spent on mail by the public (excluding businesses of course). Business mail accounted for 89% of Royal Mail's income. Of course today, the decline in letters has been compensated for by the blast from ebay and Amazon et al. Small packets and parcels now account for significant chunks of Royal Mail business.

The decline in mail only really started from 2005/06 and in fact, decline or not, if the investment had already been put in then costs would have been lower and new innovative products could have made more of a difference. Indeed, at every opportunity the CWU were arguing for better services, including developing Royal Mail's only interface with the public, Callers Offices where packets could be collected. In effect, Royal Mail always seemed to be behind the curve. They knew it, we knew it, the workforce knew it, Postcomm knew it (but so what) and naturally, the competition knew it and were taking full advantage.

In his final report Hoopers' conclusion would be, amongst other more benign proposals, that new investment could only be delivered by a partial privatisation. As the CWU would note, this conclusion appeared to have the paw marks of the newly installed Business Minister, Lord Mandelson all over it.

The rationale for this partial privatisation was that not for profit models like Glas Cymru (Welsh Water) or Network Rail were unsuitable as Hooper claimed that they were "natural monopolies operating in stable markets with low levels of risk, with long term investment needs funded by significant debt positions." That sounds suspiciously similar to the environment Royal Mail used to operate within up to 2000. Herein we see the remorseless logic of those determined to privatise the Company.

Hooper said there were greater risks for Royal Mail now such that only outside "risk seeking" capital was appropriate. Shall we "de-risk" the postal market then to protect the Universal Service Obligation? Clearly not. And herein lies the rub. No risk seeking capital is going to come within a mile of Royal Mail due to its pension issues and the micro managing of it by Postcomm. The astute reader can no doubt see where this is going.

What was even more disappointing about this analysis from Hooper, was that Royal Mail themselves in their own submission to his review had stated,

(our) Strategic Plan is robust, radical and funded. It assumes the current regulatory environment and funding arrangements and depends on implementing a broad range of challenging initiatives. However, the result is that the plan is constrained by the current regulatory framework and our lack of access to equity capital. Nevertheless, the initiatives in the plan will result in Royal Mail taking out an additional £1.5 billion of costs as a result of operational transformation and developing new products and services through a more commercial approach.[6]

Subsequently, Royal Mail announced in its 2008 accounts that they had secured agreements on pay, pensions and modernisation for the business (following a Government loan of around £1.2 billion in 2005/06) with the CWU after a lengthy dispute, the details of which follow later.

Now, before anyone says this still proves that outside capital was needed (i.e., privatisation) remember that the above quote from Royal Mail was predicated on Postcomm's unfair regime and the continuation of the pension liabilities. As Compass reported after the Hooper report, Royal Mail was profitable despite having to charge some of the lowest prices in Europe and coping with the "lower than cost" DSA access charges. Resolving these points together with the pension deficit responsibilities being shifted to its rightful place with Government, would, according to Compass, free up some £600 million per year. At the time of this Compass report, Royal Mail were paying some £850 million into their pension pot in the form of ongoing liabilities and the historical deficit.

Amazingly, Compass also noted that of the investment loan provided by the Government in 2005, only half of this had been invested by 2009.[7]

The Compass report also took issue with the underlying assumptions and conclusions made by Hooper around the efficiency or otherwise of Royal Mail. They found that, for example, some 88% of Royal Mail revenue's were price controlled, whereas only 37% of the German Deutsche Post's (DHL) were. They were able to show that areas such as the geographical size, shape and topography of the UK were different to its competitors. Another example given was population density. In the UK it was 252/km^2 but for TNT (the Dutch postal operator) the equivalent was 491/km^2, in addition, many European countries only delivered mail 5 days a week not 6 as in the UK.

Also noted was that in Germany a national minimum wage for the postal sector had been introduced as it was feared that without it "the postal service would be unable to cope." Both TNT and DHL had significant international markets and very different mixtures of business activities. In short, the accusation was that Hooper was not comparing like with like.

In fact, Compass uncovered further damming proof that despite the Labour Government looking to part privatise the Company on the back of the Hooper report, on a "purchasing, power parity (PPP)" index looking at Royal Mail, TNT and DHL, for domestically delivered items in each country Royal Mail had a cost per item PPP of 27p, for DHL it was 38p and for TNT, 40p.[8]

To the above we should add another quote from Royal Mail's submission to Hooper. Another one of those quotes that really ought not to be possible in any rational world,

> The universal service is at the core of the UK postal services
> industry, but is now loss making for the first time. This is the
> result of a range of challenges which threaten its sustain-
> ability.... These include the regulator's flawed assumptions in
> the current price control which will result in a cash deficit of
> £2.6 billion (a figure acknowledged by the regulator) over the
> life of the current price control because of the differences
> between the regulator's assumptions and the likely outturn,
> despite Royal Mail meeting its efficiency targets (set by
> Postcomm).

It becomes a lot easier to see now that the perennial issue of
investment need not have been a problem in the first place had
those crystal ball gazers thrown in the towel before they started,
on the grounds that surely, no sane person could predict the
workings of the free market.

It really does create a sense of complete bafflement and disil-
lusion to read such quotes. But of course amidst this gloom and
disbelief at such a shambolic mess, the reality was that the
Company was still there, still just about hanging on and all that
was needed were some simple changes to restore it to full health
again.

So, the lines were clearly drawn. Royal Mail was profitable, it
could be more so if pension liabilities were removed and
regulation made fair. This would enable more confidence to
invest the available capital, which in turn would close the
acknowledged gap with other postal carriers. This in turn would
open up huge and positive opportunities to restructure the
Company in ways to run the Company as a not for profit outfit
reinvesting profits and dedicated to the public interest. If that is
not a positive vision that the public would support, then what is?

In fact, the public weren't really asked as it was already

known from opinion poll surveys carried out by the CWU, that a sell off, partial or otherwise was not supported with only around 23% of the public being in favour in 2010.[9] Why ask if you already know the answer?

There were previous efforts to privatise Royal Mail in 2001 with secret talks between New Labour and the Dutch owned TNT, at which point Government sources were quoted as saying, "There is no longer any ideological barrier to a move (i.e., privatisation) of this sort"[10] and another attempt in 2005 with the Colleague Share fiasco, both of which failed. To everyone's non surprise then, the New Labour Government accepted Hooper's report in full and in so doing brought these previous "failures" to fruition.

In what can only be described as a pathetic "me too" attitude, Postcomm also welcomed Hooper and especially the final recommendation for privatisation (euphemistically referred to of course as accessing outside capital). The fact that their actions and failings had been so publicly aired by Hooper, would mean that perhaps they would have kept their heads down, but clearly not. Postcomm had previously said in a press release on 14 May 2008 prior to their submission to the final Hooper report, "Postcomm wants to see the Government and Royal Mail embrace a partnership approach with the private sector...." Proof, if proof were needed that the concerns the CWU had that Postcomm were not simply neutral bystanders regulating an industry but were ideologically predisposed to privatisation, appeared correct.

The poverty of aspiration from the New Labour Government, the lack of vision to operate something on a basis other than commercial profit and the ignoring of their own historical perspectives around not for profit and the co-operative movement, should have created a sense of shame amongst those Labour Ministers carrying out the policy to privatise.

The CWU had ended up arguing for a review and arguing

that the Labour Manifesto deemed a sell off partial or otherwise, out of bounds, only to find that all along the New Labour Government was not interested. The public could "go hang."

That old and well-worn adage, be careful what you ask for is regrettably apt in this case. A review was granted thanks to the efforts of the CWU, albeit with those tasked with carrying it out, having little or no sympathy to an alternative vision. Of course it was always eminently possible to have people other than Sir Richard Hooper (and his two other panel members, Dame Deirdre Hutton and Ian Smith) carry out the task, but the idea of a commission of enquiry with a wide range of participants (including, perish the thought, the workforce) was clearly ignored.

The Unions' subsequent campaign in 2009 to prevent this partial privatisation by the New Labour Government proved successful. Lobbying and campaigning nationally and by local Branches, including the use of a 20 feet high giant inflatable pillar box which travelled up and down the UK ending up at Lands End, proved that the public were in no mood for the sell-off. The memberships' subscriptions had apparently never been so wisely spent and all in a good cause, namely to enable their Company to remain public and out of the hands of those determined to make a fast buck at the expense of a public service.

For their part the New Labour Government, hampered by their manifesto commitment, simply stated over and over that the Royal Mail would remain publicly owned. The Union was in fact arguing over nothing. A partial privatisation was not privatisation, period. That view did not prevail other than in the minds of those propagating it. When the Government finally threw in the towel on 1 July 2009, their view was only that the sale had been abandoned due to the poor economic climate meaning that a good price could not be achieved for the taxpayer.

It seems completely normal now, especially given the arrogance shown to the CWU and public opinion by the

Government to look back and think, why on earth would they abandon the project by telling the public that they had listened to the arguments and understood now that there were alternatives to a partial privatisation? All they had to do was to brazen it out, state it was poor economic circumstances and restate that they were still right after all?

In fact, the lack of a principled position from the Government was encapsulated nicely by Lord Mandelson in his memoirs. Mandelson has told his readers that he thought Gordon Brown would back out of a sell off as he was "nervous of a political scrap to get the Bill through." Having been proved right, Mandelson informs us that without telling the Prime Minister he and his Ministerial team had formulated a back-up plan. "...my ministerial team and I had been careful to leave ourselves an exit strategy. It was not difficult to devise. Given the world economic crisis, these were not exactly the ideal times in which to open bidding for a private partner for the Royal Mail." So there you have it. Cynical to the end, one might say.

It does get better however. We read that Lord Mandelson had "one particularly gratifying ally ... John Prescott." Both he and Mandelson agreed that "the CWU had to accept change and modernisation and he (Prescott) agreed that it would be bad for the Government if we retreated."[11]

It would be bad for the Government to retreat from doing something that hardly anyone wanted? Such warped thinking can surely only be the product of two things. Either, one has lost sight of reality from within the Westminster bubble or you have sold out to free market ideology. I am not aware of any votes garnered by New Labour whilst it was ploughing ahead with its ultimately failed bid.

For the average Postie this time was something of a mystery. Why on earth would a Labour Government want to "sell us off" anyway? In fact on a purely "you scratch my back, I'll scratch yours" basis, the CWU had given millions to Labour and the

Unions' leadership (both national and for the most part at Branch level as well) had argued tirelessly both with members at meetings and with CWU Branches at CWU Conference, that the Union must remain affiliated. Such efforts meant that there never was any real chance that the CWU would disaffiliate from the Labour Party, but it did of course show as nothing else really could, the fragile position the CWU were in. A backs against the wall campaign over something that should not even have been thought of, never mind put into action.

Make no mistake it meant a reluctant acceptance that whatever arguments might be put forward, they would never surmount a Government predisposed to the ideology of privatisation – all that could be done was to fight to try and stop it happening. Such is the political journey taken by Labour Ministers from left to right without any coherent narrative as to why they arrived at the position of ignoring every conceivable alternative to a sell off, without so much as a proper explanation. That other obstacle, such as it was, namely policy set by the Labour Party Conference, was a mere distraction and a minor one at that.

Having successfully fought off privatisation (i.e., persuaded, if that's the right word, the Labour Government to follow their own manifesto commitment) and with a possible General Election looming in 2010, the task was now to sort out the pension issue and therefore release funds for investment and so keep Royal Mail publicly owned and restored to full health.

The Government for their part ignored this and some Labour MPs would end up telling the CWU that by opposing the partial sell off, that the public would not agree to a pensions "bail out" without a quid pro quo, i.e., that same sell off. Actually, this phrase "bail out" is used over and over, but is not helpful. There was a deficit which needed resolving by Government taking responsibility for the 13 years of pension holidays and the straightjacket provided by Postcomm which stripped Royal Mail of huge amounts of cash.

The argument that nationalising pension liabilities and privatising Royal Mail's profits would be opposed by the public was ignored, such was the ideological predisposition to focus solely on this privatisation agenda. In fact, the opposite argument was deployed – that the public would welcome such pension liabilities whilst the private sector took the profit! Naturally, there was no evidence for this assertion.

The message to postal workers was that nothing would be done to implement any of Hooper and that if the Conservatives got in next time any subsequent privatisation would be some how the fault of the Union. The ultimate insult to a proud and thoughtful Union who had battled to protect it members and their families and to ensure that the public service ethos was preserved. If nothing else, it gave the CWU a taste of the power of those, who whilst in Government could choose to sort out the Royal Mail or they could choose not to do so.

True to the best traditions of the CWU they kept trying by producing a report, "Time to Deliver" with the iconic image of a clock with the inevitable 5 minutes to midnight showing. They had commissioned pension experts to provide evidence to the Government. Hilary Salt, a Fellow of the Institute of Actuaries, showed how the mix of investments could be re-examined , how the pension deficit could be managed over 40 years and not crushed into 17 years, that a Crown Guarantee could be provided and that Postcomm should pay much more attention to the historic pension position Royal Mail had to cope with. In the same publication, Thompson's solicitors were able to give an opinion that within the constraints of the Postal Services Act 2000 and European State Aid rules, there was "scope ... to ameliorate or eliminate the RMGs pension problems."[12]

True to the best traditions of New Labour, they ignored this report as well. They also ignored the outcome of the cross party House of Commons Business and Enterprise Committee which stated amongst other things,

> ...we do not consider either the Independent Review (i.e., Hooper's report) or the Government has properly made the case that these two reforms (i.e., sorting out the pensions and regulatory climate), about which there is a broad consensus, can only be made as part of a package which includes the third reform – the involvement of a private sector equity partner in Royal Mail. Similarly, we are not persuaded that the provisions contained in the Bill allowing such a partnership are necessary or desirable.[13]

To all intents and purposes this report was the last piece in the jigsaw. If the Government had accepted the need to take on the pension liabilities at the 11th hour (this would have the beneficial effect of having around £27 billion of assets to benefit the state's balance sheet), then the finances of Royal Mail would have been transformed immediately and the arguments, such as they were to sell off the Company, would have been shown to be even more wafer thin than they already were. At the risk of again labouring the point the arguments in favour of dealing with the pension issues were irrelevant if your objective was always to privatise, partially or fully.

In effect, after years of campaigning, the CWU was so close and yet so far away from a resolution. It is probably fair to say that by this time – late 2009 – most CWU members had given up expecting anything positive. Postal staff can't be expected to follow all the twists and turns of their trade Union's campaigns, but it really was a sad end that for most, passed without comment as they went about their daily work for Royal Mail.

As for the New Labour Government, they might have come in with a bang, but they went out with a whimper.

Chapter 6

Rearranging Deckchairs and Moving Goal Posts

Of course, it's not that in the end the Conservative/Liberal Democrat Coalition were to pass legislation to privatise the Royal Mail following the eclipse of New Labour, it is that they were able to do so because of the actions of the previous New Labour Government who had so assiduously paved the way by acting on the seemingly unthinkable.

The newly elected Coalition duly published a Bill in 2010 and the CWU and its members once again had to lift themselves up for a further battle. A national briefing of CWU Branches in London in 2010 was to hear an assessment from Dave Ward, Deputy General Secretary in which he said that the Union was battle hardened not battle weary. Delegates from across the country definitely knew what he meant, but some weren't sure if he hadn't got this phrase the wrong way round. Of course what they knew, but the public wouldn't know, was that following a national strike in 2009 (more on this later) the CWU had secured a further agreement to help transform the Royal Mail. Yet again, this clearly left the arguments not to privatise as strong as ever. Battle weary or not, it's not over till it's over, although it couldn't be denied that there was a feeling of inevitability about what might now happen and with it, the worries and fears that postal staff carried with them.

An Early Day Motion was tabled in opposition to the Coalition Government's intentions. If the words are in opposition, they did offer a pragmatic response which was more in keeping with the sentiment that the vast majority of the public would concur with:

EDM 738 14 September 2010. That this House opposes proposals put forward by the Government to privatise Royal Mail; notes that Royal Mail's profits rose by 26% to £404 million in July 2010; fully supports the modernisation programme agreed by management and Unions; further notes that these modernisation plans are fully funded and require no external financial investment from private companies; believes that any decision to remove Royal Mail from public ownership would be deeply unpopular with the public; fears that the Government's proposals will result in increased prices for customers; and calls on the Government to re-examine other ways to support the modernisation of Royal Mail and in doing so ensure that Royal Mail remains a wholly publicly owned organisation.

It is fair to say that no one in Government was listening; they never had done and never intended to.

The Postal Services Act 2011 was intended to pave the way to a full privatisation and amongst other things move responsibility for regulation from Postcomm, who would be disbanded, to Ofcom. Such was the Coalition Government's touching faith in the free market to deliver a vibrant privatised Company that the Act also provided provision for a "special administrative regime to protect the continuation of the universal postal service should the universal service provider be at risk of entering insolvency provision." [1]

Under strong lobbying from the CWU the Bill also ended up containing a promise not to cut the 6 day service down, at least for the life time of the current Parliament and to prevent an alternative provider of the USO entering the market for 10 years. A further concession to the CWU was that there would be a new 10 year inter-business agreement between Royal Mail and the Post Office (the Post Office was to remain in public hands, but relied heavily on traffic from Royal Mail to maintain income) and that there would be no further programme of Post Office closures (the previous New Labour Government had managed to close a good few thousand, presumably to demonstrate that they could take the "tough" decisions required. Also known as the politics of the stupid). Finally, Ofcom would have to allow Royal Mail a "reasonable commercial rate of return" in setting prices. [2]

If the significance of these achievements was not perhaps fully recognised by postal workers, neither was it understood by the public at large. No one told them of these CWU successes and if there is one common thread that runs through the communications departments of trade Unions it is that their press releases are usually ignored.

There was also provision for the workforce of Royal Mail to receive 10% of the sale value in shares when the Company was sold, although it wasn't clear at that time whether your average Postie could get the shares and flog them off to pay for a holiday in the sun.

Ofcom's first report "Securing the Postal Service" effectively, if diplomatically shot down their predecessor, Postcomm. Whatever Postcomm thought they had been doing, it clearly had not allowed Royal Mail the ability to secure a "reasonable commercial rate of return" in setting prices.

Ofcom said that a new approach to regulation was needed, as Royal Mail's financial position was now such that the USO was at risk with a loss in the core mails business, including packets of almost £1 billion over the last 4 years alone. A small subsequent profit in this core area of £23million on a turnover of £7.2billion did not mean anything other than this was a crisis situation. In other words, to quote from their report, "There is a widespread recognition that the approach to regulation adopted in the past, has failed in the face of the particular circumstances affecting this sector." It beggars belief that such a sentence could be possible after all this time.

Their report recommended no more regulation of access

prices and allowed prices to increase instead of being stuck in a straight jacket that had resulted in the Company leaking money to the competition and having to provide some services at a loss. The following quote is instructive in this regard from their report:

> Moreover, an RPI-X approach to constraining prices and incentivising efficiency carries with it a major issue of credibility, given Royal Mail's current financial circumstances and our primary duty in relation to the universal service. If, in the near term, Royal Mail found itself unable to become profitable under the terms of a price control, it would have to return to the regulator to request further price rises. In assessing this, although we would press Royal Mail to increase efficiency rather than raise prices, we would also need to carry out our functions in a way that we consider will secure the provision of a universal service. This means that there are serious weaknesses associated with a price control formula in providing credible incentives to Royal Mail to become efficient in the near term.
>
> 1.27 A price control also reduces the flexibility of Royal Mail to adapt to unexpected changes in the market and its operating environment ...[3]

It cannot be overstated how powerful their report was in effectively trashing the previous regulatory framework and the New Labour Government. It was now pretty much unarguable that Royal Mail's position was only due to the framework in which it had to operate. A framework that paid little heed to the declining mail volumes, pretty much ignored the pension liabilities and saw only the chance to bring Royal Mail to breaking point via price caps in the pursuit of forcing it to change and modernise.

Ofcom also noted – and these are truly massive figures and show the extent of the previous regulatory regime's failure – that the Universal Service costs now exceeded £6 billion and cash flows for the Company had been £3 billion less "than antici-pated" since 2006. Those two words, small though they are, covered up a multitude of sins. Postal staff had been working for an employer who was controlled by a regulator who based its decisions on whether it could second guess the postal market in one, two or four years time. Given that Ofcom noted a 25% drop in volumes since 2006 one could reasonably have expected Postcomm to have reacted. To the extent that they did or didn't, is best summed up by Ofcom who stated that "the universal service must be returned to a sustainable basis." Quite so.

The fact that so little media coverage was provided in response to Ofcom demonstrated, as nothing else could, the reality that it never was about allowing the public to understand what was going on, it was only about providing a false narrative about the state of Royal Mail and those working within it.

However, whilst the state of Royal Mail's finances could be fixed and the Coalition Government's Postal Act 2011 allowed the Government to take away Royal Mail's historic pension liabil-ities subject to European State Aid clearance, which was subse-quently granted, this could only mean one thing. It was the culmination of a long process to privatise the Company.

Fix the finances, change the regulation after all who on earth would take over Royal Mail with one hand tied behind their backs and of course get rid of the pension liability and you might well attract some investors to buy it. In other words, we'll do the right thing for the wrong reason. Remember, this isn't about providing a service to the public. If it was, then the research documents from the CWU and think tanks like Compass would have won the argument years ago.

The fact that some modernisation has taken place is inter-esting. Royal Mail secured a loan from the Government in 2005, thanks in part to persistent and incessant lobbying from the CWU and had been investing in new machinery to improve the acknowledged efficiency "gap" of some 40% between them and their competitors. The loan was for five years at commercial rates of interest and was some £1.2 billion. A further £1.8 billion since 2001 had been provided via cash previously made by Royal Mail and provided to them in the form of gilts. To the extent that such amounts sound huge, it is important to recognise the scale of the task that Royal Mail had of overcoming years and years of under investment.

If this investment had been given against the back drop of a fair regulatory climate, then perhaps more could have been done over a quicker timescale. Indeed, the impression could easily be gained that in fact some of this money simply disappeared into the black hole that was Royal Mail's cash deficit, which in 2008 was some £2.6 billion due to what Royal Mail said were flawed assumptions set by Postcomm based on mail volumes and projected savings.[4]

Of course not all the money disappeared and in fact the investment to date has, according to Royal Mail, been impressive. Their 2012 accounts mention that, "early in 2012 we completed our automation programme for letters." Moreover, they said that 75% of all letters were now automatically sequenced (i.e., to the correct address) as against only 8% in 2009/10 a year after the programme was originally deployed. The Company now has some 7500 new vans and some 22300 trolleys for postal staff to use when out delivering mail. In fact the news all seemed pretty good all told.

Donald Brydon, Chair of the Group was able to state, "Years of restrictive regulation, a declining traditional letters market and out of date technology had all taken their toll on the Business." Interestingly, nothing was said that led one to think that a sell off was now required. It seemed that the Government loan from 2005/06 had just about delivered after all, coupled with Ofcom reducing price controls to just 10% of the mail handled.[5]

Indeed, such a swift loosening of the regulatory straight jacket even led the Company to advise employees that a £157 million loss on down stream access in 2009/10 and a £105 million loss in 2010/11 was now a profit of £80 million. Whether a profit of this magnitude based on around 50% of volumes going by downstream access is sufficient was perhaps a sign that all was perhaps still not well. As far as can be made out a figure of 50% would suggest some 7.5 billion items being sent in a single year.[6]

From the perspective of those working in Royal Mail though, their experiences over the last few years have boiled down to a culture of cuts and aggravation. Cuts that have gone far deeper than the reduction in mail volumes; cuts that preceded the introduction of new investment (in other words, cutting staffing in advance and expecting people to do the work anyway); cuts that have been achieved in part through what is commonly referred to as bullying and harassment (which is also known under its more benign heading of "performance management") of their own employees in ways that have become truly staggering and cuts known to all as being a "slash and burn" approach.

Royal Mail were also to demonise their own workforce by chastising them as being more concerned with operating "Spanish practises" and telling them that they were not flexible. Such a culture of "blame" would inevitably mean employees did not feel valued. To the extent that Royal Mail never themselves acknowledged blame on their part, meant a destructive mind set that simply could not see what it was doing to its own workforce. This pattern of blame has been a recurring feature within the Company.

So, to get back to those Royal Mail surveys, does the instability caused by the regulatory framework put in place by Postcomm (now Ofcom, since 2012) provide a meaningful explanation for such discontent amongst its workforce over the last decade or so or does it go deeper than that. Is it really impossible to go through change and carry your workforce with you? Or is it, as now seems to be the case, we can all get along fine now the pain is over?

Sadly, the reality for Posties is that if they thought it was now ok to pop their heads above the parapet, they were to be asked to think again. If there is one thing that has characterised the last 13 years or so it is that change has become a permanent feature of Royal Mail. If it is possible to have continuous change for such a period of time and then find that in fact all that has happened is that the changes to date have led to the need to change again albeit in a different way which in turn has triggered other factors requiring more change, the recognition begins to dawn that one could be forgiven for thinking that those implementing the changes are either behind the curve and being driven by events or, alternatively, on a different page from the rest of us.

So, we find as stated above, a Royal Mail happy with the current situation. The comments above about making a profit on DSA mail was in a direct response to further concerns by the CWU that we were entering yet another period whereby the future of Royal Mail was now jeopardised by, you've guessed it – or perhaps you didn't, no matter – the lack of regulation. Yes, the lack of regulation was now a clear threat.

In December 2012 the following Early Day Motion was launched by sympathetic MPs working with the CWU. This is what it said:

That this House expresses its alarm that the regulator, OFCOM, has failed to register the dangers to Royal Mail's provision of the universal service obligation; in particular, OFCOM has allowed the introduction of delivery competition without putting into place any safeguards to ensure that Royal Mail can fund the universal service, in the event of the loss of a substantial amount of delivery work; further, notes that OFCOM has placed no obligation upon competitors to meet Royal Mail delivery standards, or even to publish details of delivery performance in a manner accessible to customers and the public; therefore, calls upon the regulator to reconsider its decision, and ensure that Royal Mail is not subjected to unfair competition in delivery provision.

To the uninitiated this means that the next big threat is no longer DSA whereby Royal Mail had been subsidising the competition, but what is referred to as "end to end" competition. In other words, an alternative postal carrier doing exactly what Royal Mail does but without the same obligations to ensure the service they provide is compliant with the USO.

Of course for Ofcom to allow Royal Mail the ability to operate to achieve a reasonable commercial rate of return did provide for postal workers the sense that some normality might be restored to their daily working lives, but no. Fault lines set by Postcomm, which were criticised by Ofcom, would now be replaced with direct competition without apparent safeguards. And let's be clear here. This doesn't mean that a competitor like TNT will deliver mail to everywhere 6 days a week. Quite the contrary in fact. Why? Because TNT couldn't possibly replicate what Royal Mail do. It is far better to "cherry pick" the type of markets to operate within, leaving Royal Mail to deal with the conse-quences.

As a quid pro quo Ofcom were allowing Royal Mail more freedom from price caps and DSA access arrangements. For the long suffering general public this freedom also meant that stamp prices would increase and of course a first class stamp now costs 60p. The regulator saw such a price as being within the threshold of people's willingness to pay and so was allowed. For many, such freedoms would do nothing more than a raise a few extra millions whilst at the same time, encouraging people in their droves to increase their use of email. So yet again, far from competition reducing prices the exact opposite happened.

In fact those consequences of end to end competition (i.e., by-passing Royal Mail completely) had been apparent since around April 2012 when Royal Mail had felt forced to issue a statement in response to a "pilot" by TNT of end to end postal services in London. The issue had been bubbling below the surface ever since, and the CWU, by raising this in Parliament and elsewhere, showed that they could see the dangers ahead.

The issue of TNT would subsequently be picked up by another Channel 4 Despatches programme. Undercover again, the reporter would see that even though cherry-picking was the name of the game by delivering mail in London, conditions were shoddy, wages appalling (why would they be anything else?) and employees were on zero hour contracts. So, a huge Company like TNT can choose to run its affairs in this way and no one bats an eye-lid. And Royal Mail have to compete with that. The under-cover journalist would note that on his zero hour contract he would be forced to "hustle for my next day's work on an almost daily basis.... I was advised by several colleagues that I should be ready and available for work whenever called upon if I hoped to get more regular shifts." As for the wage for central London, TNT apparently paid £7.01 per hour including London weighting. It was mentioned that TNT hoped to expand in the next five years and employ up to 20,000 workers, all on zero hours no doubt?[7]

The statement from Royal Mail said they supported "fair competition" which to them meant no cherry picking. They also noted that the costs of providing a universal service were £6.7 billion against the backdrop of increasing delivery points (i.e., addresses) and falling mail volumes in the order of 25% since 2006. The Company also added succinctly that, "(end to end) raises the prospect of competitors cherry-picking the profitable high population density routes around the country whilst also being allowed to deliver fewer than six days a week. This could potentially challenge the sustainability of the six day a week universal service which Royal Mail must deliver."[8]

In other words, "here we go again." Same argument, same issues and the same message to the workforce. How many more times...?

How many more times, indeed. This really was ground-hog day for real. In a letter to members in November 2012, the CWU General Secretary Billy Hayes and Deputy General Secretary Dave Ward, stated as much when they commenced a letter to members by saying, "You maybe thinking, is change worthwhile? The Union is asking all its members to engage in a fresh debate about what's currently happening, what the future holds and what our plans are to address your workplace issues, unfair competition and privatisation."

The letter went on to mention managers stuck in a "command and control" mindset with many of Royal Mail's workplaces no more than chaotic in operation and that "The Company must also acknowledge that they have been caught out by the growth in packets and are not taking proper account of this." And so the letter continues in a similar, but predictably depressing vein. A picture that the public were certainly not aware of and a picture the policy makers were turning a blind eye to.[9]

As if to emphasise yet again, the disconnect between workforce and Royal Mail, the Company's own Corporate Responsibility Report for 2010/11 stated that they had missed their targets for employees experiencing bullying and harassment, "largely due to dissatisfaction with the Transformation Change Programme." [10] Perhaps an exclamation mark should have been inserted at the end of that quote. This bizarre world of positives one minute and gloom the next really was the actual lived reality for postal workers and their families. It is a fair bet that nothing, absolutely nothing could surprise any postal worker anymore.

In fact, if it was thought that the new concern about TNT was the only issue and that a six day mail delivery service was still sacrosanct, then such people may have to think again. The European Postal Directive only dictates a five day service. We could, of course, end up with yet further service reductions for the public so as to reduce the burden on Royal Mail of running a six day operation. Well, let's rephrase that shall we? The "burden" caused by Ofcom allowing unfair competition.

In October 2012, Ofcom raised the spectre of a reduction to a five day delivery via a consultation with the public. In a press release on the 16 October 2012 Billy Hayes, CWU General Secretary stated, "The Union is concerned about how the Universal Service Obligation (the six days a week collection and delivery service on a one-price-goes-anywhere basis) will fare beyond this Parliament and argues that it is central to maintaining service standards for consumers.... We want to see innovation not cuts, in order to maintain and improve service standards."

The jury is still out despite a decision not to proceed with a reduction in early 2013.

If it had taken years for Postal staff to get their message across that regulation was unfair and was damaging the postal market, there was now the prospect of even worse to come. The following press release was issued which to all intents and purposes fired a warning shot across the bows of the Government that the CWU were not going away:

Embargo: 00:01 Tuesday 4th December 2012
CWU launches campaign to protect the post
The Communication Workers Union is today (Tuesday) launching a major campaign to highlight the threat to the UK's universal postal service and jobs within the industry.
Key messages:
- Unfair competition is threatening the universal service
- Ofcom must step in to address unfair competition
- Competitors should match Royal Mail pay, but be forced to pay Living Wage as minimum
- CWU will arrange boycott of competitors' mail if nothing is done

Billy Hayes, CWU general secretary, said: "Today we're launching a major initiative to protect postal services in the face of mounting threats to jobs and services.

"Under unfair competition we've seen prices rise, services diminish, closures and job losses. Competition and privatisation are old-fashioned theories which have had their day. What's important is decent services and jobs and that's what we're standing up for."

Concern for jobs and services

CWU is concerned that unfair competition is undermining the sustainability of the universal service (and) at the impact on jobs ... in particular the quality of pay and conditions for postal workers. Private postal Company mail makes up **45% of letter volumes** delivered by Royal Mail (i.e., DSA), a figure which has consistently grown under competition arrangements. New end-to-end competition is a worrying expansion further undermining the USO.

Dave Ward, CWU deputy general secretary, said: "What we're seeing is private companies being able to do what they want with little concern for how it affects postal-services.... For example, TNT is conducting end-to-end deliveries without having to meet any quality standards while paying people little more than minimum wage. That will lead to a race to the bottom on pay which will be bad news for the economy in general and postal workers in particular.

"It's not a coincidence that thousands of Royal Mail jobs have been lost and mail centres and delivery offices closed since the UK postal market was opened up to liberalisation ahead of the rest of Europe in 2006. If it's not addressed, the effects on postal services for everyone could be catastrophic. We can't have competition being driven by poverty pay and reduced service standards.

"We want a fair deal for all workers across the postal sector with decent pay and conditions, but current competition means cutting costs at the expense of decent jobs. TNT competes by paying poverty wages. When TNT boasts of creating 20,000 jobs over five years, this means 20,000 jobs below the living wage, not on full-time hours and reducing fairly paid jobs elsewhere in the industry. We need fair competition between postal operators not competition at the expense of living standards."

CWU is calling for the postal regulator Ofcom to step in and redress the balance of unfair competition to:

- Protect the universal service and end cherry-picking in delivery
- Maintain quality, affordable postal services
- Prevent competition on the basis of low wages, insecure jobs and poor conditions

CWU will hold a consultative ballot of its members in Royal Mail in the New Year with the intention of boycotting competitors' mail. This would mean that any mail sent via a Company other than Royal Mail would not be delivered. If no progress is made by the regulator then the boycott will be put in place.

Dave Ward continued: "We're not prepared to stand by and watch ... jobs ... ruined by unfair competition which could be avoided. Boycotting parts of the mail which are damaging services is a proportionate response to the threat posed by unfair competition."

The problem:

Competition in the postal market has been unfairly set up and mismanaged. Downstream Access (DSA) arrangements allow private companies to cherry pick profitable bulk mail contracts, taking vast revenue streams away from Royal Mail. They sort and transport mail to a local Royal Mail office where they pay a low access fee to get Royal Mail postmen and women to walk, drive and cycle up every street in the UK to deliver that mail, what's known as the 'final mile'. That's the expensive part. TNT has also been allowed to undertake end-to-end deliveries in some urban areas, further eroding Royal Mail's volumes and revenue. AT THE SAME TIME, Royal Mail is obliged to meet strict quality of service standards and deliver to every address in the UK – regardless of how remote or expensive it is. This is the Universal Service Obligation which means all people in the UK enjoy equal treatment and high standards of service regardless of whether they live in an urban or rural area. The USO is in effect subsidised by Royal Mail's profits in areas such as urban and bulk mail. There is only so much revenue and mail traffic in the system. If unfair competition is allowed to continue unabated, it could destroy the high service standards we enjoy, the USO could collapse and that would be a disaster for post services and all who rely on them; both the public and – crucially – small businesses. Private companies will not set up deliveries to all parts of the UK, only to densely populated urban areas where they can make a return. The profit for a few private companies would come at the expense of higher costs for all consumers, small businesses and services for rural communities.

The campaign was launched at The Future of UK Postal Services Conference, DoubleTree by Hilton Hotel – Tower of London, London...

Ends

The question on no one's mind at the end of 2012 was therefore whether the above press release, for the most part ignored by the mainstream media, would be shown to be an accurate predictor of the future.

For postal staff, the reality was that they weren't especially exercised by this possible catastrophe. In fact, who could blame them? Just how many times do you have to either be briefed by your manager or read about it all in your Unions' magazine? Get on with life and leave it to others to sort out. How many potential disasters have there been over the last decade for employees to deal with? The lyrics from those rock giants REM probably – at least up to the end of 2012 – summed up the general mood, "It's the end of the world as we know it and I feel fine…" and whilst we are on the subject of dodgy rock quotes to make a point, 'Another Brick in the Wall' by Pink Floyd may be more apt.

Another question therefore on no one's mind was just how many bricks would be required before the wall was complete and the end of a great public service was finally signalled once and for all?

For the poor long suffering and under-valued postal workers the CWU would feel compelled to approach them yet again, with the message that not only was the new Coalition Government racing ahead to try and privatise the Royal Mail but that this could mean the ultimate break up of the Company with discrete parts sold off, that new employment contracts could be intro-duced – inevitably to facilitate a cheaper workforce, that there could be the franchising of delivery rounds and that the pension scheme would face a fresh assault.

If this seems too much of a "big picture" perspective to the extent that some thought it wouldn't affect them, the CWU reminded their members about their own daily working lives. Specifically, "…the cycle of unrealistic local budget/performance demands and the chaotic managerial approach to lapsing and absorption." That such a picture was barely appreciated never mind understood by the proponents of the regulatory framework and Government, demonstrates how little the lives of those in the industry are thought of.[11]

Meanwhile, the Government would press ahead by engaging UBS, Goldman Sachs and Lazards to advise them on the privati-sation process and similarly, Royal Mail would engage Barclays Capital to advise them. It would be reported that "large buyout firms" were examining Royal Mail and there was renewed interest from CVC Capital Partners, a large private equity firm which controls Formula 1 motor racing. It seemed their interest was predicated on whether the subsequent sell off was a failure. To which presumably the response is, "thanks for the concern, much appreciated." The CWU would kick start a coalition of concerned groups under the banner of "Save Our Royal Mail."

The seemingly endless cycle would repeat itself again. A dispiriting ground hog day process, but one driven by ideological free marketers. A quote from a postal worker back in October 2010 that reached the press is very apt. "It's all jiggery-pokery, ducking and diving, like old barrow boys. Sure they're suited and booted barrow boys, but they're still just barrow boys."[12]

Chapter 7

You Own It Already, Don't Buy It!

It has always been the mantra of those opposed to state sell offs, to try and persuade people that in fact they already own the asset, so why would they allow it to be sold off, only to then think about buying back a little bit of it in the form of shares. Such logic failed to persuade chunks of the electorate during the mass sell offs of the 80s and 90s as the Conservative Governments of the day looked to engineer a popular capitalism, following on from their social experiment of selling off council houses. Of course this would not tell the whole story. You could buy shares only if you had the money to do so.

More to the point, if you are going to sell off the Royal Mail, how much is it worth? In March 2012, the Daily Telegraph, amongst others, quoted Government sources saying the valuation was around £4 billion.[1]

By mid 2013 that valuation would be down to around £2.5 billion.[2] Price the Company too high and the markets might not be too impressed as they wouldn't be able to make the sort of "killing" they would look to make as they bought at the sale price and sold again at a higher price. Price the Company too low and clearly the profit making might appear, shall we say, a little grubby. As for who decides on the price, well there is always well-paid advisors to hand. Goldman Sachs, UBS and Lazards amongst others would be in line for a pay out of around £30 million if all went well. No, flogging off a treasured asset is clearly a tricky business.[3]

As if to emphasise the trickiness point, the share owning democracy that was to have been the saviour of the working class, would now be the subject of caution. The Sunday Times would speculate that possibly only 25% of the shares would be available to the public with the rest going to the big institutional investors and hedge funds (in the end, the percentage was just 33%). Such speculation gained substance as the Minister responsible, Michael Fallon, said that overseas buyers had expressed "significant interest" and that CEO Moya Greene had commenced a global road show to promote the Company to buyers. The phrase used by Fallon was that Royal Mail had been "testing investor appetite." Could he have been subconsciously relating "appetite" to pigs feeding from the proverbial trough?[4]

Inevitably then, the "ducks" were beginning to be lined up. The regulatory framework, as we have seen, was more benign and the price of a stamp went up significantly. It seems unbelievable, but the increase between 2011 and 2012 was 30.4% for a first class stamp and 38.9% for second class[5] and buyers were being sourced and the pension liabilities had been taken over by the Government and as if by magic the subsequent profits made by Royal Mail Group for 2012/13 would turn out to be a record £403 million with an operating margin of some 4.4% on a turnover of £9.15 billion.[6]

Not only that but clearly (and how could it be otherwise?) someone had to be rewarded for such magnificent work. The Sunday Times and others would note that Moya Greene, CEO since July 2010, would receive a pay packet of around £1.5 million as the business had "been transformed under her stewardship."[7]

Posties would understandably wonder whether in fact her contribution was as monumental as was being claimed. In relation to the regulatory framework operated by Postcomm, Moya Greene would tell the Financial Times, "Nothing like this existed in the world and it had brought the universal service in Britain to its knees. There was no way for the Company to ever be successful if we couldn't sweep a lot of that away."[8] And in one fell swoop, a quote that says so much about how history can be re-written and credit claimed for changes that Posties and their Union had been arguing and campaigning about for years.

However, amidst all the salivating at the prospect of a privatisation, there was the looming and ever present matter of the CWU's opposition. Michael Fallen, the Business Minister would up the ante and be widely quoted as saying that if the Union continued to fight the privatisation he would sell the Company off to sovereign wealth funds or other foreign buyers. Fallon would also be quoted as saying that the privatisation was "not based on ideology" and was so the Company could borrow on the private money markets, for "every £1 it borrows (whilst in the public sector) is another £1 on the national debt." It would be deliberately ignored that in fact any money borrowed from the Government by Royal Mail was at commercial rates of interest. In other words not only was borrowing possible but the public actually made a profit from it as the terms to date "would almost make a New York hedge fund blanch."[9]

Also ignored, according to the General Secretary Billy Hayes, was the fact that a model for borrowing cheaply already existed in the form of Network Rail "who had borrowed billions on the private markets without affecting ... debt or depriving a hospital of an intensive care unit."[10] Keeping Royal Mail in the public sector and converting it into a not for profit enterprise, that "in line with practise elsewhere in the EU, such borrowing would not be counted on the public sector borrowing requirement."[11]

So, only the CWU stood between success and failure for the Coalition Government? Well, not quite. Public opinion, so often ignored was still there in the background with a YouGov opinion poll in July showing 67% opposing a sale and 79% reckoning that prices would go up. As for an improvement in the service just 13% thought things would get better. Proof if it were needed that years of privatisations in so many other areas of life had clearly not brought improvements that had been promised by previous Governments. By September, some 70% would oppose privatisation.[12]

Small businesses were also unhappy with the sell off

proposals. Hooper's report in 2008 had stated clearly that liberal-isation had not benefitted small businesses and now a survey of on-line companies showed that 87% used Royal Mail and that of those, some 80% said that they feared privatisation and 70% felt that it was a "stealth" privatisation and that a referendum ought to have been held to see what the public wanted.[13]

Another aspect of the debate that was genuinely unexpected for the Coalition Government was the intervention of the Bow Group. A very traditional and long standing Conservative think tank said that the sell off should be "postponed". They asked rhetorically whether the sale was "popular with the public ... is it the best deal for the country ... is it politically beneficial to our Party (and) has the case for privatisation been made?" They concluded that in all cases the answer was "no." In an echo of the mid 1990s when the Tory Party last tried to sell off the Royal Mail only to decide against thanks to the concerns of rural MPs, the Bow Group talked about the dangers of a sell off to rural commu-nities and were blunt in pointing to the roots of conservatism by saying that "we interfere with institutions that are sacrosanct to British life and the grassroots of the Conservative Party, without considered national debate, at our great peril." Hardly a ringing endorsement of state control but nevertheless the point they made, namely that the sale would lead to a "poisonous legacy for the Conservative Party" was a serious warning shot across the bows for Ministers.[14]

So, the CWU (and their campaign arm Save Our Royal Mail coalition, formed of voluntary organisations including the National Pensioners Convention), the public and Conservative political strategists were not so keen.[15] More tellingly for the Government, the hostility of postal workers was causing great concern. Investors quite rightly began to worry that industrial problems would mean that any investment could become a poisoned chalice.[16] This view was also put by none other than the CEO of Deutsche Post DHL, Frank Appel, whose industry was privatised whilst mail volumes were still buoyant, said, "I can't see how you can privatise the postal operator now. Why would you invest in a postal operator without a clear growth strategy? It is a huge challenge in my view because how do you explain that this is a good investment going forward?"[17]

Such a view was not universally held however and Martin Gilbert CEO of Aberdeen Asset Management reckoned that industrial unrest was just "Union noise."[18] Perhaps Mr Gilbert knew something no one else knew? Whether he did or not it would be Private Eye magazine who looked to try and predict where this sell off was actually going to end up :

As with other modern feats of financial engineering, this one will almost certainly come back to bite the tax payer. Like the privatised utilities and the private finance initiative, the Royal Mail will soon become highly leveraged, paying large amounts of interest, almost certainly offshore, to investors who make a killing, avoiding tax in the process and forcing up prices for the customer.[19]

Whilst the markets may have been speculating on likely outcomes, the CWU were marshalling its members and the public. We have noted that they had formed an umbrella campaign body, Save Our Royal Mail (similar campaigns had been used in the past) and in addition to this they began to organise members towards voting in a consultative ballot in order to gauge opinion on four crucial areas, which were put in the form of four questions during June 2013:

Do you oppose the privatisation of Royal Mail? 96% said yes. Do you support a boycott of competitors' mail? 92% said yes. Do you support the CWU pay claim? 99% agreed, and finally, do you support the policy of non co-operation? 92% said they did.

This last vote was to gain support to oppose cuts to staffing levels. It had been clear for some time that Royal Mail had been continuing to cut staffing at any available opportunity regardless of any national agreements in force or impact on the service. The turn-out for the ballot was a healthy 74%.[20]

The boycott issue potentially had the ability to cause massive contractual uncertainty for Royal Mail. If CWU postal workers refused to handle DSA mail the knock-on effect on the privatisation process could be terminal. Royal Mail would subsequently seek an injunction to prevent the CWU actioning the boycott aspect. Such a resort to law was always going to succeed, but the CWU view was that they had a mandate and they began to discuss with their legal advisors how the boycott might be put into effect following a legal industrial action ballot.

The success of the consultative ballot – and it should be seen as such especially given the huge pressures and uncertainties facing postal workers and their families – would be coupled with a very high profile campaign in which the Union would hire an open top bus to go around central London calling at Royal Mail HQ, Ofcom and the Business Department. Thousands of postcards would be distributed to CWU members and the public to send to their MPs and at Westminster a huge lobby of Parliament on 2 July 2013 attracted some 60 MPs.

A petition was also launched by a local Postie in Exeter, Darren Rowbotham. From small beginnings, around 160,000 signatures were quickly obtained and with Billy Hayes General Secretary and others he handed them into 10 Downing Street on 4 September.

The Labour Party at last began to get the message and their Shadow Business Minister Chuka Umunna stated that Labour was opposed to privatisation and that it "makes no sense to me at all to privatise the profit and nationalise the debt of Royal Mail." The reader will recall this same argument falling on deaf ears when Labour was in Government. No matter, the CWU needed all the friends it could get and would ensure the pressure was kept on Labour by submitting a motion to the Labour Party conference opposing privatisation and demanding that a future Labour Government renationalise the Company if it was sold off.

Billy Hayes the General Secretary of the CWU would wryly note that the Minister responsible for the sell-off, Michael Fallon was also Energy Minister and was paying very close attention to pay talks as well as spending his time "fracking (up) the country!"

Behind the scenes though serious discussions were beginning to be held between the CWU and Royal Mail. It cannot be overstated that a national strike could potentially mean a sell off would have to be postponed or even abandoned if investors took fright. What few had anticipated however was the pulling of yet another rabbit out of the hat. This time it was a return to the vexed issue of pensions. If the removal of pension liabilities had made the Company an attractive prospect, Royal Mail was perhaps about to over egg the pudding. They announced a consultation on ending the link with a postal workers final salary.

This caused understandable outrage given that it was only some 12 months previously that the historical liabilities had been removed and all was supposed to be well with the scheme. Some £2.2 billion in assets had been left with Royal Mail (and Post Office Limited, who were now a separate entity) and the scheme going forward was in surplus. What could possibly have happened in 12 months that Royal Mail was unaware of when the deal with the Government was done?

In short, a quid pro quo had effectively been negotiated between Royal Mail Group and the CWU for moving from a final salary scheme to a career average pension. The agreement reached was that service prior to April 2008 would remain linked to final salaries. This had been a hard fought concession from the Company following a national strike in 2007.

Did this mean that the £2.2 billion in assets that the Government ensured remained with Royal Mail Group was simply insufficient? No. The assets had been calculated on covering pension rises going forward based on the Retail Price Index + 1% for each year. Additionally, the Company had around £300 million extra per year in its coffers due to the Government decision taking over the liabilities.

Instead, Royal Mail were arguing that gilt yields had been falling since the last actuarial review and that this could not have been predicted at the time the Company and Government sought state aid approval from the EU for the liabilities to be shifted to the Government. Their concern was that yields had fallen due to quantitative easing by the Bank of England as part of the policy to stimulate the UK economy. In a leaflet to employees, Royal Mail would produce a simple graph which purported to show gilt yields going down since 2009 and Company contributions going up by £300 million as a consequence, from £400 million per year to £700 million in 2012. Royal Mail's accounts for 2012/13 in fact showed a pension contribution of £429 million.[21]

Amazingly, any postal worker making the connection would see that this graph was apparently showing a problem that was in full swing at the very point in 2012 when the Government took over the historic pension liabilities when everyone was told their pensions were now sorted out once and for all.[22]

In the words of the CWU to its members, "...what the Company (now) want to do is use £2.2 billion of further assets that were set aside to fund the final salary link to instead lower their own contribution and subsidise privatisation."[23]

Such an angry opinion was given more traction some weeks later when it was revealed that the "Royal Mail has set aside an extra £90 million for (their) Senior Executive Pension Plan." Despite a decision being made in 2008 to close this scheme to new entrants and from December 2012 to future accruals, decisions were being taken to make special one-off deficit correction payments until 2018. Whilst there may have been an element of legal obligation to do so, workers were left with was a sinking feeling that there was one rule for them and one rule for the bosses. In other words Royal Mail management would "look after their own."[24]

Of course if there was such a massive and looming problem that required an immediate £300 million per year, one could have expected that some comment would have been made in the report and accounts which preceded the announcement. Postal workers (at least the vast majority anyway) and the author are not pension experts, however in the report for 2011/12 the Chairman, Donald Brydon would state that the decision by the Government to take over the historic liabilities would "improve our future cash generation as we complete our modernisation programme, reducing costs and improving the efficiency of the network."

The accounts would also note that the Company's pension contributions were set at 17.1% in 2010 (the Royal Mail plan for senior executives was 35.9%) and that "this rate is not expected to change materially during 2012/13", perhaps because the pension scheme assets had increased each year since 2008 from £23.934 billion to £30.745 billion in 2012 prior to the Government taking over? In other words, a leaflet to employees telling them of the dire situation which had apparently prevailed since 2009 was to all intents and purposes not mentioned. The accounts for 2012/13 equally would not provide any sense of an ongoing disaster, although they did point out that proposals would be put to employees on changes to help secure the Pension Plan.[25]

This pension proposal however had two "strings" attached. Firstly, any offer on pay, terms and conditions was conditional on Posties accepting the worsening of their pensions. Secondly, if they did accept the worsening of their pensions, Royal Mail was only promising the Pension Scheme would definitely remain open until the next actuarial valuation in March 2018 due to caveats, notably that the Pension Plan remained above 100% funded, that any interim valuation did not mean a requirement to put in any more than £50 million per annum and that there should be "no changes in investment market conditions, new legislative and regulatory requirements and/or other factors outside the Company's control, causing a materially adverse impact on how the Plan must be recognised within the Company's financial statements, or on profitability and/or the Company's net assets."[26]

If this spelled uncertainty for postal staff it was, however, a message likely to go down well with potential investors. The CWU would inform Royal Mail that there would be no agreement whatsoever on such a pension proposal, never mind the fact that it was linked to pay.

In another ominous sign of things to come, Royal Mail also tabled a proposal to the effect that they would agree to keep existing terms and conditions for the workforce for a minimum (or should that be a maximum ?) of three years. On this point the CWU would have, if it had agreed to this, effectively given a green light to a worsening of terms and conditions after three years, including the real fear that the new owners would also start to dismantle and sell off parts of the Company. It was be noted by the Union that this three year term was effectively "not worth the paper it was written on" as it wasn't legally binding.[27]

All in all, this was an employer limbering up to make themselves as attractive as possible to outside investors by minimising their wage bill going forward. As for the pay offer, this was 8.6% over three years. [28]

Royal Mail would be quoted as saying that "this is a good deal – good for Royal Mail and good for our people." Subsequently they would look to revise their pay and terms package in the light of the rejection of it by the CWU, but the link with the pensions remained and the Union decided to ballot its members in September for strike action. In its determination to persuade the workforce to accept its offer, a lump sum of £300 payable in December (part of the offer) would be taken away from anyone going on strike to help their Union secure improvements. The threat centred message was not a surprise.

Dave Ward, Deputy General Secretary stated in a press release that, "…we do not take the decision to hold a strike ballot lightly. However, we will stop at nothing to ensure the future of our members' jobs and of the services they deliver, are protected." [29] As for the members themselves, free shares and the prospect of losing £300. Maybe a "no" vote was on the cards then?

This strike threat clearly had some impact. Having said their pension proposals were vital to their commercial viability, Royal Mail suddenly did an about turn. The Sunday Times would describe it as a "cave in" to save the privatisation by continuing to allow Posties to maintain the pre-2008 link with final salaries. For their part, the Company said it would absorb the cost of this reversal but wouldn't say how much it would be. Clearly not £300 million then?[30]

The real and substantial fears that thousands of postal workers had were based on huge chunks of evidence from across the world. A report by Union Network International in October 2012 looking at global trends showed that the liberalisation of postal services, including privatisations had delivered reductions in jobs, wages and conditions. In fact in a throwback to earlier comments by Royal Mail to its staff that they were being paid some 25% more than the private competition in the UK, it would be noted that this situation was actually prevailing in other countries to the same extent, but with the appalling prospect that some national postal carriers were paying less than the competition to survive.

Other evidence was showing that Unions elsewhere in the world were having to negotiate new contracts with lower wage levels which meant two tier workforces, in some cases the working week had been increased, there were huge increases in part time employment and, as we have seen in the UK, private carriers like TNT operating by using zero hours contract.

In Germany, for instance, privatisation had resulted in an exponential increase in what the report described as being "marginal contract" workers in precarious working conditions with poor wages: part time, agency and self employed workers driving vans as owner drivers with all the attendant risks involved.

In other words, as the CWU had said, this was a race to the bottom. UNI again: "competitors will compete on the basis of lower employment and labour conditions where they are not prohibited from doing so by minimum wages, sectoral wages, collective bargaining agreements or social regulations."[31]

Now it would be possible for postal workers to read that sentence and think that they would be protected from the harsh competition by Government, the regulator Ofcom or their Unions' negotiating prowess. In the real world, a privatised Royal Mail will be the play thing of commercial interests. It would be the "tail" of Royal Mail wagging the "dog" of the public interest. In other words if you want a postal service you'll have to do it "our way." The guarantees that Parliament put into the Postal Services Bill 2011 (for example a six day a week service) could soon end up disappearing as harsh commercial realities and falling mail volumes, not to mention dividends for shareholders, held sway.

As for Ofcom, it had announced in March 2013 that it would seek to intervene in the postal market if the "unfair" competition that it was allowing, came to adversely affect the USO. This though, was a different issue entirely to whether a privatised Royal Mail would start to demand a re-definition of the Universal Service Obligation on pain of disaster for the postal service if it didn't get its way. Ultimately, the problem with assurances, is that circumstances can get in the way.

The phrase "it's not over 'till it's over" was never more apt as the final battle – a culmination of failed attempts over some 20 years to privatise this great British public service – moved into a final phase. With the fear of the unknown round the corner what other alternative did the CWU and its long-suffering members have other than to ballot for a strike? Pay, pensions, job security and terms hanging by a thread.

As for the alternative, it can be seen from the foregoing that investment can be easily secured from within the public sector. The CWU view was that a pragmatic alternative was a "not for dividend Company" with profits reinvested back into the service and its workforce; that if capital was required it could be accessed on the commercial markets without this contributing to the national debt (e.g., like Network Rail); that there would be a charter set out in legislation that would confirm Royal Mail as the USO provider and set out ethical principles by which it would operate; that governance would be overhauled with Board representatives having social, commercial and ethical responsibilities and there would be fixed differentials between what workers received and what Directors and Executives got with single status benefits covering everyone in the organisation.[32]

This vision, eminently something that could be implemented, would receive no response from the Government to say it was in some way unrealistic. After 20 years of effort to sell off Royal Mail, it really was the same argument that was being trotted out. Ideology would trump pragmatism and a public service ethos.

And so it came to pass.

Despite the Labour Party Conference unanimously demanding a re-nationalisation, Labours' Chuka Umunna said it would be "completely irresponsible (and) like writing a blank cheque."[33] That is a hell of a green light to buy those shares, although you would need a minimum of £750 to do so. Disappointingly for the CWU and those 70% of the public who opposed the privatisation, it was not even as if Labour had finessed the message by sending a signal to the markets that it was not ruling it out and or that they might at some point look to retake a 51% stake.

By early October the press was full of speculation that investors would make a healthy profit with an apparent "frenzy" taking place with pre-trading "grey market" betting that shares would rise to around £4.00, some 70p more than the Government's own maximum.[34]

Perhaps this betting was understandable. The Sunday Times had noted that Royal Mail had built up around £2.8 billion worth of tax losses. This money could be off-set against future tax bills and may mean no taxes to pay for between 5 and 10 years.[35]

To this could be added the Company's intention to pay out a £200 million dividend in the first year. And to think, the Company's viability was at stake if they didn't get their pension changes in? Money too tight to mention?

Applications for shares closed at midnight on 9 October for the 60% of Royal Mail that was being sold off. If the Government had spent millions seeking the best advice possible on what valuation should be placed on the Company, such advice was out "by a mile."

The share price was fixed at the upper limit of Government expectations at 330p per share, valuing the Company at £3.3 billion. On the first day of trading the share price closed some 38% higher at 455p. Such was the greed displayed that within the first thirty seconds around 10 million shares had been traded with huge and instant profits being made of around £300 for each £750 worth of share allocations. Around 700,000 individuals had the chance to rake in such profits. To such people, lest we forget, is now entrusted the Universal Service Obligation.[36]

The Financial Times would note that this was a loss to the tax payer of around £750 million. They would also report that far from this being a surprise to the Government (none of us were born yesterday), the indications had been present for some months that the price was undervaluing Royal Mail. Was this rectified?

In the first sign that the private sector would start to call the shots, it emerged that the big institutional investors had threatened the Government with pulling out if the price was increased beyond 330p.[37] The mark-up of 38% on the first day of trading was the highest for any previous sell off, perhaps no surprise given that the shares allocated to the institutions were some 20 times over-subscribed, implying that around £28 billion was chasing some £1.4 billion worth of shares.[38]

The Coalition response was to blame some politicians and the City for raising expectations. Another way of looking at this would be to say such a view borders on a dereliction of responsibility given the millions handed over to their advisors, the decision to introduce a more benign regulatory framework and remove the pension liabilities, not to mention the £200 million dividend in year one and as we have seen, some £2.8 billion of historical losses to offset against future tax liabilities.

On the other hand, this was not about value for money, this was about getting the sell-off completed, period. This was aptly shown a week after the floatation when the Financial Times reported that in June the Company had a £5 billion valuation according to at least two of the investment banks bidding to get the contract to advise on the valuation. The FT quoted Government officials saying that the "higher bids came from banks that were ill informed about the Company..."[39] Of course they were ill informed. What on earth did the Government think, allowing such institutions to express opinions? No, they must have got it wrong, having come up with the valuation on the back of a cigarette packet apparently happy to risk their reputations with such sloppy work. If only that were the case. It soon emerged that Deutsche Bank valued the Company at £6.9 billion, Citi Bank £7.3 billion and JP Morgan between £7.75 and £9.95 billion.[40]

Of course another way of looking at this is to say that the

valuation may well be as stated, but if it is sold at that price, none of the investors would make any profit, so the decision made is to sell low, allow profits to be made to ensure a successful sell off and then assume that subsequent future share trading will ultimately reflect one of the original valuations. There never was going to be value for money for the taxpayer.

So we have a clear indication of the probable value, subsequently we have threats from institutional investors to pull out if the price goes above 330p and now it is clear the Company was worth much more anyway. As for the share price, that would shoot up to 500p after a week of trading leaving the taxpayer out of pocket by around £1.7 billion.

Vince Cable, Business Minister would say in response that, "Delivering value for money is about more than just the level of proceeds received on day one." What a squalid end for such a national treasure.[41]

Much was made by the Coalition that Posties were getting 10% of the shares, around £3,000 each, but if they wanted to make a quick buck this wasn't open to them, unlike the speculators who could immediately buy and sell. Posties have to wait 3 years and who knows what state the Company will be in by then? As Billy Hayes General Secretary of the CWU would say, "It was flourishing in the public sector (but has now) been thrown an uncertain future based on profit margins not services." And did every Postie take the offer? No. The Guardian reported that around 368 workers had refused their allocation and all power to them I say.

Whilst the point scoring over the sale price was plastered over the TV and press, it would be noted beforehand that if the Government were to hand the City a windfall that this would be a "disgrace" given that the country couldn't afford to keep some services to vulnerable people going, but by implication could forgo millions to ensure the sell-off wasn't a flop. The idea that the Government could intervene and alter the price or even temporarily pull the plug, whilst always possible was never going to happen in a month of Sundays. Such are the values of those presiding over the sale. For the vulnerable there are of course plenty of food banks scattered across the country these days.[42]

It may not have escaped the readers' notice that if the sale was so "successful", with money available for dividends, that there should self-evidently be plenty left over to deal with the unresolved issue of how much postal workers are to be paid and for how long their terms and conditions will be protected. After the flurry of the sell-off, the CWU announced the result of its strike ballot, including this time not only workers in Royal Mail, but also those working in Parcelforce who were similarly affected.

Against a barrage of propaganda from Royal Mail, free shares, threats to their jobs from the competition, not to mention the possible loss of the £300 lump sum, the result was yet another Yes vote for strike action. On a 63% turnout, 56339 (78%) voted yes and just 15624 (22%) said no to a strike.

A date of 4 November was set for a 24-hour strike and the Union immediately asked for talks in the meantime. Additionally, a further ballot was announced to boycott competitors' mail, ban overtime and "work to rule." In other words, do the job properly!

The CWU was blunt, but in the circumstances who could blame them. Were they asking for the earth? Dave Ward Deputy General Secretary said,

We want a ground breaking, long term, legally binding agreement that not only protects job security, pay and pensions, but will also determine the strategy, principles and values of how Royal Mail Group will operate as a private entity. This means ... no further break-up of the Company, no franchising of offices or delivery rounds, no introduction of a cheaper workforce on two-tier terms and conditions ... and no race to the bottom to replicate the employment practises and service standards of their competitors.[43]

At critical times in the past postal workers have peered over the cliff edge and wondered if they weren't facing Armageddon, but each time a deal was reached. As we shall see later on, their demands have never been outrageous or irresponsible. Rather, they have put the ball into Royal Mails' court with the message, "treat us as equals and properly value our contribution."

As we have seen, some 13 years previously the CWU saw the need to stake a claim to protect its members as Postcomm commenced its tenure. Now, in the hands of a newly privatised giant, that stake would have to be hammered deep into the ground again to prevent that race to the bottom, feared by so many in the industry.

It is my hope that the following chapters will help to look at some of the consequences that have emerged for postal staff and their Union as they have coped with the choices made by Government, Royal Mail and the regulatory authorities and in so doing provide a look at this large and newly privatised organisation from some angles not usually examined.

PART 2

Chapter 8

Reality Check

Royal Mail has always been Unionised. Let's get that out on the table before we go any further. To those who say, "there's your problem", ask yourself how many times has a local Union representative put their heart and soul into sorting out all manner of problems with the local manager.

In fact, given the huge number of managers in Royal Mail – some 14923 as of May 2012 – you'd think the place ran swimmingly. You'd think there was a great rapport with staff, you'd think that managers themselves had support and yes, you'd be deluded if you thought any of that represented the whole picture. Of course, to those who say the Company should be privatised, this only serves to make their case. Thousands of managers and still there are problems. In case anyone is wondering the ratio of managers to staff is around one manager for every 10 workers.

Would these workplace problems not exist then if there was no Union? Whether there is an independent trade Union like the CWU or an in-house association, the reality is that input from those who do the work is invaluable.

Today, Union density is around 86% on average for the CWU and most see the Union as being a positive influence. No one really knows what is round the corner and so if nothing else, membership of the CWU is protection from the perils of being "stitched up", bullied and the only way a pay rise can be obtained.

Of course, the idea that a postal worker could be stitched up or bullied, is not something people think about. The prevailing discourse whenever the Company hits the headlines, is to read about a militant Union with feather bedded pensions in common with every other public sector worker who ever walked the earth. It never ceases to amaze me that at Christmas time, MPs from all Parties are out and about visiting local delivery offices and praising their local Posties, but can then take part enthusiastically having a pop at these very same people. "They need to shape up and modernise and get rid of their out dated working practises" etc.

And yet, the reality is that whilst there is a Union, people will join it and they will look to it to sort out problems for them. They will elect their workmates to represent them and these people will then be deluged with problems and issues, the like of which makes you wonder why they do it at all.

But of course, this "wonder" shouldn't be a surprise. In all walks of life, people help each other and want to make a difference. And we shouldn't forget that the time these people put in means juggling around their own duties as postal workers with dealing with members approaching them with problems, going into the office to see the boss and representing people on anything from a grievance, to conduct, to sickness.

The role can be thankless as they are caught between their members – their own workmates and friends – and the demands of the local manager.

This all means that the role of the CWU is embedded into each and every workplace in Royal Mail and if the discussion isn't about Fred's grievance, then what else is there to talk about? The mail has to be sorted, prepped and delivered every day, so can we all please get on with it? One of the most colourful of Chairmen of recent times was Allan Leighton who said we shouldn't get bogged down in the "treacle". And what exactly is this treacle analogy about? How's this for starters:

How many staff are needed in a workplace? How long have they got to sort the mail? How much mail is there on any one day? How many addresses will actually get mail today if there are say 700 addresses on one delivery – shall we say 90%? Shall we argue over whether it is 80% or 90% on average? If it is 80%, then how long shall we give the postal worker to complete their job? How shall we establish the percentage? How long does it take to deliver to a row of terrace houses or a street filled with long gardens? How fast should someone be expected to walk to get the delivery completed? Shall we allow extra for a route that is hilly and if so, how much time? If the route is hilly can the trolley be pushed safely up the incline? How much incline is too steep? How long shall we allow to deliver an item that has to be signed for? How many of these items does an average day bring? What if there is a large number of such items, can they be delivered or can they finish on time and go home as they didn't want the overtime? What shall we do if the mail is delivered to the Delivery Office late, will Royal Mail pay overtime? Will people be told to deliver past their normal hours for nothing because a Tuesday is a traditionally "light" day for mail and so everyone should have finished within their time? What if you can't get the work done in your normal hours? What if your manager says you can deliver it because the person doing that round managed it last week? Can you use your car to deliver mail? What happens if you are told "yes" and then the mail is stolen – will you still face a possible dismissal?

If we have answered and resolved all these questions, is the result that the office budget is met or not? If not what will happen? Can we fit the life of a Postie into a budget? Can we do this by tweaking the figures so it looks as if they can now complete their delivery? More to the point are we really going to share this with the local Union? You're the boss? Would you?

If we can just sort out those problems then and follow all the collective agreements which the CWU and Royal Mail have signed and if we can do this and deal with the unfair regulatory playing field, well it's just like a walk in the park.

What the public and Governments of whatever political hue do not see is that answering the above questions means having a dialogue with the CWU. How on earth can anyone arbitrarily decide how long a delivery will take? How can you guess how long it will take to sort that day's mail? Whatever you end up with will inevitably affect the bottom line. Can you be expected to sort 10 items a minute for the duration? Is that fair? So if there are different volumes of mail each day, how can you figure out how long it will take to complete the days' work? Summer is traditionally quieter and so maybe we don't need as many people, we can share out deliveries between those who are left (known as lapsing) and they'll still be able to finish on time, won't they?

This saves the Company a fortune, but who agreed the number of people that were suddenly not required? Perhaps we can establish an average over the year and we'll call that average a "model week"? Anything above the model week will require extra. That seems sensible, although who decides at the time the beginning of the week arrives, whether it will be in excess of the model week or not? Ok, we'll look at an average based on the previous year then. Hang on though, if we do that what if the mail is dropping from one year to the next? How much has it dropped in different parts of the UK? If the manager and the local representative look at the figures together will that enable peace in our time? Does it even make any difference if the manager above them says the office is over budget?

Now I am not saying that every day a local representative deals with all of the above. What I am saying is that he or she arrives at work not knowing what they can expect.

How many times have I heard it said that we – the Union – want to "work with Royal Mail". Hundreds of times. How many times has the phrase been used after an agreement has been reached through national negotiations, that "we will be walking down the leafy lane together." That phrase has now become a bit of a joke, nevertheless both sides would apparently set out with the best of intentions before it all predictably fell apart following the actions of a rouge manager in one part of the country who, it turns out was given the green light to do so by someone else, who in turn was either pursuing their own deniable agenda, or who themselves had a more senior manager feeling their collar.

Is it really like this? Is the CWU lily white once an agreement has been struck nationally? Come on, let's all get in the real world. None of us were born yesterday, were we? Well, yes actually maybe some of us were, because local representatives are on the phone to their Area Representatives to say that the manager "isn't following the agreement." And how many times does that happen across the UK? Thousands of times, that's how many.

The role of the CWU is to protect its members through collective agreements which regulate the way in which managers can manage the organisation and yes that means agreements to cover the questions posed above.

Inevitably, this is not going to go down well with some. And to those who believe this is why Royal Mail is as it is, understand this: An agreement is struck nationally with very senior managers. It's their Company and they signed the agreements. If those agreements are honoured, then what exactly is the problem? Will the Company be brought to its knees? Hardly.

So there is a long and painful history of national agreements being ignored or broken by Royal Mail. It is all the more sad that the consequence is invariably conflict, some of which ends up as strike action. If this is a predictable consequence, which it quite often is, why not just honour the agreements reached?

The culture that has developed then is one of mistrust from the Union as Royal Mail knows that they can sometimes get away with not following agreements and so they don't. For a manager, the ability to ignore an agreement can mean the budget is met and a bonus paid.

The logic of course is invariably logical – why follow something that constrains you in some way, when you can ignore it and hope to get away with it. They know that and so do the workforce. What a way to run a much loved institution. Lord Sawyer who carried out an in depth review of industrial relations in 2001 and 2003, said during the 2009 national strike that little had changed. "....the issue is about trust. These people don't trust each other and until that is addressed ... we will continue to see ... unsatisfactory industrial relations."[1] The point being for those in the industry, is that any Union representative who actually trusted management implicitly would in that common parlance, be "seen off" or "taken for a ride."

A culture that is so corrosive that it leads to strikes and still it never changes. A question rarely put would be to ask whether in fact the agreements reached are fit for purpose given the regulatory framework which Royal Mail has to operate within. If there were no budget constraints would a local manager have any incentive to ignore agreements? Would they be receiving calls from their boss to stamp down on overtime or lapse more hours or not fill vacancies?

Let's put it just one more way shall we, "if I follow agreements will my budget be adjusted upwards accordingly?" If that's a naïve question then revisit the scenarios above? In fact, think for a moment what would happen if there were no agreements to protect the workforce and if you are thinking that budgets are set in order to ensure that national agreements are deliverable, you would be completely wrong.

So we end up with that historical clash between workers and bosses. The Union wants people treated fairly and the employer wants more from everyone. Superimpose the lack of investment, low stamp prices, unfair regulation and Government meddling and you can see how there is mutual incompatibility at the heart of the industry.

Of course many will by now perhaps be thinking a "plague on all your houses" is valid, but bear in mind the following. For any official strike action to happen, there has to be a trade dispute. No trade dispute is ever going to exist in relation to national collective agreements unless the employer has broken them. If a strike is to happen and there is no trade dispute, then it's just not going to happen. The courts will intervene if asked to do so by the employer.

There are other disputes which revolve around pay or jobs, but any examination of such disputes cannot escape the fact that some are the result of broken agreements. The last major dispute in 2009 only came to a close thanks to the involvement of an independent facilitator and yet the resultant agreement, Business Transformation 2010 and Beyond, has been the subject of disagreements ever since with unagreed management documents appearing which has led to conflict.

The reality of "walking down the leafy lane together" when unagreed documents are in use, which break agreements just signed, is something that Posties are used to as a matter of course. The question why would Royal Mail feel the need to keep doing this, is perhaps something best put to them, suffice to say that any cursory look at national CWU Letters to Branches (commonly referred to as LTBs) is littered with advice to representatives on how to deal with such actions.

This Business Transformation 2010 and Beyond agreement even had the phrase, "It is essential that everyone sets aside any negative experiences of the past and looks forward to building effective relationships based on positive expectations of the future. Central to this is a joint commitment to create a culture where we identify common objectives, align interests and always seek mutually acceptable solutions to the challenges we face."

Up to then, that was apparently not the culture of the Company. I say apparently, because such phrases had been used in previous agreements, clearly to no avail. Or perhaps, put another way, if such phrases can be used and signed up to – and let's remember these words would be discussed and negotiated, they weren't a mistake or a typo for goodness sake – how can disputes keep flaring up?

In fact many managers would say, hang on, I'm working with local Union very well and we get things done, so don't knock us. Maybe it's just the "rough and tumble" of an industry that is, let's face it, not for everyone. No one understands us, we are always arguing, so just leave us alone and we'll be right as rain tomorrow.

A quote from the dim and distant past are apt here:

> We cannot persuade ourselves that things are well managed when a whole establishment is in that state of chronic disaffection which has for some time been characteristic of St Martin's le Grand. It is not merely one man or one set of men, it is the entire body which is discontented and has been discontented for a long while past. Despite the risk of dismissal, the Post Office servants are perpetually agitating, remonstrating and memorialising their superiors. As soon as one disturbance has subsided another begins. The men have no confidence in their masters and no satisfaction with their work.[2]

Quoting from the past is fine as far as it goes, but unless there has been no attempt to deal with discontent of whatever sort over the years, and believe me there has, this would be fine as an historical footnote. But what of the views being expressed by their own workforce now, which if ignored would surely damage Royal Mail. It's alright trying to be philosophical about such a large organisation employing some 130,000+ people but the harsh reality, however, is that one is drawn inevitably to the conclusion that in fact the Company could listen to its workforce if it really wanted to do so. No one is stopping it, but clearly something is.

Of course the idea that a happy workforce needs to be achieved is one which litters any management guru book worth its name, but a glaring anomaly is apparent with respect to Royal

Mail. They figured out ages ago that a happy workforce is not actually required to get the job done. No one needs a degree to work for them and that age old employer response, "if you don't like it there's the door" is one that many postal staff will have heard either directly to them or within earshot. For those on the receiving end working their proverbial butt off, what message does that send?

A Delivery Office where people feel happy and valued is a million miles away from another one just up the road where the atmosphere is awful and people can't wait for the manager to go on annual leave and yes, these managers will have had their staff comment about them over the years and nothing has been done in response. How on earth can that be the case?

There are pages and pages that have been written about strikes in Royal Mail with a good deal of it centred around who started it and who is to blame. The idea that postal workers are induced to walk out for no reason is ridiculous. In the end the role of the Union is to reach agreement on the way in which its members are managed and paid. Posties are not about to go on strike and lose pay for a cause they have little interest in.

It was the case that for a few years between the mid 1990s to around 2002, that there were many local official and unofficial strikes. Walk outs over the way things were being run. A culture that eventually led to the involvement of Lord Sawyer, a former Union General Secretary, who was asked to carry out a review into industrial relations.

His task was not an easy one. Indeed, it was openly stated by CWU representatives, never mind Posties, that if management wanted a strike they could easily cause it. If that sounds a little bit hard to accept, it was nevertheless the case. Indeed, I recall debate at the CWU's Annual Conference whereby it was discussed how we could respond to management's ability to force change by causing strikes and then being content for those same strikes to continue. Those with a reasonable memory will recall how easy it was to have literally thousands on unofficial strike by the use of suspensions whereby a local dispute had a picket line and a worker from another area was bringing mail in. They didn't cross the picket line and instead returned to their depot upon which they were suspended for not carrying out their task. Having been suspended, all their colleagues would see the seriousness of the situation and would walk out in support. Of course being suspended immediately meant disciplinary action and possible dismissal. If no one walks out you are on your own and your chances are slim. In this way, disputes could spread rapidly across the system. Sometimes people would be deliberately sent to a strike bound office; sometimes mail from a strike bound area would be deliberately sent to somewhere else and those people asked to handle the mail and if they didn't, well they'd be suspended as well.

Why on earth would Royal Mail do that? Hence the concern in the Union that people were becoming embroiled in disputes for little reason and losing money as a consequence.

Now let's put some perspective into this debate. It was a battle in many workplaces in the mid to late 1990s up to 2001 and the Union was quite capable of organising itself in ways which led to disputes, mostly unofficial but and this is a large "but", it would be in response to an action by the Company. If the workforce do not challenge an issue they believe there is no agreement for, then that change becomes the norm. A typical example from May 2001 is indicative. Around 50,000 postal workers were on unofficial strike following a local dispute in Watford over the imposition of unagreed changes. By moving mail around the system in the way described above, thousands ended up on strike – London, Cardiff, Wales, Manchester, Preston, Teeside, Maidstone, Stockport, Cheshire and Liverpool.

It is almost irrelevant what the issue was about. There were agreed dispute resolution processes which could have been utilised by Royal Mail. The response to divert mail around their system was their initial thought. Containing the dispute, getting people back to work and using resolution procedures was also a choice that could have been made.

Postal workers were quoted at the time saying they felt sad at having to take action. One was more blunt, "We lose out and that is a concern, but you have to say you won't be pushed around. The way we have to work inside there is ridiculous. The changes they have made are no better than how things were before. They said we would go forwards but, actually, we have gone backwards. It's a bit like a Dickensian workhouse." Another said, "This is the straw that broke the camel's back.... How many times are you going to get kicked by them."[3]

Unless there is a critical analysis of why people walk out of a workplace, all we are left with is derogatory comment about the average stereotypical British Leyland worker from the 1970s being the same as a postal worker today. To put all this in perspective in 2001 there were around 355 unofficial strikes in Royal Mail. Not good by anyone's standards.[4]

So, to return to that question, why would Royal Mail engineer strikes? Without a kiss and tell from a senior manager we are stuck with speculation. Nevertheless, some of the reality lies in the need for change and the requirement to negotiate that change. If an employer in a Unionised environment does not see the need for negotiated change, then conflict will surely follow as night follows day.

Back in 2002 a former Consignia Executive was quoted as saying that "there are layers and layers of management. The bureaucracy is so entrenched that even if you come up with good intentions, you get nowhere." At the same time Lord Sawyer, whilst carrying out his review, stated that the "Post Office has a justified reputation among its staff for embarking on initiatives and then not seeing them through ... managers direct the work but they do not manage ... when asked to carry out tasks which involve leadership and communications skills they are often out of their depth." Sawyer also noted that in some workplaces he had seen posters saying to the workforce, "you are the weakest link."

If anyone is thinking that those postal workers described above didn't have to walk out and management must have been at their wits end, think again. Does the Postie have to be sent to a strike bound depot or would it be less provocative if a manager drove a van there instead? As for handling the mail, perhaps the mail from the workplace in dispute could be put to the back and sorted last or not moved at all? Indeed, the public would be amazed to know that diverted mail is supposed to be subject to negotiation as to how it should be dealt with.

The answer to both these questions raised in the last paragraph is of course, "Yes". More pertinently, if someone did return having respected a picket line, did they need to be suspended? Of course not. The choice was Royal Mail's to take. Contain the strike and negotiate an end to it as quickly as possible or allow it to escalate. The message so often ingrained into both the management and the Union was, "bring it on". Of course it was. This was – and still is – about how the Company should be run: Royal Mail's way, or jointly?

A local Scottish Branch Secretary in the CWU at the time, Tam McEwan, quoted during a local strike, stated, "...the middle managers you can sometimes talk to, but further up they are absolutely Victorian. They have no idea how to compete in a competitive market and it's the ordinary postmen who bear the brunt of their incompetence."[5]

As for the poor bloody infantry, the same article described a Glasgow Postie bent sideways by the weight of his mail bag as he struggled up a hill and another is quoted as saying, "they parachute these young guys in to ride roughshod over our working conditions. That's why we've had these strikes."

Now, there are numerous quotes from any number of press cuttings that could be used for and against anything you hear about in Royal Mail but against this backdrop it is worth recalling that in an interview in January 2002, the new Chairman Allan Leighton was able to state that industrial relations were improving and he praised the workforce as "one of the most loyal workforces you will ever find."[7]

That this interview from Allan Leighton came just a month or so after an article talking of the "farce" of the "slow motion" post is interesting. This article in The Sunday Times perhaps set the tone for the subsequent years of inaccurate narrative about who was to blame for Royal Mail's predicament. The article stated that they (i.e., the reporter) could "comfortably sort more than 1,000 letters per hour" and that "sorting offices are virtual closed shops and full time postal workers automatically have an annual Union fee deducted from their pay packets." There's more, "Postmen in Hampshire threatened to strike last month after being told to tuck their shirts in" and that "within hours of the Company announcing job losses last week the CWU had threatened to call a strike." I could go on, but the point is made, all Posties are just bolshie, aren't they?[8]

In relation to sorting speeds, I'd be amazed if someone was able to sort to a delivery frame at that rate of knots day in and day out – no doubt some such people exist. Perhaps I tell a lie. Perhaps in fact you can. You go "flat out" to prove a point for your article.

As for Union subs being deducted annually, wrong again. Subscriptions come out weekly. The CWU have to pay Royal Mail for the privilege under a process colloquially known as "check off." As for the job losses, the announcement was effectively withdrawn and from a figure of 30,000 job losses we ended up with an article in the same Sunday Times stating that the losses were projected as being "14,000 postmen and 8,000 managers."[9]

If you are a postal worker reading that and worse, it might not make you inclined to feel great about things. Such negative reporting has continued to a greater or lesser extent ever since. That it was done in the early 2000s after 20 years of profits demonstrates as nothing else can, why the press really don't want the truth to get in the way of a good story. More "heat than light", shall we say.

Of course most strikes can be resolved and an agreement is reached. The sad fact is that a strike takes place before a resolution is possible. Is there a way round this? Can both sides fashion agreements that will ensure good dialogue and shared information to get the best out of people?

To help with this we will look at extracts from some negotiated national agreements over the last few years because the general themes are extremely important in getting a picture of this great organisation and how it goes about its business. It is very important to note, such agreements cover the whole of Royal Mail, not just those delivering the mail. Of necessity then, this is about looking at the impact on delivery employees.

Importantly, it is also necessary to remember the backdrop, namely the approach taken by Postcomm, which progressively weakened Royal Mail and meant that agreements were having to be fought over against the backdrop of the regulatory framework, including price caps.

Chapter 9

Actions Speak Louder than Words: The Beginnings of Change From 2000

The Way Forward Agreement and the beginnings of change from 2000

The Way Forward agreement covered everything from pay to the way people work, to the way an employee selects his or her annual leave. It was hugely controversial within the CWU and only narrowly passed on a ballot of individual members. Here is not the place to argue who thought what at the time if only because it is outside the scope of this book, suffice to say most would say that it has stood the test of time in that it is still used today by both the Company and the workforce and of course it did deliver a shorter working week, a pay rise and other improvements. In other words a theme that the industry would grapple with and return to again and again, known simply as, "pay for change."

This agreement did herald, however, the thinking that change was needed for Royal Mail to better understand itself – better forecasting and standardisation of processes, for employees to accept changes and as a quid pro quo, there would be a new single grade set at £242.76 per week and a shorter working week as well as what ought to have been a new beginning in valuing their contribution and developing them and ensuring they were appropriately trained.

There was a new relationship with the CWU in that not every minor change had to be negotiated in a workplace and instead it was agreed what would be subject to merely consultation. Up until that time, a postal worker had a duty sheet, known as a P318. A set of tasks for each day with timings against them. You knew what to do and so did the manager. If it was on your 318, fine. If not, no can do. A working class version if you like of those solicitors and others who charge phenomenal fees by invoicing per minute. The 318 meant that your Union had negotiated what was judged as being a fair and reasonable. Anymore and the employer was getting more than they should and would need to pay for it. This system let's not forget had delivered 20 years of constant profits.

For your average Postie this daily job description meant you knew when you started, how long you had to prepare your mail for delivery, when you could have a meal break, deliver the mail and return afterwards. Was this really so bad? What would subsequently follow would be the virtual elimination of such protections and instead postal workers would know exactly what it meant to "work as directed."

There was also a far more controversial aspect for some postal workers contained within it, namely the requirement to reduce to huge amounts of overtime being claimed in mail processing centres. 80 hour weeks were not uncommon. A European Working Time Directive was coming in, so there was a need to reduce overtime, try and protect earnings and compensate for this by increasing the basic wage to £300 per week, known in CWU circles as the "flight path."

The following extracts are useful, if sparse – the Way Forward agreement runs to some 47 pages of detailed text. Again, ask yourselves if the following quotes actually came to fruition in the subsequent years. Ask yourself if the daily experience of a postal worker ought to be enhanced by these quotes:

"All employees and managers must work to a clear set of principles and standards, founded on a willingness to adapt to change through trust and respect, using agreed procedures in an open and courteous way."

"Resourcing Good Practise: Projected workload, based on accurate daily/weekly forecast traffic to shift and work area, together with historic data, will be used to establish realistic resourcing requirements for at least three weeks in advance. This information will be available on an open book basis to the CWU."

In other words staff could know in advance what they would be doing. The fact that pretty much any postal worker delivering mail will tell you that this is something Royal Mail have proved incapable of ever since, may come as a surprise.

"Both Royal Mail and the CWU recognise the importance of identifying and fulfilling training and development needs of individual front-line employees and widening horizons for employees in a whole range of new areas."

So no postal worker should go out on a delivery without knowing the delivery round beforehand? Regrettably, I think we all probably know the answer to that and to this day the Company has yet to make good on this promise.

"It is founded on the basis that change is inevitable and for this to be successfully achieved there needs to be a new approach which reflects the joint commitment of Royal Mail and CWU at all levels to making these agreements work."

We "will face new challenges in the future and must respond collectively and positively to them. If we continue in the positive direction we have adopted, we will build on our excellent record on secure employment and create an environment for new job opportunities in the future."

In deploying this agreement, it was specifically agreed that there would be, "open, honest and early communication."

Within a few months of this agreement, we had the very public announcement of 30,000 job losses. An announcement made without prior consultation with the workforce.

"If circumstances change beyond the control of the Business that require this undertaking to be reviewed it will be done with full strategic involvement of the CWU nationally."

If such laudable commitments had been honoured then the colourful history of industrial relations over the subsequent years would have ended up as a drab, grey uneventful time.

As we can see by the date of this agreement, it preceded the perfect storm referred to previously. That storm was coming quickly and took the workforce into a world where the only trade off was that there would be fewer people in the industry, but that they would (hopefully) be on better pay with a shorter working week and job security. If that seems a fair trade off, I think it needs to be explained that this outcome, such as it is, would not have happened without a Union.

The Way Forward agreement was followed by the disastrous destabilising announcement of 30,000 job losses and the withdrawal from job security agreements by Consignia and then at pretty much the same time, by a pay dispute in 2002. In effect, it was, as all subsequent disputes were to be about, a trade off – pay for change. As far as the CWU was concerned, that trade off from the Way Forward agreement was not being adhered to.

If a worker is more productive, should they get a share of that increased efficiency in their pay packet? How shall we agree how to bring in those changes? How shall we deal with pay and bonus processes already in place for savings already made? Can this lead to better job security for postal staff? This is a part of the "treacle" Allan Leighton referred to on his arrival and he would soon see that regardless of the regulatory environment building up around him, the take home pay of his employees simply had to be dealt with.

The CWU had a policy at that time, referred to as a "flight path", to secure postal staff weekly pay of £300 gross by October 2003, as basic pay was only around half the UK average. In return, change could be made, but how much change and how much sacrifice along the way? If you were a postal worker doing 80 hours a week who cares if your basic pay is low? For the predominantly delivery postal staff who did not have access to such overtime levels, the low basic pay was a big issue. Any takers for trying to square the circle?

There was much bemusement as well for employees in that

during 2002 in the course of protracted pay talks, Consignia had been investing overseas, although no one knew where exactly. A national Q&A by the Company to reassure their staff during the pay talks, posed the following questions amongst others, "Why is the business investing in so many foreign companies?" and, "How are we repaying the loans to finance the overseas acquisitions?" The answers they gave were that foreign acquisitions were "funded from borrowing against the Company's reserves" and that these purchases had little or no influence on the UK operations. Interestingly, the Business was also advising staff that they were losing £1.5 million a day and "we had no spare cash for your pay rise, so in order to fund one we tied it to improvements in deliveries and mail centres."[1] Quite so.

The same Q&A also had to explain why managers had been given a bigger pay rise than the Posties had been offered.

So, if savings were made, who would get what share? A productivity scheme was in operation but which paid out very little. Would a new scheme help towards the £300 aspiration? For those unsure of what exactly productivity bonus really means, it is an area that is now almost ended in most of UK industry. It was premised on the idea that so many workers were employed to carry out a certain amount of work and if the employer wanted less people to carry out the same work, well, they would be working harder and so deserved a reward for their additional efforts. Similarly if the changes came about through automation, then the Company could dispense with some workers and so make more profit. This additional profit should rightfully be shared amongst those left. In this way, a trade Union is able to argue and bargain for the value of its members' labour to be increased.

To the extent that Royal Mail bought into this scenario is set against the reality that there was a trade Union they could not ignore. If it were possible, they would clearly then, as they do now, pay the minimum amount they can get away with. In other words, how low does the wage have to be for potential workers not to want to work for them? This point would be fought over later as the effects of Postcomm began to bite.

The reality was that the pent up feeling amongst the workforce meant something had to give, as it was universally acknowledged that morale amongst the workforce was very low. The CWU's own calculations showed that to get to £300 per week – a rise of some 18% – could be broken down approximately so that 7% would be from pay rises and 11% from consolidating bonus into basic pay, achieved through automation and the move to one delivery a day.[2]

With the sword of Damocles hanging over their head (i.e., the job losses and Postcomm), these types of debate were difficult for the CWU and its members to say the least and would become more difficult. That said, the CWU were very keen to engage the Company. A ground breaking deal known as Managing the Surplus Framework was agreed in March 2002 which was a job security agreement which also protected allowances and shift payments for periods of time, when changes were implemented. In other words, structural blockages like people in receipt of a night shift allowance, which was about to disappear for instance, would at least find some protection for their pay packet. It helped to smooth the way for enabling change.

A two year agreement on pay and change was reached in 2002 as were moves towards changing the face of deliveries through a series of trials and working groups to make sure both the Company and the Union got it right. Such was the good work being done that the Federation of Small Business said it "welcomes the CWU's positive attempt to give customers what they need through a truly tailored flexible service."[3]

A delicate a temporary balance, if you like, had been worked at in 2002 – change, reduced overtime levels, increased pay (not yet £300 per week), a productivity scheme and co-operation on new delivery methods, buttressed by a job security agreement to help facilitate progress as the Company adapted to the new regulatory climate.

Although only a brief overview, what can be glimpsed is that change was possible by negotiation, but that these things took time. However, chuck into the mix the brash Allan Leighton fresh from his private sector exploits and this delicate balance would unravel.

Chapter 10

The Fuse is Lit: Pay and Major Change

Pay and Major Change Agreement – January 2004

The CWU have long had an overriding policy to secure the status of postal staff – their pay, professionalism and how Royal Mail treats them. As part of this there was a need to improve pay. The CWU had what was known as a "flight path" to £300 per week by October 2003. More than an aspiration, it was a policy discussed and agreed upon within the Union to enable workers in a predominantly semi/unskilled industry to increase the value of their labour significantly.

It is often forgotten that the value of a workers' labour is the pre-eminent issue for a trade Union. It goes to the heart of what was once a live issue and it is best put in the following terms, namely it is either, "I am doing you a favour by employing you" or "I am doing you a favour by giving up my time to work for you." It was this very issue of workers combining to set a price for their labour that led to the Tolpuddle Martyrs. By the same token, it was never really understood just how precarious the status of a postal workers' pay was once Postcomm and the threat centred approaches by the Company (and supported by the Government) in relation to job losses, began to manifest themselves.

Now earlier, I said we had moved from the macro side of things – huge political debates, regulatory matters, campaigning and the like – to a more micro look, namely the collective pay and terms for the workforce. Royal Mail were in the middle of a pincer – a restless workforce and Postcomm – the like of which led them to make an audacious attempt to dislodge the CWU. Their chosen instrument was the charm and likeability of Allan Leighton who would become the Government appointed

Chairman of Royal Mail Group.

As he was the former Marketing Director of Asda, many Posties wondered what he would now bring to the party. They would soon find out. Leighton's business acumen led him to adopt an approach unheard of before. If employees were taken aback, then so was their Union. Was this really to be a cultural change for the better?

A taste of things to come is best encapsulated in a letter to employees and reproduced in the Times:

Dear Colleagues
It's time for one of those Chairman's letters again!

I got into trouble last time for writing to you direct ... telling it straight. Well tough, that's how we do things round here now. I think I have either spoken to ... had emails from ... or listened to you through "Have Your Say", about 65,000 of you. Your feedback and questions have always been the same:

- Give us a fair day's pay for a fair day's work
- Simplify our bonus scheme ... nobody knows how they work or what they are for
- Give us a five day week
- Secure our pensions ... a lot of us have been in the Company a long time
- Can we have VR ... and make it quick! (NB VR: voluntary redundancy)

As always we all then get in the way of delivering this ... "the treacle" ... and everyone wants to spend months ... and ... often years ... negotiating the obvious ... making the obvious complicated when we already agree on what needs to be done. Well the good news is that we want to crack on with the obvious and therefore because the business is beginning to perform we are going to deliver you the following:

- Basic pay up by 14.5% giving everyone a minimum

pensionable basic of £300 per week, from around April 2004

- This £33-38 per week rise is new money
- Simplified bonus scheme now
- We will introduce a five day working week, as agreed *(with "job and finish" in delivery)* (my emphasis as it relates to a "Spanish practise" that Royal Mail would subsequently blame their workforce for)
- We will secure everyone's pension by putting £100 million into the fund each year until the current pension gap is filled
- A straightforward, entirely voluntary redundancy deal on the table and available immediately.

The only "string" (and forget what others might say) is that we must implement the key change programmes – that we all know about – and which I know you understand. That's it!!!

We have a real chance not just to save the Company, but to make it prosper. We're on track and if we focus on delivering the plan, then next year your "share in success" will pay out £800 – £1000. We can do this because the Company should be profitable … for the first time in five years. We have to keep it this way … share in success … do the right thing … look after customers … and trust and respect each other.

You have all said "but why should we trust you?" My reply is always, "you will know if you can trust me when something sensible gets delivered."

I'm delivering … I need your support to deliver the Company! Let's crack on.

Kind regards

Allan Leighton, Chairman[1]

That, by any stretch of the imagination was a sign of things to come. It came out on the same day as the CWU announced that this deal had been rejected as the discussions from 25-29 June 2003 had resulted in Royal Mail suddenly linking everything to major change, that not everyone was covered by the £300 and that the settlement did not flow through to overtime (including what is known as scheduled attendances – in effect, contractual overtime voluntarily entered into by an employee), that there was no shorter working week offer and that job security issues were not dealt with in line with the current agreements. Additionally, this was predicated on the introduction of a single daily delivery designed to save around £300 million per year. The change to the delivery format had already been the subject of discussion and trials had been agreed following the 2001 pay deal and known as Tailored Delivery Specification or TDS for short. Leighton's single daily delivery (or SDD for short) was just a variation on a theme.

It must also be said that these words from Leighton were unprecedented. Read them again and think about what was being guaranteed here. This was suddenly an issue of "trust me or trust your Union."

The degree of reality gap was perhaps best demonstrated in the issue of the 14.5% pay rise. The 14.5% was never on offer. The only money upfront was 4.5% over 18 months. The rest was linked – although you would never have guessed it unless you read it carefully – to change and meeting targets.

The new Deputy General Secretary, Dave Ward said to his members that the deal has "more strings than the Philharmonic orchestra (was) smoke and mirrors (and) you have to hand it to Allan he is certainly a great self publicist, a master of the hype. With him it is not so much a case of 'telling it straight', more a case of telling you what he wants you to hear ... no more carrot and stick, instead just a carrot dangling on the longest piece of string you have ever seen." It was also noted that the Consignia Board had seen its remuneration increase by no less than 320%. [2]

Of course the biggest elephant in the room was the glaringly obvious, which was that if there was a 14.5% pay rise on offer, the

Union would have obviously grabbed it. By 26 August 2003 a letter from Leighton to his workforce stated that the 14.5% really was only 4.5% over 18 months.[3]

The rest was dependent on the change and some 30,000 job losses and was a huge incentive to agree with the Royal Mail stance for those wanting to leave. It was also the toxic ingredient that would quietly nag away at postal staff. Would their job really disappear?

Subsequent negotiations between CWU and Royal Mail meant that at each occasion the Union obtained a concession during the few months leading up to the industrial action ballot, Royal Mail would trumpet each as their own and as another indication that you could trust Allan Leighton to deliver.

Part of the approach adopted by Royal Mail and Allan Leighton in particular was to get all of his managers away to a huge conference venue. The whole organisation was gripped by these events. The phrase "Nuremburg rallies" inevitably reared its head. Nevertheless, managers had a day off and they came back, psyched up to deliver the message from Allan. And deliver it they did, but with varying degrees of success.

In parallel with the letters from Leighton to the workforce, unagreed change was happening in relation to redundancy preferences around the 30,000 job losses the Union were expected to agree to, and there were also efficiency targets cascaded out to workplaces. Royal Mail had claimed to the Union and its employees that targets wouldn't change but once the detail was out, the Union noted to members:

It would seem that there is some fancy footwork going on, in an effort to make the managerially imposed targets look more realistic. Several representatives have reported that they are being informed by their local managers that the targets on display are not all they seem and goalposts are being shifted by drawing a distinction between 'work hours' and 'gross hours.' The net result being our members facing a more difficult task than that being displayed. We are also aware that .... in some areas, revised targets are being re-calculated as this LTB is written.[4]

The Union were saying one thing. Leighton was saying another and the actual organisation was pressing ahead with unagreed initiatives, which to many seemed to put a "coach and horses" through the position set out in his missives to employees.

The ante was soon upped considerably. A letter from Allan Leighton dated 26 August 2003 declared, "If you vote with the activists amongst the Union against the deal (or don't vote at all) we begin the process of commercial suicide. We are prepared for months of strikes, costs/losses will mount up at £20 million per day and competition, which is now a reality, will come marching in."[5] A message to put fear into many poorly paid staff and a message that if the CWU were pictured as being suicidal in not agreeing to Leighton's plans, then of course the Company itself was quite prepared to ignore the wishes of its staff, should a Yes vote be delivered, and instead press ahead themselves to obliterate their own organisation with "months of strikes". An approach commonly referred to as "cutting off your nose to spite your face."

It would be an approach that Royal Mail would come to deploy again in the years to come, as we shall see. To the extent that this was a "carrot and stick" tactic to persuade employees is not in doubt. To the extent that it devalued the views of their own workforce and moved to a culture of managing by fear, was a genuinely disappointing side effect.

Local bonus money for change was mentioned and this would demonstrate that national pay bargaining might just be at serious risk. As for the reports to the Union of "goalposts" moving this had *followed* the above letter from Leighton which said, "What's more we have listened to you about your targets and these have been revised to ensure they are achievable. The local targets are now fixed and will not change."

On 10 September 2003 the Guardian noted that Royal Mail had turned down an offer from the CWU for further talks to bridge the gaps. The Union noted that their view was that the losses in the Company were being exaggerated in order to justify the 30,000 job cuts and that the Trade and Industry Select Committee should independently examine the Company's accounts.[6]

Culturally then, two strong messages were being sent. Firstly, the Company will, come hell or high water, do exactly as it says and secondly your Union is actually part of the problem. If the Union wanted to talk about the treacle of the deal, then this would be glossed over as the workforce would be enjoined to "crack on" and get the job done to save the Company.

Behind that was the inevitable logic of the situation. It was Royal Mail who employed the workforce, not the Union. It was stated quite often in the run up to the strike ballot by some postal workers, that the best way to "take the money and run" was to vote no. The ballot result when it came was either a relief or a disaster, depending on your point of view with 46391 for and 48038 against. A Yes vote from postal staff in London over London Weighting was overlooked in the aftermath, but nevertheless this affirmative vote would prove crucial.

Suddenly Royal Mail saw an opportunity to marginalise the CWU in relation to pay and change in the industry.

Royal Mail advised the Union and the workforce that, "the world has changed." Immediately unagreed changes were being made with some who signed up to the unagreed changes and others who did not. In some cases the Company organised workplace ballots or had a quick show of hands (including Union and non-Union workers). If you were missing for whatever reason, too bad. The CWU view was that the standard of the ballots left much to be desired with workers not being given the full story and being "bounced" into voting outside of the established and agreed procedures.

The Company would try and let people know and in one letter stated that 428 delivery offices had put in the changes to move to a single daily delivery (up until then, the public had enjoyed two deliveries). In reality no one was really sure who was signing up, such was the confusion, only that it was reckoned to be a huge exaggeration. Soon though, there were strikes across London, Kent, Scotland, Oxfordshire, the North East and North West in response to this unagreed change. Around 25,000 workers were on unofficial strike.

Now this explanation doesn't quite sum up what happened. If the CWU had often spoken of the way in which Royal Mail could provoke strikes, this was to come true once again. The apparent spark for the above walk outs came after management took a decision to discipline drivers in Southall, West London following a day of official strike action over the London Weighting dispute. Such swift action only really makes sense in such a volatile situation if there is another agenda.

The decision of how to end the walk outs was of course with the Company. Would they look to resolve them or let things develop. The Guardian gave the public a taste of what happens when decisions are taken to let things "develop." Mail is moved from the strike bound London offices to adjacent areas and those hundreds of miles away. The paper reported that mail was sent to Oxford. The local Union is apparently told they will not have to process the mail from London – after all, once processed, who was going to deliver it? What happened was that mail was "slipped in". In other words hidden amongst other mail. When spotted, this triggered a walk out in Oxford.

The Guardian also quoted a postal worker saying, "The managers are in your face all the time. They stand over you with their arms folded and even monitor how long you are in the toilet for. The shaved head seems to be the managers' standard look."

Needless to say, Royal Mail issued a denial.

Such a denial looked threadbare when a management document was leaked showing plans to break the walk outs by identifying ringleaders, to follow Union representatives surreptitiously and note who they spoke to, picket lines would have CCTV trained on them and managers were urged to buy disposable cameras to photograph workers.[7]

Of course elsewhere, Posties saw that Royal Mail were attacking all national agreements and prolonging unofficial strikes by insisting that local agreements were null and void. How was this communicated to employees? Royal Mail stated that, "...we will not change our position however many strikes take place."[8]

So on the one hand, the Company has a secret document telling managers to undertake an operation, "unprecedented by a big public employer since the 1984/85 miners' strike" to try and stop the strikes, whilst at the same time prolonging them by telling those workers that all their collective agreements were scrapped.[9]

Moreover, it soon became clear that Royal Mail were promising managers around £1,600 bonus for getting changes in outside of a national agreement and changes were being pushed through at opportune moments, such as when the local CWU Representative was away on holiday.

While all this was going on the CWU and Royal Mail met to discuss formalising an agreement on pay and major change in the industry. That such talks were taking place after the strike ballot had been lost, indicated that culturally, the pendulum was swinging back. Why? Because trusting Allan Leighton was a different matter to having terms and conditions either imposed or taken away. In other words, Royal Mail had pushed things too far. The world had not changed after all.

Royal Mail agreed to finalise a national agreement on a single delivery by 10 December 2003, preconditions for getting workers off strike and back to work were withdrawn, ceasing local agreements in strike bound workplaces would be withdrawn and Posties would not be targeted for disciplinary action as a result of the unofficial strikes unless there were serious cases involving threatening behaviour. More positive still, talks would resume on 4 November 2003 with ACAS. One can only wonder at why preconditions were ever put in place for those on strike, when the purpose should have been to get the Company working again and customers happy.[10]

The following extracts are useful in setting out the broad commitments made in the final Major Change Agreement:

> The Future for Delivery/Delivery Improvement Project: This is a major new business/CWU initiative, as part of the commitment to significantly increase the status and professionalism of the delivery job. It will focus on further improvements to terms, conditions and improving business profitability. The national parties will oversee the project including establishing the involvement of CWU, employees and managers.

There would be a "menu of proposals" which would cover "scope for imaginative attendance patterns", "continuing to support full time employment", achieving "a better working environment", "more family friendly attendance arrangements" and "improving the development of and support for young workers." "Single deliveries will be introduced to provide all delivery employees with a fair and manageable workload whilst fully safeguarding welfare and safety." This list is not exhaustive, but you get the picture.

This manageable and fair workload would be facilitated by "...jointly reviewing all aspects of Pegasus (and used as a) planning tool that can assist in developing ... routes with a balanced workload." Pegasus is a software programme to assist with plotting delivery walks. We shall see later whether fair workloads would be churned out of Pegasus or not.

"RM and CWU are committed to maintaining national pay bargaining. The parties will re-examine the pay bargaining process to ensure that pay deals are always delivered on time ... reaffirms the MTSF Agreement." This stands for Managing the Surplus Framework and is designed to ensure compulsory redundancies are avoided at all costs through voluntary redundancy terms, pay protection for people moved from one part of the business to another (a rock bottom essential if for example you end up moved off a night shift to a day shift with no night allowance) and the payment of excess travel if a postal worker had to move workplaces.

Also included was an 18 month pay deal of 4.5% plus an additional £26.28 per week as part of local efficiency changes and savings. The mechanisms to ensure these savings were fair and deliverable was spelled out and agreed. "Let's crack on", now actually meant something and moreover, the savings demanded would be "reduced by approximately 30%."

The overall message to the workforce after all this, was regrettably for Allan Leighton that perhaps we can't really trust him after all and should have led to a reassessment of the way in which Royal Mail related to the workforce. If they thought they had the Union on the run, then clearly their own employees going on strike proved otherwise.

In fact, the portents were good when Leighton arrived to the extent that The Times in an editorial noted that he had "begun to tackle the ... appalling management. He noted recently that there were probably more bullies in the industry than in any other large organisation."[11] This suggested that he really did want massive and fundamental change in cultures, it was just that this necessarily involved a much reduced role for the trade Union.

And yet, he had taken a decision after the strike ballot had returned a slim No vote, to press ahead with unagreed change in the knowledge that almost half those voting were clearly not with him and then allowed his senior managers to deliberately prolong unofficial strikes. If it doesn't make sense to an outsider, then I think it can be said that many if not most postal workers, especially those employed at the time, saw that this type of stance made perfect sense. It was just what the workforce had come to experience. There is a phrase that is perhaps apt at this juncture, an iron fist inside a velvet glove. In other words, we'll be all sweetness and light to try and persuade those restless Posties, but if this fails, then the gloves are off. Was it possible for the Company to move away from such a mind-set?

Peace in our time then or conflict deferred?

Chapter 11

False Dawn: Shaping Our Future 2006

Shaping Our Future Agreement – August 2006

Regrettably for the workforce it was conflict deferred, for in the Company's panic (or deliberate intention to ignore the CWU) at facing full deregulation, yet again they reverted to type. It simply didn't seem to make sense to them to work with their employees and the problems were triggered to all intents and purposes by the decision to impose a pay rise of 2.9% as well as forcing through change linked to budgets. Doing more with less with no agreed process to see if the extra work was within the bounds of a "fair day's work for a fair day's pay", was the message the Company managed to transmit and most Posties thought that Royal Mail was highly successful in that regard.

It is useful to note that as well as unagreed change being imposed, there were around 20,000 casuals in the industry. A figure that would put the Company in the lime light as it appeared they had no control over who they were employing, such was the drive to reduce the headcount of directly employed people, whilst still trying to keep the show on the road. In reality this meant that such people were actively preferred to directly employed staff. Again, the message to their workforce was clear. The status and value of a postal worker was not as high as many had thought if casuals could be employed and sent out to deliver the mail with little idea of where they were going.

If nothing else this pointed to what surely must have been a policy driven by panic. As for those 20,000 casuals, Royal Mail would subsequently claim their numbers had been drastically reduced to around 500. The result though was huge gaps in the workforce as vacancies were unfilled and part time employees covered full time jobs.[1]

The agreement finally reached, which included a pay rise of 2.9% and a further 1% for efficiency improvements, only came after the whole of the workforce took part in a CWU organised consultative ballot setting out the Unions' vision for the future. As always, this vision involved working together with Royal Mail and not opposing change and automation. This was vital with the full opening up of the postal market from 2006.

It was not vital though if a judgment could be made that change could be imposed and arguably this message was the one that filtered down to the workforce. It was a pattern that kept on repeating itself as we have seen and we shall see further on. A disconnect that meant on the one hand a decision to put themselves into the straightjacket of negotiations with the Union and on the other hand, a frustration at this very decision. In simple terms, if the discussions were usually civilised at the top – and they weren't always – at the shop floor it was something akin to a jungle as managers sought to by-pass agreed commitments by imposing budgetary savings regardless, e.g., replacing staff with casuals, vacancies or part-timers.

Of course however placid and reasonable a senior negotiator might be to the CWU when signing up to a commitment, the Royal Mail's top down command and control approach would mean that it was extraordinarily easy to "put the word out" to managers in the field at the same time as being "sweetness and light" to the Union nationally. This was the message the Company seemed all too willing to give and it would lead to the inevitable response from the CWU to refuse to co-operate with this or that initiative until a national agreement had been honoured. It was this mind set that the Shaping Our Future Agreement was supposed to dispense with once and for all. If it wasn't possible against the backdrop of competition, then just when would it be possible?

The Agreement had a powerful opening statement which ought to have provided some genuine reassurance to employees that things would improve: "This agreement is a defining moment in the relationship between the Company and the Union ... about all of us doing things differently. It's about setting the clear direction we must now take to achieve real success for the Company and the workforce."

There was a commitment to "develop high quality managers and representatives by investing in joint training on the skills necessary to understand the business and do their jobs ... ensuring that our managers and representatives demonstrate full support for national agreements and work together to implement them through constructive and positive relation-ships."

These powerful words would be put into practise by trialling new delivery methods, the success of which would only be possible if "our people's views have been taken into account" and that "new ideas will be sought from the national and local parties. Nothing will be ruled in and nothing will be ruled out."

"We must modernise the Company. Investment in our people and automation are central to this aim. We will work together to ensure that we become the most efficient, customer focussed and flexible Company in the market place and at the same time raise the value and status of a postal workers job. We will reach agreement that takes these issues forward by no later than April 2007."

In other words, job reductions dealt with by natural wastage or voluntary redundancy; No worker will be forced from full time to part time; The pensions deficit would be tackled without increasing contributions from members or delaying the retirement age and there would be investment in people and machinery, all subject to Government assistance via a commercial loan of around £1.2 billion – a loan, it has to be said that came about thanks to intensive lobbying by the CWU.

The Agreement was subject to a national briefing of the Unions' branches. The view was positive and the phrase used by many present was that the agreement "ticked all the boxes". Let's restate for a moment that this meant, yet again agreement from the CWU to changes that would involve job losses and investment in new machinery. Let no one think this agreement was signed through the gritted teeth of the CWU. The quotes above are powerful words and should have, once and for all, meant that changing cultures was about genuinely engaging with the workforce and their Union.

In a final letter to members the Union said that the Royal Mail were,

determined to ignore the Union and impose their plans for major change on the workforce. Denying you (i.e., the members) a say on pay typified their approach. The Union responded by gaining massive support for our vision through a consultative ballot. Then at Conference we left Royal Mail in no doubt we were prepared to call for industrial action if we could not reach an acceptable deal. Under the terms of this agreement the Union will now be fully involved in shaping your future job through negotiations due to conclude by April 2007.... Everybody knows we are operating in a different environment and that future change is inevitable.... Crucially Royal Mail has now signed up to continuing to raise the value and status of a postal workers' job and investing in people. The Shaping Our Future Agreement gives us a real platform to move forward with confidence.[2]

Peace in our time now...? It ought to have been. The Government loan provided a fantastic opportunity for the Company to develop and move forward. Crucially, it was a time to take the workforce with them as well.

Chapter 12

The Gloves are Off: Pay and Modernisation 2007

Pay and Modernisation Agreement – October 2007

A national strike took place – just a year or so after the previous agreement was signed.

No pay rise was offered, there was change being introduced without agreement, job cuts, changes in start and finish times and many staff having no idea what they were doing from week to week. Another bone of contention was the prevalence of what were known as buy-downs. Full time staff were offered a payment for converting their contract to part time. Of course, if someone reduces their hours, who will pick up the slack? Everyone else? Perhaps it will be claimed that the reduction is reasonable? Whatever the answer, the normal process as per those inconvenient National Agreements, would have been a discussion with the Union representative to see if in fact the cuts were reasonable.

Of course we know where this is going by now. In many cases no proper discussion took place and someone was happy to get a few thousand pounds in their back pocket without fully realising the consequences, both to themselves (including pension implications, as of course little advice appeared to be on offer by the Company) and their workmates. In other words, there was a "slash and burn" approach to the service the public were receiving and as a leaflet to the public stated at the time, the CWU wanted, "Royal Mail to enter into meaningful talks with the CWU on resolving pay and major change and to honour the 2006 agreement which committed both parties to agree a joint approach on pay and modernisation."

In fact, although the public would not realise the full

enormity of the above statement, a Union research paper was stark in its assessment: "Regrettably, Royal Mail do not wish to honour" the 2006 agreement anymore. "Indeed, to date not a single proposal has been tabled by them concerning automation and the introduction of new technology."

The question to be asked, was how on earth could such a situation come to pass? Was it the fear of investing in machinery when they had no effective control over pricing and regulation? Was it simply incompetence on their part despite having the Government loan in their back pocket to invest? Was it that they wished to progress automation without the involvement of either their staff or the CWU? The view of the CWU though was clear, they had "consistently pushed Royal Mail to introduce new and improved products and services ... and to also provide better equipment and automation for the workforce."[1]

The regulatory climate was such that the CWU were also asking for:

"A Government review of the damaging impact of competition on Royal Mail to date, in line with Labour's manifesto commitment."

"An immediate change to Postcom's competition rules and a fairer pricing and access regime that gives Royal Mail the revenues it needs to support the universal postal service and post office network."

The issues around the unfair regulation were put bluntly to the public:

"A combination of Royal Mail's 'slash and burn' strategy and rigged competition rules now threaten the future of Britain's universal postal service. As competitors queue up to cream off the most lucrative work, Royal Mail is facing a financial black hole and proposing a swinging round of cuts both to postal services and to our members' terms and condition."[2]

The battle for public support meant a national petition was circulated addressed to then Business Minister, John Hutton which said, amongst other things: "We the undersigned condemn the plans by Royal Mail to cut the service provided to the public by introducing later deliveries and less frequent collections...." As with many such petitions, it would be left to gather dust in an archive somewhere instead of being a wake up call to those tasked with ensuring responsive postal services for the customer.

The Union didn't want a strike, contrary to the opinions of those numerous self appointed experts in Parliament and parts of the media who, to be frank about it, genuinely had no idea what they were talking about, but whose opinions nevertheless seem to plaster the front pages of the tabloids from time to time. Think about the situation facing postal workers and their families. Would you go on strike when even your own Union is saying that Royal Mail is in dire straights?

The pressures on the CWU to balance out the need to have change negotiated – it's not as if the Union was opposing change – whilst protecting pay and jobs in such a "rigged" postal market was brave but necessary. Foolhardy it was not. The alternative would have been the probable end of the Union as a force capable to negotiating change and protecting people. Additionally, into the mix was Royal Mail's contention that postal workers were some 25% overpaid compared to the competition, more of which later. To suggest that this wasn't used to try and reduce expectations on pay amongst their workforce would be delusional.

By April 2007, just 8 months after the hopes of the 2006 Shaping Our Future agreement, the Company would offer a pay freeze and a lump sum payment of between £250 and £400 to employees in exchange for making some £350 million of savings in the coming 12 months.

Now that was a drastic and unsettling message to employees. Some thought this would be money saved through automation that everyone was hearing so much about at that time in the guise of compact and walk sequencing machines which needed maybe 2 or 3 people to process thousands of items per hour and which it was said would sort the mail out for a postal worker, negating the need to sort it themselves. This was the first sign that automation would potentially cause huge job losses. It was almost, but not quite, the instruments of torture being laid out before the hapless victim. That the CWU were on record in supporting the need for such change, surely should have been embraced by Royal Mail?

If the initial thoughts of postal workers were that the £350 million was coming from automation, they were to be sorely disappointed. This £350 million was on top of the expected savings from automation. This shock was compounded by the failure of the 2006 Agreement to deliver payments to employees for making savings. April 2007 saw a payment of some 92p being consolidated into basic pay.

As for the £350 million of savings, fully £55 million would come from ceasing what was a payment for delivering so called "junk mail". The phrase in the industry was "door to door" (D2D) or "household delivery". This "junk mail" was over and above the normal workload, so naturally people got paid extra and had a week to deliver the items to each address on their delivery. They received 1.67p per item. Now if you are delivering these items and you have perhaps 500 delivery points then this is a handy sum to go into the family budget, in this case £8.35. Stopping payment was nothing more than a pay cut. What else could it be?

Some £67 million would be saved by forcing postal staff to deliver their colleagues mail during summer and for short term sickness, for example five people would do the work of six. This might or might not be fair, but if nothing else someone would have to decide if this extra could be done in the time the postal worker was paid. There was no detail on this crucial point. More earnings were also identified by the intention to cut some £17 million from overtime in Mail processing centres.

Some £32 million was expected to be saved by reducing sickness through a "managerial contact strategy" and some £6 million from ceasing Sunday and bank holiday collections, having been given the green light to do so by Postcomm – so much for competition improving services. Additional headings in relation to night shifts and changes to the way first and second class mail was processed, etc., formed the rest. These were truly huge amounts of money, large chunks of which would come out of pay packets.[3]

It would not be long before workers woke up to the enormity of the calamity facing them. A strike ballot result declared on 7 June 2007 showed 66,064 voting to strike and 19,119 against. A 77.56% Yes vote.

Further issues would be added to the above list of demands . Royal Mail wanted to introduce later starts for delivery staff. On the face of it, fine! More time in bed. In reality this was yet another pay cut as employees received early start payments. The early starts also meant those with second jobs could get to them and those with child care and other family responsibilities, could carry them out. This issue was also very controversial with the public and small and medium businesses were against later starts as this meant later deliveries. Posties could be forgiven for asking why on earth would their employer do something that the customer did not want. The answer would be provided in due course with the independent review of the postal market carried out by Sir Richard Hooper in 2009, which showed that large business users were quite happy and it was they of course who were effectively calling the tune.

As for Royal Mail's stated reason for later deliveries, this was down to the nationally introduced 56 mph limit for larger vehicles. In other words, cutting millions off their wage bill by stopping the early start allowances had nothing at all to do with their thinking. The CWU would be able to state that in fact, speed limit or not, some 60% of mail was already at mail processing centres by midnight. Many postal staff would note that lorries didn't make a habit of racing through country towns at 56 mph either.

The CWU view was as always to try and secure change that would enhance and protect the service to customers and as a result of the intentions of the Company, the CWU sought to obtain agreement from Postcomm to request a postponement to allow for proper consultations with business and mail user groups. This would be yet another attempt by postal workers to protect the service provided. Was anyone listening though when it was that much easier to condemn workers for trying to prevent their pay from being cut?[4]

As for the reference above to saving £55million by stopping D2D payments, Royal Mail were now seeking to increase the number that could be done to five. What exactly did this mean then? To use the example of 500 delivery points for a delivery person, one D2D meant 500 leaflets to deliver. The maximum at that time of three items would mean 1500 items to deliver. Increase that to 5 and you have 2500 items to deliver and sort into your mail bag for no extra money and no extra time to complete the task. If there was a bank holiday that week, you would have 4 days to deliver the lot or face possible disciplinary action for failing to deliver the mail.

Even if this was possible to do so in addition to the normal workload, add in the demand to do the work of your colleagues when they are away and keep within the then allotted delivery span of 3.5 hours (as it then was, due to the need to prevent unnecessary fatigue on the physical health of workers carrying mail bags) and it can be seen how draconian the measures were. Added to this of course there would be the loss of the early shift payments, which for most was £6 per week. As a minimum then, cuts of about £15 per week. Not trivial sums.

All this was suddenly necessary or the Royal Mail would

simply become a failed Company. What a message to give to your employees. This was the politics of fear, for the most part hidden from the gaze of the public. A battering ram to batter their workforce into submission. Of course it needs to be reiterated that Royal Mail were beginning to struggle not only due to the first real signs of mail volumes dropping, but the inexorable rise in the amount of mail posted via downstream access and the increasing desire of customers to "down trade" by posting items second class instead of first class. Increasing use of email was also beginning to have an impact, price caps set by Postcomm were biting and the Company was saying that unless they improved efficiency, Postcomm would continue to squeeze their profit margins. The CWU were not unsympathetic as we have seen. Huge efforts were made by the CWU to discuss with the Government the need for a full and open review of liberalisation and across the UK, local CWU Branches were campaigning to get the message across to MPs and the public.

And yet, did this mean their adopted approach was required? Hadn't they just signed an agreement just a few months before? Perhaps the Directors woke up one morning and in a blind panic realised that the agreement reached was not fit for purpose and that they had not been paying attention to any of Postcomms' directives? Was this really a Company panicked into such changes at short notice or were they the inevitable result of agreeing something in bad faith?

By June there was some movement. There was now a 2.5% pay rise in return for delivering change or an unconsolidated lump sum of £600 (the CWU had already been asking what this change was – presumably later starts for instance and more budget cuts leading to less staff to carry out the work?) and a payment of £800 if a Royal Mail imposed target was met and a 50% share of savings made above the local office budget. For the vexed issue of D2D the offer was that the first three items would now be paid at 1.67p with anything above this carried out within normal workload for no payment. The letter from the Company concluded by saying that their negotiating team "will be available to explain any of this to the Union at any time."[5] The concept of a negotiating team simply explaining something may have been lost on some employees, but it was not lost on the CWU. It was a message that said, "go ahead and do your worst."

In response and in order to get a deal without the need for any strikes, the CWU responded. They said there was "hostility" towards postal staff who will no doubt remember some managers gleefully stating that "this is your miners' strike." Of course it is difficult to understand from the outside what "hostility" actually meant, but whilst postal staff were on the receiving end, it was the Union who, in a letter, diplomatically stated, "Royal Mail must be more realistic about what can be achieved in advance of automation. It will be the agreed introduction of automation that can reduce costs whilst at the same time improving service and properly rewarding staff. This means you must step back from the current damaging cost cutting frenzy taking place in every office" and "reflect on your position and engage in ... talks before any strike action takes place."[6]

There can be little doubt that Posties had their fingers crossed that the straight talking Allan Leighton would do the right thing. In fact, what else would be sensible given the huge pressures on the Company? An offer from one of the most militant and organised Unions in the UK to talk rather than strike, protect the customer rather than engage in an industrial battle.

If this letter was sent in the full knowledge that it would make no difference, then why send it? Was it a cynical ploy to get Royal Mail to lose face by backing down? Whatever the arguments that had preceded the letter from the CWU, the offer not to strike in favour of talks was surely something to be grasped. Wasn't it? Apparently not. For Royal Mail it was only about explaining a non-negotiable offer.

The Daily Mirror would describe the attitude of Royal Mail as "sordid" and suggested that "....this act of bullying management is a set up – a deliberate trap to starve postal workers into submission by driving them into a stoppage they can ill afford. The way would then be open to privatise Royal Mail, with multi-million pound pay-offs for top management." It was in truth difficult to see what other description could usefully be employed.[7]

The Company was apparently content with strikes and it was therefore time for postal workers to "put up or shut up." Tragically, and yes this may be the right word here, an assessment of the strike and its aftermath would state that "for the business, the direct costs of the dispute have been estimated by senior sources within Royal Mail at over £200 million."[8]

Two hundred million pounds and loss of reputation as well. If nothing else, this estimate demonstrates that if Royal Mail say to their workforce: you can go on strike for however long and we won't change, there is clearly some suicidal truth to it. In other words you can wreck your own industry by going on strike or you can do it our way. Alternatively, those in charge are prepared to wreck the Company on the grounds that they aren't prepared to negotiate any more with the CWU.

Such a mind set as the CWU saw it was encapsulated in the public comments from Tony McCarthy, then Group Director for Royal Mail who was quoted stating that postal staff were paid 25% more than postal competitors and that Royal Mail had a 40% efficiency gap in comparison with the competition. This was quickly translated as, "you lot are 25% over paid and 40% under worked." Now, Royal Mail did seek to nuance that message by claiming that the 40% was due to their competitors already having modernised, but nevertheless, the original utterance stuck, due in no small part to its repetition by local managers.[9]

Of course if one steps back a moment to look again at the list of cuts demanded of the workforce, they were to come in as soon as the Company could make them happen and would therefore effect change before automation came in. In this way, the message was that the 40% efficiency gap would be closed as far as possible by employees working harder and their pay would be reduced to close the 25% pay gap with the private postal carriers who were content to pay just the national minimum wage. To the question, how can you get people to work so much harder the answer would come to be seen as bullying or "performance" management. At its most blunt, the ruthless rationale of the free market says that Royal Mail could cut the wages by 25% and still find enough workers to work for them, hence any pay above that level is simply not required.

The position of the CWU was inevitably to secure higher pay and a shorter working week in exchange for the increased efficiency and profitability that automation would bring. All postal workers recognised that automation would lead to job losses and some were quite happy as they could leave on voluntary redundancy terms. We have already seen how postal workers were paid below the average workers wage and therefore the aspiration was to seek to get to the average UK wage, to around £395 per week from the then average pay of £323 per week, hopefully within five years. This would be translated by Royal Mail and chunks of the media as being a demand by postal workers for a pay rise of 27%. The actual breakdown according to Royal Mail was 22% on pay, 4% for a shorter working week and a further 1% on overtime rates.[10]

Some readers may also remember during this time the re-emergence of that loaded phrase, "Spanish practises". Adam Crozier then CEO was widely quoted and probably interviewed on TV for all I can remember stating with absolute certainty that there were 1442 Spanish practises a few years ago and now there were apparently only 92 left! Are you serious?! Ninety two ways for the workforce to skive off and take the Royal Mail for a ride.[11]

Amazingly, one of those so called practises was that people didn't work the hours for which they were paid. This was the big one. How on earth does an employer allow that, never mind advertise its own apparent inability to sort itself out you may wonder. Crozier was quoted as saying Royal Mail were only trying to make people work the hours for which they were paid.

Now, to the untrained, this seems eminently reasonable. If you were then told that this practise had actually been introduced by Royal Mail then you would have to suspend your disbelief as it is true. It was Royal Mail who, after the Major Change Agreement referred to above, brought in "job and finish" as an officially sanctioned working practise. Race around, get the work done and off you go, job done! And if your manager then said, by the way I need you to do some more work, what would your answer be then? Think about it now...

Yes, of course you are ok to help out but as you have raced around at top speed to get an early finish, you are ok to do this extra work for overtime only. Now, let's not get too far ahead of ourselves now. Is this a reasonable response? Would you adopt that approach or would you say to your boss, that's fine I'll do that extra work for no payment at all because I am still within my normal working hours?

Now, even if you are inclined to do that, would you keep on rushing around knowing that you would be asked to do some more work? Suddenly things aren't quite so clear cut anymore. They are certainly crystal clear though if Allan Leighton has told you it's ok. In fact, it was and is widely known that job and finish actually enabled cuts to be made. Running around demonstrated that the job could apparently be done with fewer hours. Of course as hours were removed from workplaces, this threw up the inevitable crush. Suddenly you are rushing round and still not finishing. In fact from being a sanctioned perk, what you are now doing is coming in early just to finish on time. Amazingly, if you came in early and got the work done, this fact was invariably ignored. To the Company, the job could be done and so the hours would be cut.

In fact a good number of those rushing round were part time employees with other jobs to get to or child care responsibilities. For newly employed part time employees, the fear of not having a contract renewed was enough to get you to do what was necessary to keep the show on the road. Add to this the impending move to later starts demanded by Royal Mail (and later finishes of course) and the crush was that much bigger for many vulnerable employees.

Another of these Spanish practises was apparently the nerve of postal staff not to work in different areas of the Business. Again, for the unschooled, what could possibly be the problem with this? It's a given that in Royal Mail as with any employer, if you are asked to do something else then you need to know how to do it. Ok, that seems fine. Did Royal Mail train people then as per the Way Forward Agreement, mentioned above? You begin to get the message that training was not high on the list of priorities. So, was it the case that people refused to move? If there were cases of refusals they were few and far between whether you were trained or not. In fact, what you did come across was the reality of an employee wanting to move and being stopped!

Royal Mail is split into "functions" – delivery, distribution and processing. This was done to assist with the intentions of the previous Conservative Government in the 1990s to privatise either all of Royal Mail or discrete bits of it. So, Royal Mail is functionalised and there are management structures and staffing proper to those functions. Not the idea of the CWU. They don't run the Company. If you want to move then you have to apply to get in. If you are told to go to another function then you affect the staffing and earnings of those already there. It's like three separate employers – but not quite!

No, the issue was not people refusing but the crisis slash and burn approach which meant people having to do whatever they were told whether trained or whether it made any sense. A Spanish practise, it was not. As for the other ninety Spanish practises, it is doubtful in the extreme that anyone within the Company would have any idea at all what they could possibly be. Presumably if there really were that many Adam Crozier would have advised his staff of this situation and told them to shape up or else. In fact, the whole list in all its gory glory would have been in the hands of those elements of the press happy to see the back of a bunch of militant, no good postal workers. The supreme irony of course to all this is that in the good old days when that mythical number of Spanish practises was in full swing the Company made substantial profits year after year!

Of course the Spanish practises apparently endemic within the Company could not easily be squared with the actual experiences of postal staff of the "slash and burn" approach, but it was yet another disconnect between employer and employee that Royal Mail chose to focus on to the inevitable detriment of that elusive goal of valuing their staff.

This elusiveness would be cemented thanks to their decision to plough ahead with introducing later starts without agreement and continuing with a policy of cutting hours during the dispute itself. A process that will be discussed later on, but which at its height involved, amongst other things, employing part time staff, sometimes on contracts of five hours per week or less, and allocating them to full time vacancies. In other words, you would be regularly doing 35 hours overtime each week and getting 5 hours pay when you were sick or on annual leave. Other hapless individuals would be on 20 hour contracts and be expected to do pretty much what a full time person would do or face the possibility of their temporary contract not being renewed.

Strikes commenced from 29 June 2007 and not surprisingly were solidly supported. As the dispute would progress workers would take strike action in different parts of the Business, for example Mail Centres would be on strike followed by Delivery Offices. In this way it was hoped that the impact on the Company would be more severe and ensure a swifter return to the negotiating table. Additionally to try and bring the Company beyond merely explaining its position, CWU members were implored to "work your proper hours" and to "do the job properly." More Spanish practises? Not quite. This was far more prosaic. Come in on time, have a meal break, deliver the mail, not take out overweight mail bags, not use their own private car to deliver the mail and finish on time.

Any postal worker then and now will state with absolute certainty, as would any Royal Mail manager that if such a practise as doing the job properly caught on, the whole edifice of the Company would come crashing down. The terrible dark secret the Company and all in it knew was that the show was only on the road because literally thousands of postal staff would come in early for nothing or carry on after the end of their daily scheduled duty for nothing to get the job done. This view is as much relevant then as it is today.

By the beginning of July, the media was full of reports at the bonuses being paid out to managers totalling some £40 million. Postal staff would question their manager on what they had been given to which many would deny it! The amounts were said to be between £1500 and £10,000 with Adam Crozier pocketing around £370,000. Royal Mail would be quoted as saying that bonus was paid "if targets are hit or exceeded." That would be the slash and burn approach to which their employees were being subjected to then?[12]

Further strikes took place and in Glasgow there were unofficial strikes due to Royal Mail demanding that postal workers there handle the mail from other places that were on official strike. This was a perennial tactic that was employed for reasons that are frankly impenetrable unless the view taken was to get people out on strike. There would also be reports of the Company bringing in "hundreds of Polish casuals" to try and break the strikes. Choices freely made by Royal Mail and all in the light of an earlier offer by the CWU to talk rather than strike.

It was a mad world that postal workers had been plunged into.[13]

There is one thing that goes with being plunged into a mad world and that is to ask when or if, it is possible to emerge from it. The CWU would tell its members that there was no real vision from Royal Mail. That it was a race to the bottom and, more tellingly perhaps, that,

> these people are supposed to be managing the Business and providing inspiration so that postal workers want to do that bit more to make things work ... what incentive is there for those working in the Business if they are told there will be pain this year, pain next year and pain the year after that, and if you are still here in four or five years' time that terms and conditions will be worse still.[14]

As part of this mad world, we not only need to take stock for a moment and recall the offer made by the Union not to enter into any strikes, but to note that although no positive response was received to that letter, Allan Leighton asked his CEO Adam Crozier to reply. This is from an open letter addressed to the CWU which whilst explaining the Company's position also said that change was vital and that, "the Union could and should be playing a positive role in this." This letter would also make reference to the Company contacting ACAS. A positive sign without doubt.[15]

In fact, on the basis of actions speaking louder than words, the Company would candidly tell their staff via the good offices of ACAS that change and cuts and later starts would continue to be imposed.[16]

Into this heady mix of demands from Royal Mail, came changes to the pension scheme in which the Company wished to end the final salary scheme link; these were leaked to the Daily Mirror. The Mirror would note that existing Royal Mail pensioners and senior management would not be affected.[17] For their part the Company would claim that the Union knew all about this leaked document and that it had actually been discarded. Of course to the extent that discussions on the future of the Royal Mail Pension Plan had been taking place, they were against the backdrop of an employer out to beat the Union in an industrial dispute by prevailing with their own plans. In other words what had started out as discussions some months previously, had mutated into something much bigger and the idea that Posties would be able to engage in a rational and reasonable negotiation on pensions when they were fighting for their lives on so many other fronts was unrealistic. More to the point, what deal on pensions could possibly be achieved if the current industrial dispute was lost by the CWU?

By August Royal Mail had made some conciliatory moves in relation to allowances/shift payments and executive action to implement later starts would be put back. Strikes were suspended as a result as the Union offered a period of calm. A letter to the CWU from the Company confirmed this point. Changes to start times would be done by "consider(ing) people's personal circumstances such as child care responsibilities and second jobs before we confirm the new duties" The letter also said that later starts due to the 56mph limit would "not impact" on the current service specification.[18]

Negotiations took place with the assistance of ACAS and the TUC. Those talks proved unsuccessful and further strikes were announced as the Company changed its final position just prior to talks concluding.

Royal Mail wanted much of their original financial savings but they had added that staff would be liable to have their duty time each day changed by up to plus or minus 2 hours, at seven days notice – people on different hours or different days of the week, delivery rounds would be collapsed during the summer, people could be made to change their finish time at 24 hours notice by 30 minutes each day as required, later starts would be in from 17

September 2007 (the pill would be sweetened by the early shift payments remaining as "grandfather" rights, in other words paid to those in receipt of them on a permanent basis) , "cutting off" would not be allowed if there were late arrivals of the mail to a delivery office (cutting off means a postal worker brings back mail they can't deliver within their normal paid duty time) and people were liable to be moved to any job that required covering if the person had current or historical experience of that task, annualised hours would be in so that people worked more hours in the winter than the summer – all this to enable the Company to become "dynamic (and) flexible."

If any of this was deemed to be unreasonable, then Royal Mail would allow a worker access to the grievance procedure, but they would have to do as directed in the meantime. All this would be backed up by having a "mature relationship" between manager, worker and the Union. This "agreement" would come in from 1 October 2007. In other words, in less than one month time. So much for working with employees to help them with their personal circumstances.

Another bomb shell was also dropped. The national job security agreement would be ceased from 1 April 2008 to be replaced with one that "manages headcount in a commercial but sensitive way". And another... any, pay rise would be conditional on accepting "all aspects" of change and conditional on accepting the Company's pension proposals to end the final salary scheme – never mind that the Scheme covered workers who did not work in Royal Mail such as Parcelforce and Post Office workers. And there was more. The fear of D2D payments going from the pay packet was to be realised, instead this would apparently now be done within normal workload.

There would be a bonus too. A postal worker could get 50% of any savings made over and above those of the office budget. There would be Colleague Shares contingent on the overall profit of the Company and for achieving unit cost budget. The package had to be agreed in whole or no payments of any kind would be made, to which a rational response might just be, "I'll take a rain check on that if it's all the same to you."[19]

This document would regrettably pave the way for more strikes. In the mad world to which postal staff and their families were now stuck in, a widely available Royal Mail presentation to senior managers would say in respect of the document, "In an attempt to find a resolution we started to widen the debate and bring some other issues onto the table, e.g., pensions and MTSF", (aka that job security agreement known as Managing the Surplus Framework that the Company didn't want anymore).

The question to be asked of course is whether anyone at the top of Royal Mail honestly believed that such a document, never mind the disingenuous phrase above, would lead to an agreement or more strikes. The Company had always claimed support from their "stakeholder" (i.e., the New Labour Government) so this widening of the debate, as Royal Mail put it, can arguably be seen as a deliberate decision to up the ante by piling on more issues in an attempt to get as many concessions as possible regardless of the wider impact on their workforce or their professed view of valuing that same workforce. In other words a resolution would come by making things very much worse and through that, force the Union into having to agree to what was never even supposed to have been part of the dispute in the first place.

To ram home the point, in response to the CWU advising its delivery members that there was no agreement for later starts and for them not to co-operate, the Company wrote to their "people" to remind them that, "....your employment contract does allow Royal Mail to change your hours of working as long as we have given you reasonable notice. This means that lawfully you are not in a position to refuse to comply and if you do so, you will be in breach of your contract with Royal Mail. I would ask you to reconsider your position and confirm that you will be working in accordance with your new notified start time, with effect from 8 October 2007."[20]

The same old approach. Say one thing and then, if it doesn't quite go your way, force it through. How things had changed from valuing employees. This was executive action across the UK from 8 October in the middle of a national dispute in which ACAS were currently involved. It was change customers didn't want, was based on the "discredited" 56mph argument and ignored the inconvenient fact that according to the CWU at least 60% of mail was at a Mail Processing Centre by midnight anyway. It also ignored proposals put to them by the CWU which was to take the 60% figure and use it to provide employees with the choice of working later or remaining as they were.

It also appeared to make little sense to their employees who were by now very agitated, with many who had family responsibilities and other second jobs, at their wits end and liable with seven days' notice to have their daily start and finish times changed by plus or minus two hours.

The Government "stakeholder" support would be encapsulated in a phrase used by the Prime Minister and echoed by the Secretary of State John Hutton, that "the dispute should be brought to an end on the terms that have been offered as soon as possible." During a Trade and Industry Select Committee hearing on 22 October, Hutton would respond to the charge that the Government had taken sides, by saying, "I think what we were trying to do was speak up for the public in all of this (and that the offer) was a genuinely fair and reasonable one and affordable for the business and therefore for taxpayers."

Strikes took place in October and Royal Mail decided to ban those striking from any overtime to clear up the backlogs. A typical "cut off your nose to spite your face" response. We can't reward strikers with overtime, then again our customers want their mail – what to do? Customers can wait, although in some areas it was reported that casuals would be used.

However, after the strikes an agreement was reached and yes, in the end Allan Leighton did get his hands dirty by meeting with Billy Hayes, General Secretary and Dave Ward, Deputy General Secretary to sign a document stating that they would not introduce unagreed change and the Union would suspend any industrial action. This, to allow for talks facilitated by ACAS and the TUC. Implicit in that agreement however, was a recognition that Royal Mail had been introducing change without agreement or buy in from their own employees. That unagreed change again. Why keep doing it? Why on earth keep on antagonising "your people"?

Perhaps the message was that if the workforce know their employer will do what they want come hell or high water, then everyone will slot into line and oblige. If this was the philosophy then ultimately it only succeeded in alienating people. Perhaps we are simply back to that question again, whether Royal Mail is institutionally incapable of valuing its own workforce. If this poses a thought that maybe the pudding is being over egged, then the above quotes from the Shaping our Future Agreement show how far the Company had come from those thoughtful and considered commitments.

In fact, so difficult was it for Royal Mail to re-establish contact with its employees after the agreement was reached (with the help of ACAS and the TUC) that the CWU was dealing with subsequent attempts by the Company to press ahead with later starts, by having to consider additional local strike ballots. What sort of message was this providing to their workforce?

As for the pension bombshell, that would be formally separated from the agreement, to be known as Pay & Modernisation and instead a formal consultation would be undertaken and balloted on separately by CWU members from all parts of Royal Mail Group. The subsequent ballot of postal workers across Royal Mail Group would see pension changes agreed, which involved, amongst other things, a move to a career average scheme from the then final salary pension and a normal retirement age of 65, up from 60. Additional safeguards negotiated would sweeten the pill with service prior to 2008 remaining as a final salary and allowing the option of continuing to pay in after the normal milestone of 40 years had been reached, up to a total of 45 years' worth of pension (very sadly there was no room for new entrants to join and they would be left with an inferior defined contributions scheme once 12 months service had been achieved). The huge issue of job security was also resolved with the Company withdrawing their intention to cease MTSF.

The potential for huge pay cuts from the later starts and the absorption of door to door work was dealt with. D2D would continue and be subject to separate talks and later starts would see those affected paid the allowance in perpetuity.

To the extent that the public would be affected, was the reality that later starts, which resulted in later deliveries, would be introduced from October 2007 subject to agreement locally on the implementation arrangements.

Amongst a good deal of text, the following extracts from the final Pay & Modernisation Agreement:

"October 1 2007: A pay increase of 5.4%.... April 2008: A 1.5% increase...."

"In order for Royal Mail to thrive as a Business and to ensure that it remains able to compete efficiently it is recognised that change is going to happen at a scale and at a pace never experienced before. Both Royal Mail and CWU are jointly committed to working together to deliver that change by agreement, continuing to protect jobs in line with our commitments in MTSF) and provide high quality terms and conditions for all employees."

"New Ways of Working – Employees will be treated fairly, with respect and will be expected to be flexible. The opportunity to perform more flexible attendance patterns will be introduced to improve workload, increase efficiency and provide a better work-life balance for employees."

"It is all about managers, reps and employees working together sensibly with a bit of give and take, applying equally to all. This is not about employees not knowing what job they are on or when they start and finish from one day to the next. Nor is it about anyone refusing reasonable requests. Account should of course always be taken of individual circumstances."

There were four phases. Phases 2 and 3 for example concerned new ways of working. Amongst other things, it said:

"New arrangements to cover for one another and develop sensible options to absorb absences and increased workload where time exists within normal hours."

"To ensure all paid work hours are utilised" (NB in other words, the end of Royal Mail's job and finish concept) and to create "a working environment where (everyone feels) valued and motivated."

"Both parties recognise that a fresh start is needed and are committed to moving away from the adversarial relationships that persist in too many parts of the business. This needs to be replaced by respect for different viewpoints and a determination to work together to find common sense solutions...."

As for the demands of Royal Mail to make people work plus or minus two hours per day at one week's notice, this was wisely removed. Instead we had a commitment to reduce agency and casual staff. Workload alignment would be crucial and as well as a weekly meeting with the local CWU representative and manager there would be the introduction of "longs and shorts" and we are not talking about trousers here. Mail volumes (i.e., traffic) would be tracked and on quieter days duties would be set for fewer hours, so that for example a Tuesday would be say 7 hours attendance and a busier day, say a Friday, would be a 9 hour attendance.

There would also be the ability of a local manager to ask an employee to vary his or her hours by plus or minus 30 minutes if there was an unexpected problem, for example late arrival of the mail. Such a request was not compulsory but the idea was that there would be an adult to adult conversation to enable the request to be fulfilled or not depending on the circumstances of the individual. In other words if an employee could help they really ought to do so. The fact that staff helping out was a fact of life anyway, was missed in the rush to claim a huge change in working practises had just occurred. Indeed, as some Posties would no doubt recall, some managers would see this provision as being a waste of time as they couldn't actually force someone to stay on. It was safe to assume that such managers did not bother themselves unduly with the introduction of a new culture of valuing their staff.

The contentious demand that postal workers cover for each other was agreed with the pill sweetened with a concession that lower summer mail volumes could mean more people able to have annual leave at the same time.

As for Phase 4, this was, "to assist development of a fourth phase of modernisation, consultation and negotiation [that] will now take place...." There were three groups. The first on Relationships would look at improving industrial relations, how change was managed and "practises covering issues like attendance, conduct and performance management." The second group would look at a new pay and reward package, examine annualised hours, flexible working and making attendance patterns to benefit people in line with Royal Mail's family friendly policy etc. The third group – Future Working – looked at mail centre, delivery and network strategies (in other words, the door was opening to discussions around rationalising the number of workplaces, i.e., closures to you and me), developing proposals to capture the benefits of automation (for example issues around a shorter working week and continuing job security), job design and product strategies to develop and grow the business.

And finally, "This agreement lays the basis for changing how we work to ensure a successful future for the business, its employees and how the business and CWU will work together." In this case working together would be to pull all the aspects of flexibility and new ways of working and agree for each office a local flexibility plan.

The above words, selectively quoted but nevertheless representative, covered as they say, a multitude of sins. Sins of an adversarial environment, bullying, a slash and burn approach to staffing and of course the perennial fall back position which the Company as we have seen, inevitably took, namely to introduce change without agreement if they possibly could.

What was missing perhaps was any sense as to how exactly Royal Mail would implement a culture where people felt valued as expectations were so low as to be bordering on the nonexistent. Royal Mail knew this of course as its employee surveys were telling it so. This Agreement, coming as it did just after the full market liberalisation and on the back of a Government loan, was the perfect time to really engage staff and get people on board. If not then, when?

Enough said. Peace in our time then for employees and managers alike. At long last something to crow about. In other words, an agreement reached in the teeth of opposition from Royal Mail, but which nevertheless enabled some sort of normality to resume. Regrettably for many postal staff though, the peace hoped for never arrived. As was noted by Europe Economics it would be "conflict deferred rather than resolved."[21]

"Conflict deferred" however, really should not have been an opinion even remotely worth expressing if the harsh realities of Postcomm and liberalisation at the forefront of everyone's minds had been allowed to inform the need to work together.

Indeed, to their credit the CWU would look to tackle this issue head on. During the ballot process to ratify this national agreement, it issued a Q&A for members. Question: How can we trust Royal Mail? The CWU view to its members was unequivocal. "Lack of trust can never be a reason to vote against any agreement – in fact the reverse is true. This agreement offers the best chance for everybody to regain trust and build a better working environment." Allowing mistrust to dictate would mean, "...a self fulfilling prophecy and means we just go round in circles and never move anything forward."[22]

For Royal Mail's part they would in due course issue a briefing to managers known as "Myths and Facts" in which it was stressed that people would know what they were doing from one week to the next (in fact the Pay & Modernisation Agreement gave employees the right to know two weeks in advance what they would be doing, proof enough that the good intentions of the 2000 Way Forward Agreement had still not been realised in ensuring employees knew what they were doing) and that people would not be forced to work the 30 minutes etc. Everything seemed set for a period of calm for managers and representatives to "walk down the leafy lane together."

Added to this was the very public and positive comments from Allan Leighton and Adam Crozier in that years' report and accounts. Calling the agreement a "major milestone in the history of Royal Mail...." The Colleague Share scheme which remained in place would play a "significant role in ensuring our people are rewarded for their efforts ... the first batch of Colleague Shares has just been issued (which is) demonstrating to our people the tangible effect of their efforts to modernise the Company."[23]

It should not be underestimated though how the pressure on the CWU mounted enormously once Government became involved. We have seen above the comments from Hutton that the CWU should accept the terms put forward at the end of the sessions with ACAS and the TUC. At this same Trade and Industry Select Committee Hearing John Hutton would add that the final agreement was pretty much the same as the rejected one in that it contained only "a number of small changes...."

Such a comment demonstrated how great the support really was for Royal Mail's position as well as being a rather arrogant attempt to make it appear as if the rejection of the offer had in fact lead to hardly any further concessions. Nothing could have been further from the truth. Indeed in that same hearing, John Hutton would find himself unable to state that management was even partly responsible for the dispute. More philosophically, Hutton stated that,

I do not accept the criticism that the Royal Mail has acted like a bully boy in this case; I do not.... The fact that they did not reach an agreement I think cannot fairly or exclusively be laid at the door of management. I just think that is an unreasonable analysis. I think it is a flawed analysis and I think it does not take into account the complexity of the package of changes that the management were trying to get through the business in a short period of time to meet the challenges of competition as they see it.

Hutton also added that Royal Mail were "behind in terms of the modernisation they wanted to see...." A comment the CWU would agree with, but with a cynical twist. Hutton said this was only to do with the strike.

Now such opinions may or may not be reasonable, but in order to test them out, clearly there is a need to go back some few pages to look at what the Company were actually doing in reality, including turning down an offer of a period of calm in order to prevent a dispute commencing in the first place and not following on their solemn commitments from the 2006 Shaping Our Future Agreement in relation to new investment and automation. As the Conservative MP Brian Binley would point out to John Hutton during that session with the Trade and

Industry Select Committee, "During the first six weeks of the postal dispute Royal Mail refused to negotiate with the CWU and that resulted in four bouts of industrial action."

Chapter 13

The Gloves Stay Off: Transformation 2010

Business Transformation 2010 and Beyond – March 2010

The lead up to this agreement was to be littered with what can only be described as imaginative versions of what "flexibility" meant. That plus or minus 30 minutes was now suddenly to be used whenever the manager said there was an issue so that for some offices it became a tool to use to compensate for the lack of staff or to prevent the need to pay overtime. To the extent that it was supposed to be a voluntary provision guided by an adult to adult conversation, was too often interpreted as being a "reasonable" request which can't be refused.

Posties coming in early to try and get their work done were now stuck with a later start and a provision that was bordering on the compulsory. If working an extra 30 minutes one day seems eminently reasonable, it isn't so reasonable if you can't complete your delivery in time in the first place. Nevertheless, such practises would inevitably generate savings as by hook or by crook, more was done with less.

As for the "longs and shorts", this soon mutated into a full on drive by some parts of Royal Mail management to adopt a variation known as "swings and roundabouts." In other words, the manager told the employee that they had an early finish on a Tuesday and he would sort things out so they could get the time back some other time. In some places employees were persuaded that swings and roundabouts were better than longs and shorts. As would become clear, those stuck with swings and roundabouts would see that this was a way in which overtime could be negated and you never quite knew if in fact you were losing on the swings and losing on the roundabouts. New entrants and part timers were particularly vulnerable to pressure in this regard and would either be known as "runners" or as workers to be pitied as they had to come in early and finish late just to get the job done to ensure the manager kept them on.

The impact on the workforce was again completely predicable. There was confusion and/or anger at other colleagues who supported one or other system and a management that was content for that picture to prevail as there was no incentive to do otherwise as long as the work was done.

As for the system by which staff covered for each other in the summer this soon became a mandatory requirement with employees being faced with such arrangements long after the summer had finished and long before summer had started. Other variations involved employees being told to cover for colleagues on the first one or two days of any sickness or annual leave, again regardless as to whether it could be done or not. Many Posties found their offices short staffed as a back door way of making savings, although in truth Royal Mail had been operating this type of approach for some years. In other words, the "trust" issue at the heart of the last strike, was again comprehensively trashed by Royal Mail.

It was soon clear that the flexibility arrangements were a cover to be abused to square the circle of office budget cuts as the Company struggled to deal with the impact of Postcomm and the then lack of modernisation and investment.

One particularly pernicious abuse was against those who could not complete their delivery on time but who didn't or couldn't do overtime. Such people faced harassment. On the other hand if they agreed to do overtime, then there was no problem. The idea that a delivery that could not be completed should be examined and altered to allow for the workload, was anathema to a budget driven process.

In another office it was the exact opposite. An employee putting in an overtime claim would find it was refused and they would be subject to numerous tests of their sorting speed. Any sane outsider looking in would probably say that someone should go out with the Postie on their delivery to see if it could be done or not.

At that time and for reasons of the health of an employee, there was a maximum delivery span of 3.5 hours per day. In other words you were expected to walk for 3.5 hours maximum delivering the mail with your first mail bag having to weigh no more than 16kg. Try lifting that and putting it on your shoulder? That's your first bag of mail. Others will follow, the second and third of which should not exceed 16kg and 12kg respectively to be delivered out to you by van or quite often, to be shoved in the back of your car. Your fourth and fifth bags are to weigh no more than 10kg's each. And so it goes on with each bag having to weigh less.

A culture of harassment and bullying prevailed as managers focussed on meeting budgetary targets. The reader may well be thinking that there were surely enough national agreements to mean that the Union would engage the Company and common sense would prevail, after all the commercial climate was grim and unpredictable and there was an investment programme to implement. The only answer to give is that such national agreements became superfluous to requirements. In fact many CWU representatives would quote the Pay & Modernisation Agreement to their manager only to be told, "We run the business not the Union." How on earth then had matters come to this? Yet again an agreement is signed, positive words are used and then, back to square one.

Inevitably then, by early 2009 just 13 months or so after the Pay & Modernisation Agreement there were local strikes as Royal Mail sought to make change without agreement on the back of what was seen by postal staff as a culture of bullying.

These strikes did not bring about a solution and even though the CWU offered a three month no strike deal to resolve the issues, it made absolutely no difference at all. National strike action followed in October 2009 against the backdrop of a strategic decision by Royal Mail to push ahead with their plans without agreement.

It is worth just looking a little at this offer of a no strike deal. The CWU had their Annual Conference in early June. The no strike offer came on the back of an emergency motion to the conference by the Unions' leadership. In short, although there had been discussions with the Company on 3 June, these had made no progress. With this being the case, the CWU would try again, but to do so they had to persuade the Union activists – yes those very same people who had been forever castigated as "wreckers" and only out for strikes, to forego the same. The result was a huge and overwhelming vote to offer a three month moratorium on strikes in return for the Company not continuing introducing unagreed change. The motion even had provision to agree ground rules for dealing with any flashpoints and challenges during this period. A hugely positive message to give to worried and stressed out Posties and their families.

Regrettably, the Company rejected this and for months local strikes flared up. The view taken by the CWU for some time was that if their members locally rejected unagreed changes, that in the end this would be enough for the Company to rethink their strategy due to the reputational damage of local disputes and instead reach an agreement around the issues at stake.

If nothing else, it showed the restraint and efforts on the part of the CWU not to use the "nuclear" option of a national strike ballot. It also showed that the CWU was rightly concerned to get the outstanding issues from the Pay & Modernisation Agreement resolved so the industry could move on.

The CWU stance was that the Pay and Modernisation Agreement contained four phases, the last of which was not honoured by the Company. This concerned improving industrial relations and negotiating on the future of deliveries, mail processing centres and the introduction of automation. Of course if you are going to ignore the part of the agreement which talks about the future of the industry, what did Royal Mail think would realistically happen? What exactly was the calculation? Dave Ward, the CWU Deputy General Secretary stated that Royal Mail had effectively abandoned Phase 4 so they could press on with the unagreed changes.

If the decision to press ahead in this way was Royal Mail's to make, how would the CWU respond? At the same time you are discussing Phase 4, unagreed changes are being made across the UK. Is it reasonable for Royal Mail to act in this way as they have a business to run and a regulator to cope with or is it reasonable to challenge that mind-set?

It is a sad truism that many Posties were of the view that Royal Mail "wants us out on strike". Stop to think about that for a moment. Thousands and thousands of Posties had this view. Unbelievable – or at least it should be in any sane society.

Re-wind back to the 2003 dispute with Royal Mail and the Company's chosen method to introduce unagreed changes was to by-pass the Union and have their staff gather round where upon it would be explained to them the importance of making change and that if they did, extra money would be forthcoming. Often a quick show of hands was enough. If this "quick show of hands" had been held in the car park (and for all I know, maybe some were), you could be forgiven for thinking that the bosses had used the very same methods which they and probably every other employer in the UK had condemned when deployed by a trade Union.

So, a show of hands in many workplaces (some also had Company workplace ballots, but with no independent scrutiny of course and some left out who might have been on sick or holiday. Oh and of course, such ballots included employees not in the Union) led to changes in some places.

Back to 2009, and the chosen method this time by Royal Mail was to either implement change by executive action, i.e., with no one's agreement but theirs, or carry out a sham process, generally referred to as "running it through the process." In other words, the established procedures for dealing with disagreements and proposals would be subverted. This process, known as the Industrial Relations Framework has three stages and only if there is absolutely no other option after that, is change implemented without agreement. In other words, every effort must be made to avoid conflict not only because this is good for customers, but because using the procedure to its fullest provides opportunity to reach a deal.

The other point to note is that this Industrial Relations Framework includes text, which can only be described as being helpful, to enable dialogue to remain open with a provision for the "status quo" to be respected in the event a disagreement is lodged by either side. In other words, the existing situation prevails until agreement is reached or the procedure is exhausted. Looks like a solid agreement already exists to prevent disputes then?

Generally, if local requests are made of the Union for strike ballots, there are always further efforts made to hold last ditch talks to resolve things. This is crucial. Customers don't want disruption and employees don't want to lose money going on strike. Sometimes, both sides play "hard ball" and no talks take place until a ballot has actually taken place and both sides can see the strength of feeling. Then further efforts are usually mounted to bring people round the table for discussions. In other words, anything that can be done to stop a dispute must be done. That is the only responsible way to proceed. Given the backdrop of unfair regulation and the understandable fear of postal workers for their futures, such responsibility was needed as never before. Of course, there is another way.

Royal Mail decided on their course and they stuck to it. This was not unexpected. The Company had a well publicised policy, shown to best effect by the use of a graph – known colloquially as the "change curve". In short, it purported to show how sticking to the path was right. At first the work force are unhappy but unsure. They then become angry and are in denial about the changes. This is then followed by a recognition that change is happening whatever they do. Finally, an acceptance of change and peace and harmony is once again restored.

If there were strikes then, Royal Mail's view was so be it. In the end, their workforce would turn on their Union for delivering nothing but conflict and would also see the dire shape of things to come with the competition and would decide to knuckle under, be more accepting of the vision of Royal Mail and the changes that were apparently required. They'd also be more amenable to the argument that they were 25% over paid in relation to the minimum wage competition and would lower their expectations accordingly. By accepting this perspective, this was the way in which a postal worker could best protect their own personal future employment security. Wasn't it?

Now, this approach of introducing unagreed changes, comes after previous national agreements where solemn undertakings have been signed up to by Royal Mail. Undertakings that themselves took place against some very difficult trading conditions, so surely it was even more important to ensure change without conflict. It's their Company. These are choices for the Company to make. If you are an employee, what message is being sent by your employer? Are you valued or not?

Of course it is important to understand the obvious point here, which is that Royal Mail publicly didn't see things in this way. As the situation worsened, Mark Higson, Managing Director for Royal Mail explained to his staff that "all of these changes are in line with existing agreements and we have announced that no more will be made until the end of the year so we can concentrate on delivering a successful Christmas for our customers."[1] Mark Higson was also quoted at the time in the press as saying that Royal Mail had met the CWU more than 70 times in recent months.[2]

The difficulty with Higson's comments was that to most, change was being made outside of national agreements. If it were not so, then it is difficult to see why they did not seek to stop the strikes via the courts or in line with established dispute resolution procedures.

Another difficulty with this disconnect, was that in August 2009 an email from a senior manager was leaked to everyone, thanking managers for their efforts. The email begins as follows:

> It has been now 10 strikes (soon to be 11) since we started on this long, exciting and challenging journey. I have been reflecting myself over the weekend of the past 5 months or so and wanted to share with you my heart felt feeling of the significant changes you all have made; and when you read below and wake up every morning taking a decision on whether to roll back over and pretend it isn't your issue or as you all do, which is jump out of bed and rise to the day and the challenges it holds before you. I thought you would like to take a look at the below and take a few minutes just to reflect on your achievements.

These achievements were amongst other things: "Who delivered the 1st Pegasus walk revisions in xxxxx without CWU or local involvement? You did." (NB Pegasus is a computer software system to assist with plotting delivery routes and the time taken. It all depends on what is input as to what the outputs are. Naturally.) The letter continued:

> Who took their efficiency savings through the IR Framework at pace and then delivered it? You did.
>
> Who started to make indoor savings by absorbing the indoor element? You did.
>
> Who stated to make outdoor savings by absorbing this

with staff from your unit? You did.

Who delivered change through executive action? You did.

Who introduced less than part time working? You did.

...I have never seen this amount of unprecedented change in this short period of time. You should all be extremely proud of your achievements ... and I hope you will feel the same warmth of pride when you look at what you have achieved as a team so far this year.

...I know we haven't delivered everything yet. I am absolutely convinced you will and to the timescales we have agreed.

You get the message. The email closes of on a congratulatory note, in capitals: "A MASSIVE THANKS FROM NOT ONLY ME BUT THE DIRECTORS TOO."

Now this email is going out after ten one day strikes with more to follow. In fact, the number of requests from local CWU Branches would reach almost ridiculous proportions to the extent that in the end the CWU decided to cease all further local ballot requests and instead reluctantly move to a national industrial action ballot. Gloomy and depressing for some but this was about Royal Mail creating "facts on the ground." Perhaps a useful stance from which to negotiate, should that time come? In the meantime, the Company would press on with change in the knowledge that for anyone involved the only option they realistically had was to "put up or shut up."

It is well known in Royal Mail that as with an employment contract, if you disagree with it you must object or else you have agreed to it by default. Hence, for some Posties a considerable sacrifice was being made by having to take part in numerous one day strikes. Keep in mind again, these are strikes to make Royal Mail return to a position of negotiating change. Nothing more and nothing less.

As for the customers, well, the less said about them the better and those facts on the ground would hopefully mean that workers would simply accept the changes as strikes wouldn't change things. A month after this email, Paul Tolhurst Operations Director was quoted as saying, "It is now more clear than ever that the CWU is focussing all its efforts on strike action and political posturing. Their claimed support for change is no more than lip service.... Royal Mail is getting on with modernisation in an entirely fair and reasonable way which is completely in line with our existing agreement with the Union on flexible working practises."[3]

The disconnect between Royal Mail wanting to get its staff to work together to protect their futures was put into sharp relief by the same Company apparently content to see numerous disputes all over the place and it again begged the question whether they were simply incapable of valuing their own workforce never mind their customers.

At this juncture it would be helpful to briefly look at the headlines of the CWU stance. That there was widespread bullying in the industry was now clearly in the public domain, that the Company were making record profits (£321 million for the year 2008/09) but had offered no pay rise, that a bonus scheme for sharing in savings made had been abandoned, that managers were still getting bonuses,[4] that there were issues around the methods used to calculate and plan staffing levels and that pretty much no one anywhere in the UK was being employed on a full time contract.

The CWU wanted to see change, they a pay rise, they wanted automation which would help the Company and would at the same time allow scope to protect jobs by introducing a shorter working week and definitely a move away from the culture of bullying by managers, themselves under orders from more senior managers to meet budgets. Finally, they wanted agreed planning standards in delivery offices which were transparent and allowed for a fair workload. In other words, "...the pace of change can only be dictated by what people can cope with and workload must be based on agreed standards – not unachievable budgets."[5]

By September a letter from Billy Hayes General Secretary and Dave Ward, Deputy General Secretary to their members was able to state that Royal Mail had reverted to the attitude from the 2007 dispute of, "we make the decisions, you do as you are told."[6]

This decision to hold a national strike ballot had come after the offer of a three-month no strike deal made in June and repeated in July and August, had been ignored. Not that New Labour or Royal Mail were listening. In fact this approach of a no strike period of calm was a repeat of the CWU's offer prior to the 2007 national dispute. The national ballot would produce a three to one vote in favour of strike action – 61623 (76%) to 19207 (24%).

But just what were these unagreed changes anyway? What was going on to precipitate Posties going on strike when they were being told that strikes would damage their futures? For "changes" read "modernisation", or so the public would have thought. In fact, for modernisation, read: "...budget targets mean some postmen are unable to complete their deliveries in the allotted time and are forced into unpaid overtime or faced with disciplinary action."[7]

A postal worker in the Guardian's Comment is Free forum said he was striking

one day a week for months now. We are doing so in response to the imposition by executive action of massive changes such as job cuts, increases in workloads and the replacement of overtime by compulsory coverage for absent colleagues for no extra pay. Sometimes the changes plainly don't even work, but management presses on regardless in order to meet demands coming to them from higher up.[8]

For the keen eyed reader the above may trigger a thought that perhaps refusing to cover for absent colleagues in the way described is one of those Spanish practises? Well, yes you'd be right, but only in that this so-called practise was named as such by Royal Mail from the 2007 strike. The CWU had already agreed that the work of absent colleagues could be covered. That has gone on since the beginning of time. The issue is to ensure that such extra work can be fairly absorbed into a Postie's daily duties. If it can, fine. If it can't then that would mean this person was out delivering mail long after their duty had finished for the day.

That such a common sense approach was now apparently a Spanish practise is something that will be explained later on, suffice to say that who decides that the work cannot be done in the time allowed? If the postal worker says it can't, will anyone believe them? You begin to see the reality of having fair and transparent standards for deciding on workloads because there were some managers' content to throw around whatever weight they had. If there are no agreed standards or if staffing has been cut back or if the staffing base has to fit the budget, then you will be left to bully your workforce by hook or by crook, to get the work done. And so it came to pass. In fact there is unlikely to be any postal worker in the United Kingdom who would not recognise the picture painted.

In other words, a process would commence whereby staffing levels would be cut in order to meet a predetermined budgetary outcome. At the same time, start and finish times were often changed. Postal workers today do not now generally start work at the crack of dawn. The modernisation so beloved by everyone covered a multitude of sins of course. Modernisation through new sorting equipment actually meant later deliveries (it always will now), meaning later start times, meaning a huge impact on many postal staff with family and caring responsibilities. As for the customer and small business owner, later deliveries weren't popular either unless you happened to be a large business posting millions of items as late as possible the previous day.

As for the New Labour Government in September Lord Mandelson was quoted as saying that the Union were, "essentially boycotting the agreed processes for making change in the Royal Mail." It is doubtful if Lord Mandelson even today would acknowledge that postal workers can be forced to work for nothing and one can only assume that he didn't believe a word of the CWU in August 2009 either when Dave Ward Deputy General Secretary was quoted as saying, "We are repeating our offer of a no strike deal to Royal Mail to avert current and future action." All Royal Mail had to do was to stop implementing unagreed change. Instead they carried on. It was a calculated decision and the reader would be foolish to think otherwise. [9]

A document from Royal Mail was subsequently leaked to BBC's Newsnight, it demonstrated that they were yet again looking to try and break free from the CWU. A Letter to Branches by the CWU described the document as coming as little surprise. It sought to "actively down dial the role of the Union", to get an agreement on their terms and if this couldn't be achieved Royal Mail would put in place "a framework for delivering change without agreement" and would "serve notice on the current industrial relations framework and facilities/release arrangements and substitute the legal minimum." The document also assumed "shareholder support", i.e., the Government.[10]

This assumption by Royal Mail seemed well founded as Mandelson was quoted as declaring himself, "beyond anger" at the CWU. However, The Guardian noted in an editorial that "Lord Mandelson and the rest of the Government cannot evade responsibility for this debacle. For years, Labour Ministers have been hell bent on privatising the service." It is perhaps too much to ask of a Minister predisposed to a privatisation, that they should analyse the situation before pronouncing upon it.[11]

Mandelson would also be quoted in the same article as saying that the strikes were, "self defeating" and he would not condemn the use of 30,000 temporary staff to help fight the strikes.

Of course these 30,000 workers were to enable Royal Mail to deal with weeks of strikes as opposed to settling the dispute. Why on earth agree to some Union "no strike deal" when you can prolong the agony with casuals? Some were employed at special warehouses such as at Severn Beach near Bristol. Mail would be trunked in and a parallel operation would start up. If a processing centre was on strike, then places like this would do the job instead.

The Mail on Sunday sent in an undercover reporter who witnessed "unpleasant confrontations between Union members and temporary workers" and that staff had "refused to speak to us" (the temporaries) in the canteen. He also described having to endure "taunts of scab, scab, scab!" as he crossed the picket line. One wonders what reception he expected. Perhaps it would have been best for pickets to have welcomed everyone to the warehouse and expressed to them the hope that they would have a long and fruitful period of employment carrying out the work of those in dispute.[12]

In the event no more than "a few hundred" of the 30,000 started when required, due to backlogs with vetting.[13] It should not be forgotten that there were laws to prevent the employment of temporary workers to substitute for striking workers. By employing so many and doing so before national strikes took place Royal Mail hoped to usurp the effectiveness of the law. They would also claim it was simply a matter of ensuring that the impending Christmas period had extra helpers. It would be noted however that the previous Christmas just 15,000 were temporarily employed. As a result the CWU began to commence legal action against the suppliers of temporary workers.[14]

On the 2 November Royal Mail wrote to their staff to advise them of the damage being done to their futures. Whilst the CWU was now determined to get a deal the view was that after months of unagreed change, any deal really had to be honoured. For their part Royal Mail advised staff that, "In London your colleagues have already lost 20 day's pay with no end in sight. They have taken action to avoid working as you do, are you sure you are not on strike to help keep poor working practises?"

What were those working practises? Postal workers sitting around, just doing a bit here and there? If some were actually doing the work of their colleagues for no pay – in other words they were doing what they were told – by working beyond their normal hours or by coming in early, then was that a good working practise? What about staff reductions meaning that delivery staff were out walking the streets for more than the then agreed 3.5 hours or staying past your time because the manager said he could make you under the terms of "flexibility?" Did it matter that this was all outside the 2007 Pay & Modernisation Agreement?

The reality was of course that some ended up working for nothing and others due to perhaps a stronger local Union could actually come in on time and finish on time. To think that it takes a strong Union to try and enforce what anyone else would simply take for granted? In truth, Royal Mail had always tried to play the "London card". Workers there were a nightmare and ruining it for the rest! To suggest that postal staff in London were not equally affected by the unagreed changes was of course untrue, but inevitably the truth should not be allowed to get in the way of providing a barrage of propaganda to Posties working outside of London.

Thankfully an Interim Agreement was reached soon after in early November which allowed for talks under the auspices of ACAS, the TUC and an independent facilitator, Roger Poole.

But what of this Interim Agreement? Well, there would be a period of "calm". No strikes and no executive action. A tacit admission that the Company had been taking such action was encapsulated in the phrase, "Royal Mail have committed that no further change will be imposed during the course of these negotiations."

As for the places where unagreed changes had been made, "the local parties will undertake a review (and) in offices where change has been implemented without agreement the local parties will engage in genuine negotiations to reach local agreement."

As part of Royal Mail's attempts to force through change, they had introduced a practise by which employees were taken off pay if deemed not to be working "normally". Normally, was defined by the local manager and generally involved carrying out extra work that the manager deemed could be done. Whether it could actually be done in someone's daily time was of course immaterial. This practise was seen as a punishment for opposing unagreed change. It was yet another way in which the Company were able to endear themselves to their workforce.

The Interim Agreement stated that "Royal Mail confirm that the process of taking people off pay is a response to industrial action and is not a measure to deal with individual performance issues ... where there are disputed cases of individuals who have been removed from pay these can be raised by the Union and will be reviewed."

In respect of the disputed Phase 4 situation from 2007, a joint commitment was reached to "accelerate and complete the modernisation programme by jointly resolving all outstanding issues from Phase 4..." This covered all aspects of Royal Mail from delivery staff to those in mail processing centres to those trunking the mail around. For Deliveries the vexed issues of delivery spans, work measurement and revision processes and tools, would be resolved.

Ironically given the clear decision of the Company to force in change and allow the resultant disruption to continue, it was agreed "to deploying change and resolving disagreement without service disruption." If Lord Mandelson was "beyond anger" before, then for many Posties who had lost money, they could perhaps be described as being in the same frame of mind.

In a period of months we had gone from managers taking "pride" in pushing in unagreed change to an agreement that commenced the process of unravelling some of those very same changes! It is impossible to really understand the worry for many staff caught up in a battle some did not fully understand, but was this really a sensible way to run things? To plough on in the hope workers will give up only to have to change tact because they didn't?

Thereafter negotiations continued until a final agreement was reached in March 2010. A pay rise was obtained (6.9% over 3 years), as was an hour off the working week (by mid 2013 not fully implemented). There would be some quid pro quos – the delivery span would increase beyond 3.5 hours but there would be more vans and electric trollies to take the weight "off the shoulder" and employees would get one Saturday off in four if they wanted it (this subsequently proved easier said than done – some didn't want it and Royal Mail said it cost more so they would try to actively discourage it). Importantly there would be agreed planning standards and tools (something which is still being discussed at the time of writing) and job security would be enhanced.

As for that "junk mail" mentioned earlier, this would now go into normal workload so that extra workers might be needed to deliver it. The loss of the payment for delivering this mail was compensated for by a weekly payment of around £20.60 for a full timer paid 52 weeks of the year and which would increase with normal pay rises. Many Posties were very unhappy with this as some had been able to receive payments above this level and the CWU struggled to explain that as this was now in normal workload, if it couldn't be delivered in duty time, don't deliver it or claim overtime.

It must also be said at this point that this agreement also paved the way for the removal of what was known as "cars on delivery", whereby some Posties used their own cars. This practise required strict insurance obligations but managers turned a blind eye knowing that this would get the job done. In its place would be van deliveries – two workers sharing a van, parking up delivering mail and then driving off to another part of town.

The agreement showed that with both Royal Mail and CWU working together to secure a vision of new ways of working more safely and efficiently, improvements were possible and was intended to demonstrate to Government and Postcomm that modernisation was happening before their very eyes. For postal workers the hope was that a sell off of their industry would now not take place and the Pension issue would be taken on by the New Labour Government.

The CWU said, "We now have a shared vision on modernisation with powerful statements covering customers, employees and the future ambitions of the Company.... This will hold us in good stead for the future." [15]

As for the agreement:

This agreement reaffirms the 2007 Pay and Modernisation Agreement, concludes all outstanding Phase 4 negotiations.... Royal Mail has a proud history of being a trusted Company with deep rooted public support. It ... performs a valuable social and economic function across the United Kingdom. Its employees are respected and valued members of the communities they serve. However, Royal Mail is facing challenges on an unprecedented scale. The digital revolution, pension deficit, competition and volume decline means that to secure our future everybody must work together and fully embrace radical change. To signal a fresh start Royal Mail and CWU have developed a shared vision of modernisation.

Royal Mail wanted a workforce "that feels valued and is

genuinely involved in making Royal Mail a successful business ... that supports ongoing improvements to employee terms and conditions, greater long term job security and which sets the benchmark for our competitors to follow."

Royal Mail would "provide the CWU with genuine engagement at the development stage of key business policies supported by transparency and good information share."

Also, "A new relationship cannot develop overnight and it will take commitment and time from everyone to build trust and confidence.... It is also essential that everyone sets aside any negative experiences of the past and looks forward to building effective relationships based on positive experiences of the future. Central to this is a joint commitment to create a culture where we identify common objectives, align interests and always seek mutually acceptable solutions."

To support this there would be a "deployment engagement framework" which must ensure that "All Royal Mail managers and CWU Representatives ... are responsible for transforming and improving relationships in a way that is visible to all employees." Initially the ACAS Chief Conciliator would be present, as would the independent facilitator Roger Poole. Both individuals had played a huge part in bringing Royal Mail to a position where they recognised an agreement was necessary.

Yet again, I will use the phrase, peace in our time. Surely this time a national agreement would be honoured in full and relationships all changed for the better?

Sadly not. The agreement, whilst providing a strong commitment to work together, did not cover many of the nitty-gritty issues, in other words, how is some of this change actually going to be implemented? The Company would quickly move to try and introduce change at an efficiency rate of 100 BSI (British Standard Institute). Such a level of performance means everything in a workplace is ideal and there is a motivated workforce with no interruptions to the working processes. Additionally, planned rest and relaxation breaks have to be built in and normally a productivity bonus is paid according to the ACAS code of practise. There is more: 100 BSI in the context of Royal Mail would have to mean every letter requiring sorting by a postal worker would have to be the right way round, no letter must have stuck together against another, there should only be one address per slot on a delivery sorting frame and no necessity to have to sort between fittings.[16]

This wasn't part of the agreement reached, but that was irrelevant for Royal Mail. Local CWU representatives quickly found different versions of planning documents circulating with Planners coming in to ensure changes fitted around these ungreed documents and to fit in with budgetary requirements. For their part the Union would engage the Company and try and retrospectively agree revised versions in line with the Agreement.

One area that soon became conflated in the way that swings and roundabouts had a couple of years before (and still does to some extent), was the idea of the "model week." How many hours on average were necessary to fulfil the USO? As with any employer, they need to understand their business and Royal Mail is no different. A model week meant a set number of workers would be needed depending on the average volume of mail over the previous 12 months. Anything over this would mean extra hours were required. So far, so sensible.

Previously, the issue had always been dealt with by "lapsing". In other words, a duty would not be covered, e.g., if six people were on annual leave, not all their jobs would be covered and those left would take up the slack. This then was a system to cut staff numbers if mail volumes fell whereas the model week was set at a low average across the year and staffing would have to be added if the mail was above the model week.

Forget for a moment that this is purely to do with mail volumes and instead add into the mix that most contentious of subjects, budgets and you can see where this is going. Apply the model week approach strictly and extra hours would have to go in, which may of course bust the local budget. If it is possible to get employees to work above the model week without extra help, job done. How this is done is another matter entirely.

This 2010 Transformation agreement then ended up as a process to rejig delivery offices (and other parts of the Company), introduce a shorter working week, one in four Saturdays off and plan to ensure staffing was appropriate if model week volumes were exceeded. To complicate things though, Royal Mail had a separate intention to identify those delivery offices in the top 10% of performers and get everyone else to that level.

The hope that a workplace could introduce change, free from budget interference by only using agreed planning tools turned out to be pie in the sky.

For Posties working in delivery offices and having seen major agreements reached, there was by this time supposed to be "adult to adult" conversations about what was achievable, clearly defined flexibility to ensure no unfairness, weekly meetings between the local Union and manager to ensure planning of staffing, people knowing at least two weeks in advance what they would be working, everyone having one Saturday off in four and fully trained for what they might be asked to do. All of which should, if implemented properly have led to a genuinely well motivated workforce. That was what Royal Mail desperately wanted to see, wasn't it? Why was this so difficult to achieve?

So this agreement is concluded in March 2010 and by 2013 Royal Mail have been able to deliver such stunning staff satisfaction survey results as mentioned earlier. For such a huge organisation, battling to survive isn't that just a fantastic environment for creating an "all pull together mentality?" People motivated to get stuck in to the job knowing that at long last they are now being valued?

Now, as stated above, the foregoing is far from a comprehensive look at what went on. It is a potted set of quotes and comment to show that the question posed at the start, namely is Royal Mail institutionally incapable of valuing its own people, is perhaps beginning to be seen as having some substance after all. Look again at some of the themes above. Jointly working together, valuing people, developing them, finding mutually acceptable solutions to problems etc.

How can it be possible to commit to such words and then – and yes let's just say it from the point of view of the average Postie – break those same agreements so that by April 2013 such was the situation that the CWUs members saw only budget driven change and a chaotic approach to running delivery offices that led to the CWU seeking from Royal Mail talks to "put right failing delivery revisions."[17]

There is an overriding thought that must be articulated, namely that there has been a pattern of behaviour from Royal Mail. They need change, they try and impose that change, there is a dispute, there is a subsequent agreement and there is relative peace for a while. Then, the cycle starts all over again as they ignore previous agreements.

Is it that they simply don't trust the CWU or is it that the whole process of talking to a trade Union when there is action needed to respond to the commercial environment is just too much effort. Well, if their intention was to run the Company without the CWU then they kept on trying regardless of the effects on their customers or their own employees. All that is required is to reach an agreement, honour it and then if it becomes unfit for purpose, approach your staff and Union and re-negotiate. Is that really too much to ask. The truth is probably that the Company just gets fed up being in a straightjacket and wants the freedom that non-Union employers have to pretty much do as they please. And that leads us back to the fundamental point of the purpose of a trade Union to protect its members.

The critical point in all this is not that the Royal Mail are and were facing huge problems, but that at each stage they saw – in fact they must have, as no other explanation fits – the CWU as an obstacle to get round, hence the inevitable move to introducing changes without agreement.

If this sounds a little unfair and your thoughts are that there must surely be more to it than meets the eye, then amongst the examples and anecdotes that could be provided, it should be noted that having signed the Transformation Agreement in early 2010, by September 2012 the CWU would be noting the following in advice given to its members and representatives,

> We have been in discussion with Royal Mail regarding what appears to be a centralised move to undermine the national agreement ... .and other national guidelines and joint statements. The falsities that feature most at the moment are: Delivery spans must be at least 4 hours long, start times must be no earlier than 0700, indoor performance (i.e., the speed of sorting all the mail for delivery) must be 100 BSI and a revision must deliver at least a 5% savings target.... None of the above has been agreed ... .and all are contrary to the national agreement. Our advice to representatives is to register disagreement wherever this becomes an obstacle, unilaterally if necessary and get the problem into the Industrial Relations Framework.[18]

It is of course open to me to labour the point again by asking what the Company must think their workforce thinks of them. As valued employees or just a number? By May 2013, Royal Mail would find themselves signing up to a Joint Statement designed to ensure that the Transformation Agreement was delivered. A National Delivery Transformation Resolution Group would assist to help deal with unresolved local difficulties.[19]

And did this work? Apparently not. An average month would bring about three or four strike requests, but in June and July around 40 had been made. Areas as diverse as London, Coventry, Bristol, Bridgwater, Plymouth, Truro, Edinburgh and Middlesbrough. Bob Gibson the Unions' National Officer for Delivery members would be quoted as speculating "whether there are managers who can't read the content of an agreement or there is a deliberate attempt to undermine national agreements and procedures."

The Union would see these developments as being "disappointing and frustrating." And no doubt it was. If you spend large chunks of your time negotiating agreements then if nothing else, it is not an unreasonable expectation that they would be honoured? For goodness sake, the national agreement last signed and the subject of this chapter is called the "Transformation" agreement. The public could surely have expected that with such a transformative word used, that change would be forthcoming as a consequence! Some perspective is perhaps in order at this juncture. 2013 was of course the year the Government really did look to privatise the industry and this would be cited as a possible reason. Bob Gibson again, an "aggressive management strategy (is) down to the looming issue of the potential sale of Royal Mail."[20]

Now these all these agreements mentioned above contain far more than has been mentioned and at various times involved processes around bonuses for extra efficiency, one-off payments for introducing change (i.e., for working harder) and consultation and negotiation processes for restructuring the organisation in response to the changing environment. Nowhere will you see anything other than an agreement forced on the Company by their own workforce, demanding that they be included in the changes with their input treated as valuable. The idea that such agreements would have existed without a Union or without industrial action is completely delusional. In truth however, most do want to work together to get things done fairly and in the right way, but somewhere in the mix that goal is lost sight of.

In Royal Mail's accounts for 2009/10 the Chairman Donald Brydon said, "we very much regret that CWU strike action ... resulted in Royal Mail falling short of some of its ... targets." It's a fair bet to say that most people will not read these accounts but if such a sentence was put before many of Mr Brydon's employees they would simply be unable to believe it. If he regretted the strike, would he also regret the actions of those in charge who made decisions to plough on with unagreed change regardless? Perhaps their own regret was of a more private nature. A regret perhaps that they had to reach an agreement after all, or at least an agreement that was some way from what they originally envisaged.

This then is surely a litmus test for the Company. An ability to accept some blame. A desire to level with your workforce and a commitment not to repeat these actions again. Of course whilst Brydon also wished to "record my gratitude to all involved..." in the "tireless efforts to find a mutually agreeable was forward...." in fact if no trade Union existed or if they had beaten the CWU, then the original position would have been maintained: no pay rise, no job security enhanced, no shorter working week, no fair workload performance tools etc.[21]

Of course, it cannot go un-remarked that for many workers in the UK never mind anywhere else, the idea that you receive an extra payment for working differently or with less people, is the stuff of fantasy. The Tolpuddle Martyrs were the catalyst for the idea that by banding together, workers could increase the value of their labour. Ever since, any employer will do their upmost to secure workers at the cheapest rate possible. At its most blunt, "I'm doing you a favour turning up to work for you, so pay me a fair days pay for a fair days work," "Is that so? I'm doing you a favour by employing you and if you don't like it you know where the door is."

The message is clear, if depressing. Too few employees are in a position to bargain over the rate of pay and for those in areas classed as semi or unskilled, that position is exceptionally weak unless there is a trade Union you can join.

The supreme tragedy here of course is that the Royal Mail management wanted to run it their way and the workforce and Union wanted to run it by agreements reached – walking down that leafy lane together. Of course a philosophy that underpinned, and still does, the approach of Royal Mail is the idea of what is known in the industry as "command and control". A heavily vertical organisation, with a strict pecking order and a top down approach to managing. As we saw above, this approach does enable the "same old same old" to predominate – bullying of workers, a failure to follow national agreements, strikes and finally, a poor public relations image.

Such a command and control game plan came into its own with the introduction of the Postal Services Act 2000 and the arrival of Postcomm. The last thing Royal Mail wanted was to negotiate agreements when there was work to be done. Arguably, to the extent that there were agreements reached, had more to do with the Company seeking to use the Union as a vehicle to enable change to happen, after which there was a reversion to the default stance of trying its best not to follow what it has just signed up to do. In fairness to Royal Mail though, with Postcomm strictures lapping round your ankles as water levels rise, you might well be inclined to adopt a "by any means necessary" approach. Ironically of course intrinsic to such an approach is the concept of choice. Which choice to make?

Enter Lord Sawyer.

PART 3

Chapter 14

Enter Lord Sawyer

Command and control of an organisation should enable positive values of respect and dignity in the workplace to be embedded even if it is under banner of "treat your people fairly or else!"

As far as can be established nowhere has Royal Mail sought to challenge the idea that their Company is run on such a philosophy of command and control. In fact, the more that this concept is thought about, the more attractions that maybe found, none more so than the idea of a strict hierarchy of responsibility with reporting mechanisms in place so that those at the top know what is happening and can direct things in the right way. If a culture from the top is embedded, then surely it really would be eminently possible to transform the Company (or any Company?) with inspiring leadership and a culture respectful of each employee's contribution.

In fact, to be more specific about it, corporate culture is set by those in charge, regardless as to whether there is a command and control process in place or not. We have all heard about the Boardroom excesses, but at its heart is an important principle, namely that those at the top will "walk the walk" so that their values and the example set is looked up to in a way that challenges all the old views about "them and us." More than challenge though, it would be a culture whereby those senior managers not prepared to accept the change would go.

Arguably, the issue though for Royal Mail is that it has seemingly been unable to blend in a command and control process with the equally important process of empowering those managers on the frontline. More pointedly, for postal workers they are well aware that their immediate boss is only carrying out orders from someone else higher up. Add into the mix the various tiers of the Company which in turn replicate this command and control process on a smaller scale and you are left with another disconnect. An area manager can and will look to command and control his local managers to ensure budgets are met so as to secure their place in the organisation and enable them to walk away with a hefty bonus for a job well done.

Now to assume from this that Royal Mail only have to click their fingers to get managers on-message, would be ridiculous. Or would it?

A huge and complex Company placed into the middle of a political bun fight and a regulator in Postcomm who was hell bent on stretching its remit as far as it could get away with, suggests that those charged with running Royal Mail have a massively difficult job to do. Organisations develop and mutate with internal machinations, personalities and policies all inter-mingling. Suddenly a command and control process doesn't seem to be the panacea that it first appeared, unless of course those at the top turn a blind eye to those implementing the Company's policies in, shall we say a rather robust fashion. In other words we have a centralised budget driven top down process supposedly running in parallel with an ethos which is supposed to ensure dignity and respect in the workplace.

The website run by Roy Mayall, hits the nail on the head in a section on productivity following the decision of Royal Mail in the wake of the 2010 Transformation Agreement to ensure that all workplace's and people's performance is equivalent to the top 10% of the Company:

What if one worker can't get into that top 10%? Some of us work at different speeds. Older guys just take longer to do the job, that's all there is to it.... With a bullying manager and a weak on non existent (Union) rep, I can see this turning some people's lives into a living hell.... And we all know that despite the platitudes and high minded phrases, that bullying is endemic in management culture. The Directors bully the DSMs (area managers) who bully the cluster managers who bully the DOMs (local delivery office managers) who bully us. Some people get it worse than others.... Hidden in the quiet recesses of a frame (a delivery frame where the postal worker sorts their mail into their delivery walk) a lot of threats can be made.[1]

We have seen that Royal Mail has been placed under huge strictures and has been expected to do wonders with one and sometimes both arms tied behind their back, so surely it is time to give them a bit of slack ? Well, yes and no.

Lord Sawyer was asked in 2001 to carry out an independent examination into industrial relations. For some two years prior to this, the CWU had been seeking an independent enquiry into industrial relations within Royal Mail due in no small part to the number of disputes taking place and to the large number of conduct code cases being prosecuted by the Company against CWU representatives, amongst other issues. Indeed, in 2002 the CWU stated that "it was quite clear that for a sustained period the employer were singling out CWU activists for disciplinary and dismissal action." More serious than this comment was the picture in 2001 when the Consignia Board advised the CWU that they were now intending to "proceed with summary dismissal where activists were alleged to have acted unlawfully and outwith their terms and conditions of employment." Such an intention, if enacted would have precipitated an immediate national strike (ballot or no ballot) and this message was relayed to the Board by the then General Secretary Derek Hodgson and the Deputy General Secretary John Keggie. That the only response to the strife was to summarily dismiss employees, was reason enough to let someone from the outside have a look at what was going on.[2]

In campaigning for such independent input, the CWU were

arguably showing that they had nothing to hide and wanted to see change for the better take place. No other explanation could realistically be put on the Unions' position as no one could predict the outcome. In retrospect it was brave of both parties to allow Lord Sawyer in.

His two reports would provide neither the Company nor the CWU with any real excuse to continue with the same old adversarial environment that had prevailed since goodness knows when. The fact that the Company had been continually making good profits during the previous 20 years showed in one way that adversarial relationships need not lead to years of losses and Government bail outs, but the question for those who saw the need for Lord Sawyer, was whether he could help the Company make change in a different way now that doors were to be opened to let in competition.

Royal Mail had previously approached the consultancy firm Organisation Consulting Partnership and through this link was born the "Creating Our Future Project" which both CWU and Royal Mail bought into; and out of this mix came the approach to Lord Sawyer, formerly the General Secretary of the Labour Party until he became a life peer in 1998.

The following look at Sawyer's report can only give a snap shot of the issues covered, but the crucial issue to bear in mind is that this report was at the exact time that Postcomm was starting its work. The stakes could not have been be higher and the task of those responsible for running Royal Mail was to follow up on the brave decision to bring in Sawyer, by ensuring that change really did happen, and for the better. Six areas of the UK were examined, Oxford, Cardiff, Liverpool, Glasgow and Reading (which had been involved in disputes) and Tonbridge and Leicester which had not. Interestingly, the focus was not on delivery offices, but on the huge mail processing centres, sites with up to 1,000 people working across 24 hour shifts.

The good news first. Sawyer noted that whilst some "failing" mail centres had been chosen to focus attention on, this did not mean that all workplaces were failing. Indeed he went further and said, "It would be unfair if the parts dealing with those Centres were taken as condemnation of all ... managers or all CWU representatives.... We repeat that we met many managers and Union representatives who were showing both leadership and vision in a time of real difficulty."

However, it was not all good. He noted previous initiatives such as "Teamworking" from 1991, which foundered on mistrust over its ultimate purpose. At the time there was a feeling that with Teamworking the best could be got out of people and they would feel more valued. On the other hand, it was a way by which a trade Union would be sidelined as the boss would go to the staff first and get them to do x y or z with no independent look to see if it was in their interests. The example was given of the Japanese production methods (for the most part, from the car industry with videos such as "Nissan – We Are Driven", providing the backdrop to what the ultimate purpose of team working might be) which showed how employers could get far more out of workers for no extra pay and with fewer people. In other words, the nightmare was a group of workers ostensibly happy enough but who were in effect being exploited without them fully recognising it or being able to do anything about it. For Royal Mail, it was nothing more than a way of getting people to work together. The workforce would respond by asking, "oh really?!" Hence no progress. This was followed up by a national strike as Royal Mail pressed for a variation in 1996. Again, no movement.

Other previous initiatives were the Agenda For Leadership in 1995/96 to deal with the quality of front line managers and tackling cultural issues over the way people were managed, spoken to and trained. A subsequent review stated that, "the task of delivering change within Royal Mail was underestimated. The constitutional style of management which exists is deep rooted within operations management and this is compounded by the mutual lack of trust between managers and front line staff."

The conclusion was sobering, but in a way positive. The Company had genuinely recognised deep seated issues and could now sort them out: "Agenda for Leadership has made a start ... significant improvement in attitude and behaviours will be dependent upon long term emphasis and business commitment."

There was also the concept of Strategic Involvement which existed within the internal industrial relations machinery and was designed for a free flow of information and dialogue on the basis of "no surprises" over initiatives or business thinking with an emphasis on sharing and developing ideas. Sawyer would note that implementation was "patchy." It would remain so thereafter.

In 1999, Sawyer noted the "Creating Our Future" project set around two Mail Centres with a brief, amongst other things, to create a culture of dialogue and problem solving which could be rolled out across the UK. It was noted that the project was abandoned after 12 months.

In 2000, Royal Mail and the CWU involved ACAS in Scotland to review industrial relations around the misuse of the conduct code, leadership behaviours of both managers and Union reps and working towards a Code of Practise on how each party should interact with the other. Sawyer would note that this last initiative would seem to have borne some fruit.

So, a history of efforts made but no real solutions. Sawyer would state at para. 104 of his report, that "Royal Mail has a justified reputation among its staff for embarking on initiatives and then not seeing them through. It has been suggested ... that our report will have a similar fate." Given the subsequent events and national strikes, it would appear that the doom mongers were more right than wrong.

The terms of reference for Sawyer's report involved looking at the extent to which procedures and agreements were kept, whether structures were working well and used properly, whether managers and employees understood the commercial realities and constraints under which Royal Mail operated and whether the application of individual procedures against individuals such as the conduct code and attendance procedure (a process for managing sickness based on the issuing of three stages of warning with the third being a consideration of dismissal interview) was being applied fairly.

Unsurprisingly, the report concluded that there were serious issues where dysfunction was considerable. He would note the increasing number of strikes in 2000/01 both official (25 strikes) and unofficial (330 strikes). Sawyer noted that some strikes would be spread on the basis of Union members coming out on strike in sympathy, but *typically* the spread will result from employees in one workplace being asked to do additional "breakdowns" or to handle diverted mail as a result of industrial action elsewhere." In other words, without actually saying it, Sawyer noted that Royal Mail were sometimes apparently content for strikes to spread, rather than contain and resolve the problem in the locality where it originated.

Amongst other things he noted that morale and motivation needed to be maintained, but that front line managers saw their role as "authoritarian and purely directive", that managers were seen by some in the workforce as "body watchers", that procedures against individuals were applied "mechanically and to ignore the emphasis on correction and counselling which have been deliberately written into them" and that these same attitudes "can be found in more senior operational management."

A further damning quote was that, "many senior managers, like their front line subordinates, often have little concept of how to deal properly with their employees or their Union representatives. Many used the language of "management control" –

reflecting a prevalent "command and control" attitude.

Sawyer noted also that managers were up against a strong Union and that this accounted for "part" of the problem. There were threats of industrial action and that some felt "beleaguered and under threat." They would even note that they had "heard of, and accept, instances of both threatened and actual physical assault on managers." Significantly, the report would not produce one incident by way of evidence to suggest individuals had been disciplined or dismissed. This suggests probably no more than aggressive finger pointing of which both sides could give as good as they got.

However, against the prevailing ethos it would be correct to think that if such acts occurred then this was in effect managers and reps "fronting up" on the basis of the Company demanding that something be implemented and to that extent the report noted that "the essential approach (of managers) is to defeat or outmanoeuvre the Union rather than develop a constructive working relationship." One Union rep would be quoted in the report as saying in his mail centre it was a "dictatorship based on a climate of fear."

Now this is about rows and arguments over most aspects of working arrangements. As we have seen that there was an Industrial Relations Framework Agreement in place already, only demonstrates the depth of the problems. More to the point, it was noted that at Tonbridge and Leicester the picture was entirely different between management and the Union. Sawyer could have done no worse than to demand that this Industrial Relations Framework Agreement be followed every time and indeed his report quoted this agreement as if to demonstrate the solutions were there. Page after page of depressing reading then and yet the problem was at least out in the open in a way it had not been before.

There was though a surprising failure to fully understand the Industrial Relations Framework. The document itself is a procedure and once completed, there is no further recourse to negotiation unless both parties agree. What happens then is down to the Company and to the Union members in a particular workplace or workplaces. Will change be introduced without agreement as the procedure is at an end? Will the workforce accept he change or will they oppose it? Another fault line was the way change could be brought in without agreement. The phrase executive action is used to describe such actions. The Company claim an overriding need and the procedure allows change to happen. The circumstances have to be exceptional and for many it was clear that Royal Mail would try and seek change in this way. Sawyer says as much himself when he refers to managers trying to defeat or outmanoeuvre the Union.

Sawyer also noted how Royal Mail knew empowering managers was critical, yet they seemed incapable of it as more senior managers would direct what should happen. The effect was a deskilling of the front line manager role. Employees would complain they did not know what was going on even though an established arrangement was in place known as "Work Time Learning" (WTL). In the years to come, such WTL sessions would be applied in a patchy manner and in many cases ignored in the rush to get the work done.

There were issues raised around training, over-management of the workforce, promotion arrangements and all the internal machinations that one could expect from such a large employer. The CWU was also enjoined to ensure it trained its own repre-sentatives, asserted itself on "wayward" Branches and moved towards an acceptance of the necessity of change, including dealing with a Royal Mail view that the CWU had in Sawyers' words, "shown indifference or inertia in the Strategic Involvement process; we were told of a litany of cancelled meetings or non-attendance by key officials." History would subsequently show that the tables would be turned as the CWU would have to go to extraordinary lengths to talk with someone who could make a decision.

It was though in the area of dealing with its own employees that change surely had to come? The report mentioned concerns about procedures being used unfairly against people with mitigation sometimes being ignored and a strong perception – denied by managers – that sick absence warnings were being given automatically in order to reduce absenteeism.

Of course the impact of the recently signed Way Forward Agreement, loomed large. It had to be implemented and yet to do so meant that workers, especially those in mail centres who had been used to working long hours on overtime, were to see maximum caps put on the number of hours as part of the implementation of the Working Time Directive. This Agreement was also designed to free up the potential to allow resources to be moved to where they were needed in consultation with the Union. Any move to change the existing order however, meant employees losing overtime. It was a structural problem with acknowledged high overtime levels going hand in hand with a low basic wage. A complicating factor was an existing scheme known as the Performance Bonus Scheme. Although designed to reward change, it would have to compete with how much a postal worker would lose when off set against a potential bonus once the change had been made. Sawyer's response was to set up a small expert group from the CWU and Royal Mail to help mediate and generate solutions.

Numerous recommendations were made covering the above issues and for there to be a period where both sides would not look to implement change without agreement, nor to stage strikes. A "big idea" was proposed, that of Partnership Boards. A facility which would not replace collective agreements, but would rather encourage a different mind set to encourage joint problem solving.

Sawyer would return to produce a final report in March 2003. Strikes were down, there were some Partnership Boards up and running and the new Chairman Allan Leighton had introduced an initiative to make Royal Mail a "Great Place to Work". Additional good news was in the formation, though patchy, of Dignity and Respect at Work (DRAW) groups, where volunteer workers met to see how this could be implemented in their workplaces.

However, he would also note that "the general feeling amongst employees I have spoken to is that very little has changed since my first report. I can't disagree with this." Also, that the Partnership Boards meant change was happening but that "these changes are yet to touch employees."

Ominously, he would add that "almost every indicator points to the potential for a worsening industrial relations situation within Royal Mail." And so it would come to pass. The Partnership Boards and even the DRAW groups would not be rolled out across the whole of the UK and good intentions would fall by the way side. It cannot be ignored that due to a deterioration in the industrial relations climate, a decision was taken by the CWU to suspend its own involvement in these Partnership Boards. Although in the middle of jointly implementing these Partnership Boards, the Company unilaterally announced that there would be "share options" which would be paid to workers in 2005 depending on the performance of the Company. Given the jittery nerves around the intentions of the Labour Government and the clear connotations that the phrase "share options" carried, it was no surprise that they would withdraw.

Their subsequent failure to re-emerge however, despite the CWU stance, which was that as soon as the difficulties had been resolved that the Union would resume its full participation, perhaps suggested their time had come and gone in the eyes of Royal Mail? The question was only posed as the CWU view at the time was that there had been genuine benefits but that these had only been "reluctantly acknowledged by the employer."[3] Instead, the message from the new Chairman of the Board, Allan

Leighton became to most postal workers, that things would be done his way and that it was now time to set out his stall and use such phrases as "it's time to crack on" in his letters to employees. As we have seen above, national strike action over pay, job security and change dominated instead in response to the Company's agenda.

So far as the culture and behaviours identified by Sawyer were concerned, there was clearly an issue of bullying within the Company and not only by managers on their workforce.

Here, the command and control approach came into its own. Allan Leighton to his credit introduced a 24/7 helpline manned by outside professional counsellors following a damming report from the Equal Opportunities Commission (EOC) on the prevalence of bullying and harassment within the Company. In its first year the helpline took around 4,000 calls. In the 2003/04 Accounts Allan Leighton would state that this total was "unacceptable" but that the Company was "determined to confront this issue and eliminate all forms of bullying and harassment."

The CWU also found itself in the firing line following the intervention of the EOC with some of its representatives not upholding that fine line between supporting the victim or remaining neutral, or perish the thought, coming down on the side of the alleged bully. It all pointed to a need to train representatives so that they knew how to deal with such issues and could better cope with what might be their own feelings or prejudices as to who was right or even, whether they thought that an incident constituted bullying or harassment in the first place. Mandatory Equality & Diversity training was introduced and the CWU also set up its own independent harassment and bullying helpline. Additional to that, was a process by which CWU representatives and officials would interview members who had a complaint and provide with the members' consent, an "in confidence" report to the Union Equal Opportunities Department so that trends could be tracked and potential "hot spots" raised in an appropriate way with the employer.

By September 2004, Royal Mail were claiming that "bullying and harassment is being tackled, openly and fairly." In relation to sickness absence a scheme had been introduced to provide a prize for those not taking sick leave. For employees under the then Disability Discrimination Act, it was clearly something that they would not benefit from. Similarly, if you were unlucky to have been injured at work and gone off on sick leave, the chance to win would not be within your reach. For Royal Mail however this was evidence that they "believe(d) that taking the carrot rather than the stick approach will help to reduce absence levels."

Of course it was not all prize draws. It would be noted that as part of this package, managers would be staying in closer contact with their workforce when off sick.[4]

In parallel with the Great Place To Work initiative and the DRAW groups, surely now things were genuinely changing for good? By 2005/06 Royal Mail stated in their accounts they had

achieved our target of completing diversity training of 175,000 people in just over 18 months. This was the largest undertaking of its kind by a UK employer. Our efforts in working to create an inclusive culture throughout the Company where everyone feels valued and respected were recognised in July 2005 when Royal Mail was awarded the Centrica Diversity Award in the Business in the Community National Awards for Excellence.

In anyone's book that surely is good news. It demonstrated that a command and control culture could deliver for employees. The bad old days were over and over for good. In fact, the task at hand, namely dealing with the regulatory regime set by Postcomm, was now considerably easier with employees feeling valued for their contribution. Regrettably, this is something of a fantasy.

That is not to say that Royal Mail didn't agree with making itself a Great Place to Work. That would be a trite and shallow assumption. In fact, up to a point quite the contrary. To quote from the September 2004 accounts again, Allan Leighton stated that "our people were demoralised and their pay was too low – a major factor behind our unenviable reputation of the worst strike records in the UK. There were numerous complaints about bullying and harassment and the Equal Opportunities Commission was planning to investigate Royal Mail. No change was not an option and Royal Mail had to get out of the industrial backwater it was in."[5]

Now without wishing to state the obvious here, this was the Chairman looking back over the previous year. The sentiments though, could not be clearer. A corner had been turned albeit on the back of an enlightened approach from those in charge. Perhaps there would be no going back to the bad old days of confrontation? Of course Royal Mail's self congratulations were coming after the huge dispute in 2003 when they were content to try and force through change on the back of a national industrial action No vote and against the backdrop of some 4,000 calls to their bullying and harassment helpline. The CWU would also note that its own helpline since November 2000 had received 9,700 calls up to June 2003.[6] Perhaps this was a case of trumpeting your success too soon?

Maybe, maybe not, but the answer was surely to be found in the same command and control structure that commenced the Great Place to Work philosophy. If they could turn on the tap of respect and dignity, they could just as easily turn the tap off again to do what they thought was necessary at any given time. If that appears to be a simplistic viewpoint, the lived reality for postal workers would be the best antidote to those who think otherwise.

Chapter 15

Alarm Bells

As for most trade Unions, each year (or sometimes biannually) there is the gathering of their Branches, Officials and Representatives for the "conference season."

This is the opportunity for CWU Branches across the UK to put forward motions for debate, based on deeply felt issues that have sprung up from their own localities. Motions are debated, speeches made and policy is enacted or not depending on the way the conference votes.

Typically, a motion from one part of the UK is suddenly echoed elsewhere as another Branch will stand up to speak and to confirm that the terms of the motion not only should be supported, but that it reflects what is going in their patch too. Then another will do so. Then, perhaps a further contribution in which the point is made that the sentiments are genuine but what is being asked will not be achievable or may actually make things worse. In short, there is a high level of debate and discussion. The pros and cons of issues are examined. Branches can turn up to a conference with the motions printed out in what is referred to as the "Agenda Pad", thinking they will vote for this or that motion, only to hear the debate and change their minds when the practicalities are looked at. A phrase commonly used at CWU conferences when such problems are encountered, is "the words are the words". No matter what you want a motion to mean, it is what the actual words say that matters.

For Royal Mail's part, they attend each year and sit in the public gallery to observe the debates. Delegates to the conference will sometimes give of their own personal experiences or relay an anecdote of some abuse of a CWU member or group of members. Indeed, some truly awful stories, made suitably anonymous, are sometimes heard.

Nothing is off limits – members who have had their pay stopped arbitrarily, managers spying on sick members by turning up unannounced demanding to see employees whilst they are ill in bed, managers shouting at employees, managers seeing an employee who is on sick leave outside their home and then claiming they are not in fact ill at all as they are capable of doing a bit of shopping perhaps, managers threatening employees with various outcomes from dismissal to ill health retirement to removing them from their normal duty if they are not fast enough, compassionate leave requests being refused, employees being stopped annual leave for hospital appointments, managers threatening employees with discipline for simply "doing the job properly" and managers issuing warnings to employees for sickness when in fact by any common sense yardstick someone who is hospitalised for an operation is perhaps not in a position to attend work and should be given some slack and welcomed back once they are better. There are any number of stories and all come as no surprise to postal workers who have seen it all. For newer employees, some will come wonder what on earth they have walked into.

That these experiences and others like them keep on raising their heads is either the result of a large complex employer who cannot possibly be expected to have each and every manager (let alone employee) on-message, or it is where those at the top simply shrug their shoulders and claim that in every barrel there will be one or two bad apples.

And why on earth should Royal Mail be there in the conference hall anyway? Well, for a start it is a public conference so who is going to debar them? More importantly, it is a genuine opportunity for the Company to hear what is going on in their organisation. From such insights have come changes and progress on issues down the years – from pay to harassment and bullying procedures to health and safety matters to the rehabilitation of ill workers. So, no excuses then for the Company not to know the views of local CWU Branches. Indeed, occasionally, once motions are submitted and accepted for inclusion, it is not unknown for such motions to be shared with the Company beforehand with a view to seeking agreement on the content. Is a particular motion unrealistic or is it something the Company can live with and who knows, maybe even embrace?

Of course not all such debates are open to the public and for those involving possible requests for industrial action, the public are sent out and the debate is held "in camera." A reasonable precaution not only to protect individual delegates from possible repercussions from their employer, but also to recognise that some things really should not be in the public domain. Tactically of course, not even an enlightened trade Union wants to show its hand to the employer and so Royal Mail cannot expect to listen to every debate. It has not been unknown however for a member of management to try and stay inside the conference hall undetected thanks to a stray (or given away?) CWU membership card which will get them past any stewards checking for non members.

So, a forum with considered debate and a million miles away from a monolithic North Korean style approach as can be imagined.

For Royal Mail themselves, it must be accepted (and kept in mind throughout this book) that not all managers are bad, not every employee is blameless, not every employee pulls his or her weight and not every allegation against a manager is true, nevertheless Royal Mail are certainly aware that the horror stories sometimes mentioned are rooted in reality. More pointedly, there would be few postal workers who, given the opportunity to sit through conference would not recognise these debates as being reflective of the job, the bullying that goes on and the abuses of procedures. In other words, across the whole of the UK there is a similar story.

For an employer that claims to be trying to eliminate bullying and poor behaviours, such conference debates by now should surely be the stuff of history, should they not? Apparently not. In 2013, Royal Mail found themselves on the back foot over what was described as being a bullying culture which lead to them having to spend (yet more) time meeting the CWU to discuss a national survey of CWU members which threw up some 700 cases of bullying and harassment.

The following two examples quoted from the Unions' journal to members,

> My new manager increased my workload and when I couldn't complete in the same time he said, 'you're far too slow. I'm going to test your prep (the speed at which mail is sorted into a frame to be delivered).' I've worked for Royal Mail for 25 years, never once cut off (brought back mail at the end of a delivery which couldn't be delivered in time) and they make me feel like a piece of rubbish. I dread going to work now.

Another, from a postal worker in Northern Ireland,

> I am constantly being forced to do overtime by my manager. He has threatened to conduct me for a 'deliberately inefficient performance.' I feel that I am being singled out, threatened and intimidated. I worry constantly, I can't sleep properly and feel sick.[1]

It should be noted that in 2006 there was a huge unofficial strike in Belfast due to, yes you've guessed it, years of bullying and harassment of postal workers by managers.[2] A resolution to the dispute centred on Royal Mail agreeing to an independent body to oversee and facilitate processes to improve working relations once and for all. Seven years later and again there is a horrible sinking feeling of ground hog day. At the risk of labouring a point, we have seen above how Royal Mail were able to state confidently in their accounts for 2005/06 that all 175,000 of their people had been diversity trained. The Royal Mail accounts would have been published soon after this strike. If that is not a huge disconnect, then one wonders what is. In fairness to Royal Mail though, there was no doubt that a huge exercise had taken place, so what on earth was going on that was to deliver such a bitter strike over bullying by managers who themselves had been trained in diversity?

Of course a claim by one postal worker in Northern Ireland responding to a national Union survey does not mean every employee there is having a hard time, so what does it point to? Was this individual always in this awful situation? What changed and led to his life becoming one of misery and upset? Is he the only employee experiencing such treatment or just the tip of the iceberg and just as pertinent, if there was an independent look at what was going on inside the Belfast delivery office in 2006 to improve cultures and behaviours, why has that work ended up being unable to prevent this person from being unable to sleep due to bullying?

It would be tempting to say that the questions are unfair and that it may well be the case that a lot of good work has been done over the years, and yet we must look again. The complaint is one of being threatened with disciplinary action for *not* performing overtime, a complaint made by many across the country. For the manager concerned, they may not even recognise what their actions are doing, but one thing is certain if a culture of respect and fairness was established after the strike in Belfast, then surely this new start would have been enthusiastically relayed from manager to manager with each new subsequent manager being indoctrinated in the same philosophy of respect and fairness?

In an almost tragic-ironic sense were this worker elsewhere in the UK he might even find that far from being forced to carry out overtime to complete the delivery, the opposite is the case. They will be bullied into *not* claiming overtime for work done beyond normal daily hours.

If this doesn't quite seem to hang together, then to simplify matters, one worker may need to "cut off" and leave work at their normal time and so not want overtime (the reason could be anything from child care to having a second job), but be bullied into doing it and claiming the overtime to complete the round whilst another worker may be prepared to claim overtime to complete the round, but be bullied into not claiming it. This is the reality and it is a reality that many workers and their families will recognise, especially those on the receiving end.

Another two quotes from responses to the CWU survey are instructive in showing the vulnerability of many. It is best to read this from the viewpoint of imagining you are these people. "I used to love this job now I feel sick at the thought of coming in each morning. I hate the constant battling with a manager that thinks I am lazy." This, from someone with 12 years' service. For newer employees : "My manager says if I book overtime I'll never get a permanent contract, so I just keep my head down and never claim any overtime I work."

One further example is needed as it helps to link up an example Lord Sawyer report when he referred to a positive initiative in Scotland with ACAS, Royal Mail and the CWU on behaviours and working together in 2000 which produced a Code of Practise which was bearing fruit. Yet now, an example of a worker in Glasgow states, "You watch Gordon Ramsey screaming at people on TV and don't think that happens for real, but it does happen in our office. Every day is a battle and it's starting to wear me down. And if you do overtime, very often it's not paid." A decade or so later and a manager is able to shout at staff without anything said.[3]

As for the those discussions between the CWU and Royal Mail in March 2013, a national Joint Statement was the outcome in which the Company "reaffirmed" its commitment to treating employees with dignity, fairness and respect. Acknowledgement perhaps that they were failing to do so. That such a public statement is required is testament enough to the continuing inability of Royal Mail to value its employees consistently whatever may be said to the contrary.[4]

From such public examples however comes hopefully good news. A wake up call to try and shift the mind set once more. Postal workers would not be aware but in the background much work was going on nationally with the CWU pushing for improvements with a view to re-launching an updated version of the Company's Bullying & Harassment Procedure. A civilised dialogue nationally over how to deal with this vexed issue, which, least it be forgotten, is not just between managers and employees. There is bullying on employees by employees. Launched in July 2013, it is now part of yet another attempt to change things and of course for those Postie's and their families suffering even as you read this it must be sincerely hoped that it makes a swift and profound difference.

It is worth noting that whilst the CWU national survey during the later part of 2012 produced 700 replies which could not realistically be anything other than an underestimate of the problems, Royal Mail noted in its Corporate Social Responsibility Report for 2010/11 that some 390 formal claims of bullying and harassment had been made, down from 797 the year before. In 2011/12 this would fall again to 382 formal complaints.[5] Indeed, they could also claim that the number of calls to their bullying and harassment helpline had fallen from 40,178 in 2009/10 (the year of a major strike) to 1,204 in 2011/12.[6]

Good news, but the questions remain due to the graphic examples quoted. How can this still happen and as postal workers will generally ask themselves, how can the manager concerned still be employed, which for the vast and overwhelming number of cases, they are. Again though, a health warning: The figures do not breakdown into complaints between workers, but the Company's employee relations survey for 2013 shows that of those who had "personally been the recipient of bullying and harassment in the last 12 months", some 62% had emanated from a manager and 35% from a colleague.[7]

Given that the CWU survey uncovered some 700 cases straight off – nearly twice the number of formal complaints during a whole year – does demonstrate that there is another disconnect, namely workers who are reluctant to make a complaint against their manager (or co-worker). Indeed, the quotes above would suggest that this is the case, although there is no way to know whether those individuals who responded to the Union survey were going through the formal complaints procedure. For their part Royal Mail would undertake to investigate the complaints presented to them.

For now though, we need to go back to the internal deliberations of the CWU conference process. If it is true that nationally during the 2000s there was a huge battle raging over the future of the industry, that battle was playing out in workplaces in the form of change and whether it would be negotiated and agreed or simply imposed. Beneath that, was the daily grind of worker/management conflict and with it, the cultural mindset of commanding the workplace and implementing whatever was demanded.

These daily battles would feed through the Union's machinery to form motions to the Annual Conference. Here is not the place to have a blow by blow account of each motion to the Union's conferences, but the following snap shots are worth a mention to give a flavour of the debates that were and are taking place.

A number of motions to the Unions' conference in 2012 would graphically illustrate that there continued to be a streak running through Royal Mail which appeared to be almost impossible to erase. Take the following motions:

"This conference is concerned that Special Leave with pay is no longer being granted in cases of domestic distress or medical emergencies. We call upon the Postal Executive (that is, the CWU's nationally elected representatives) to address Royal Mail's interpretation of the Special leave policy and jointly work towards clarification of this policy taking into account each individual's personal circumstances which need to be of paramount importance."[8]

"This conference believes Royal Mail is abusing the contact strategy when members first go off sick under the umbrella of caring for their employees."[9]

Real lives and real people being put through the mill.

"It is recognised that huge strides have been achieved in this regard, (in relation to the Royal Mail and CWU bullying help lines) therefore we believe the victim bias contained within the B&H Procedure must now be addressed. The imbalance between the treatment of OPGs (Posties) and managers where conduct is recommended indicates that the B&H procedure is selective in its application. Furthermore the tendency to classify minor incidents / disagreements as falling under the auspices of the B&H procedure is further leading to the misuse of the Procedure. This results in the process being discredited in the eyes of the membership. The Postal Executive is instructed to enter into discussions with the business with a view to ... placing an emphasis on restoring relationships, rather than resorting to the Conduct Code in every instance."[10]

"There should be urgent discussions "regarding management's constant failure to observe all aspects of both the Rehabilitation process and the Ill Health Retirement Agreements (as) increasing numbers of CWU members are being unnecessarily forced out of the business, despite medical evidence from GPs, hospitals and consultants that fully support their claims."[11]

"This Conference widely believes that the employer is failing in its obligations under the Royal Mail Rehabilitation Agreement. As a result we are seeing increasing numbers ...

returning to work after long term absence ... without suitable or sufficient plans in place for their return. OHS (occupational health services) and other medical reports are also regularly ignored when, or if, these plans are formulated."[12]

There must be "adequate guidance for managers and representatives to support ... the Ill Health Retirement Agreement" because reasonable adjustments to avoid ill health retirement were not being made.[13]

"Royal Mail is continually taking steps to bully our members back to work, by threatening to stop their pay even when presented with relevant fit notes (they replaced "sick notes") and also when our members are carrying out their obligation to maintain contact with the employer. The reasons given by Royal Mail is that their policy is to take the advice of the occupational health provider should they claim an individual is fit for work. This blatant attack on our members can only cause more stress, anxiety and misery at an already difficult time...."[14]

It should be noted that if it seems reasonable to take the advice of occupational health even if an employee has a GP certify them as being too ill to work, the Royal Mail policy states that there should be a dialogue between occupational health and the physician to try and resolve any differences over the opinions given. An excellent policy but one apparently not being carried out in every case.

"CWU members are being subjected to abuse as managers are using the procedure in a mechanistic and systematic way to issue warnings ... regardless of mitigation."[15]

"This conference notes the continued number of Attendance Procedure warnings that are issued by Royal Mail. Local managers show an inability to consider mitigation raised including absences related to: The Equality Act, stress and bereavement and female related health issues. The Procedure is too often used in a punitive manner, ignoring the spirit of the joint agreement."[16]

"...as Royal Mail are constantly using an unagreed attendance procedure with threat based language it is imperative that (an appeal process is introduced at each stage)."[17]

"CWU members will not be forced to attend hospital on their day off, on annual leave or in circumstances in which they are forced to complete their delivery, or make up their duty hours."[18]

The foregoing were part of some 118 motions covering all manner of issues. Context wise, this conference is being held against the backdrop of what has been mentioned previously as the Transformation Agreement 2010, which was supposed to have heralded a new era of dignity and respect for all. Postal workers would however note that this conference formed the backdrop to new agreements on sickness absence and bullying and harassment, so perhaps the pressure from the Union to simply keep banging on about what is happening at the grass roots, could be seen to pay off.

What the CWU could not do though was to renegotiate these two procedures knowing that it would definitely lead to employees having a better impression of their employer. It doesn't need a great deal of thought to recognise that the motions above come from workplaces, from real life situations. The talk in the office of so and so who's had a family crisis and "you know what, the manager refused him paid leave for the domestic distress – wouldn't even listen to what he had to say. Disgusting if you ask me." Such conversations are the stuff of Royal Mail. And in the next town, you wouldn't believe it, but someone who had an urgent family matter was given the day off with full pay.

If we drift back another year to 2011 we come across an interesting motion. "This Conference records its concern of the misuse of the Bullying & Harassment Procedure by the Gateway Team when processing members' complaints on the H1 form (this Team are the first port of call when an individual makes a complaint on the official H1 form). The Gateway Team extract complaints with no agreed process and *downgrade the seriousness of the complaint from a claim of bullying and harassment to an individual grievance."*[19]

So the statistics trumpeted by Royal Mail may not quite be as good as first thought? That every CWU Branch in the UK could relay similar thoughts perhaps tells the reader that all is not well. In fact, what appears to have been happening doesn't bear thinking about. In a command and control culture, getting those bullying claims down is of course a priority. There is a debate to be had about whether a complaint really is one of bullying or not, but it can be an exceptionally fine line to draw when an employee feels bullied about being refused overtime and made to work regardless past their hours and someone in Royal Mail who will claim this is a grievance about non payment of overtime only.

Or perhaps that line isn't so "fine" after all. A choice is being made to channel complaints one way and not the other? We can safely assume I think, that the example just given did not consist of a sympathetic and reasonable conversation between manager and employee. Indeed, were that the case, the problems that lead to the overtime request might have been looked at properly and the overtime paid, if only on the grounds that the manager knows full well the delivery Tom is on, simply cannot be done in the time allowed.

Take the following from 2011's conference:

"On a regular basis members have been threatened with having their pay being stopped and in some cases, dismissal."[20]

"...conference agrees that it is an absolute disgrace that Royal Mail is deliberately withdrawing this right (to contractual sick pay) from certain members in order to bully these members back to work."[21]

"...the Royal Mail conduct code is being used inappropriately by ... managers ... to remove CWU members from their duties in advance of any disciplinary charges being laid ... yet it is becoming the norm for managers to speak to individuals about matters such as alleged poor performance and then remove them from their duties 'pending investigation' thereby creating a culture of do as I say or I will remove you."[22]

On the matter of sickness, from 2008: "Managers are often including accidents on duty and disability absences when issuing warnings. In addition to this mitigation is being ignored. Managers are using intimidation tactics to frighten our members to return to work prematurely when off sick. This cannot be allowed to happen."[23]

All these motions resonate across the UK. Same problems, year in and year out. One step forward and two back. Sometimes, two steps forward and just one back. Is this just an inevitable part of life for such a huge organisation? Issues are raised and talks take place to deal with the problems and then everything moves on only to reappear or on many occasions not to be resolved at all. The impact on Posties is soon forgotten about, but they would make a mental note as to whose side of the fence they were on.

Of course just because an issue is raised by a Union conference doesn't mean it is appropriate or acceptable to the employer. After all, who is running the Company and is the motion addressing a genuine issue or maybe it refers to just a problem in one locality? Nevertheless it may be useful to delve a little further back and at the risk of continued, if necessary selectivity. Motions from 2006 and 2007:

"....the increasing number of bullying and harassment cases occurring within Royal Mail Group."[24]

"Conference ... accepts that the bullying and harassment complaint form is being used to predetermine cases of harassment without any investigation. In fact, cases are being dismissed based on how articulately the complainant has completed the form."[25]

Royal Mail were, "increasingly abusing the ill health retirement procedure in order to harass and ultimately terminate the employment of our members..."[26]

"...full support will be provided to any person who complains of harassment on the grounds of unnecessary contact made by a manager or managers while that person is away from work as a result of sickness or personal family issues requiring special leave of absence."[27]

The Company will want to keep in touch with staff and perhaps a manager will pay a visit to the person's home for a chat or perhaps they'll get a letter calling them in for an interview with the threat made that of course they must co-operate or the sick pay arrangements will have to be reviewed. Oh come off it, you say, there is nothing wrong with this. Well, it all depends on how it is carried out. Too many Union representatives relaying too many instances of upsetting and intrusive behaviour from managers who are expecting their employee back at work even if the manager himself is the cause of the absence in the first place.

The 2007 Conference came before the national dispute that led to the Pay & Modernisation Agreement. By 2008, a motion from the Mount Pleasant International Branch felt that "Royal Mail no longer has an effective equal opportunities policy (and that) there is no active promotion of equal opportunities by Royal Mail."

Clearly, a motion like this would be fiercely contested by Royal Mail, but look further at the motion and it calls for the Union to "play an active role in pushing our own equal opportunities agenda with the employer ... to push for and participate in the creation of an effective Royal Mail equal opportunities policy (and) to monitor the outcomes of any such policy." Fine words perhaps which could still be challenged by Royal Mail. On the other hand such a motion might make more sense knowing that the Mount Pleasant site hosts possibly the only workplace crèche in Royal Mail, which they have sought in one way or another to either close or cut provision over a number of years in order to save money. A battle that shouldn't be taking place and which alienates the workforce, for little, if any, financial gain.

Move back another year to 2006 and a motion stated that "the employer rarely complies with the four week investigation timescale contained (in the bullying and harassment procedure). Conference also recognises the additional trauma and stress a delay in processing such cases can cause the individuals concerned", and ensure, "in particular a commitment to the timescales...."[28]

Be in no doubt. Waiting for an investigation outcome is not a good place to be. On many occasions the employee is off on sick leave, mulling things over, stressed, not sleeping and perhaps on medication from their GP. The agreement states four weeks, unless there is good reason. The motion above was from 2006 and by 2010/11 of 390 formal complaints, just 153 were resolved within four weeks.[29] Many will be able to relay instances of investigations taking weeks and weeks followed sometimes by an appeal which again takes time. The best way to keep to an agreed four week commitment is of course to act of the basis of first putting in the resources and secondly keeping in mind the mental wellbeing of all involved.

Although selectively picking out motions to a Union conference in order to "prove a point" could be seen as lazy, the stark reality is that one must ask why these motions are there at all. We have seen previously the wording from some national agreements reached after disputes and we are bound to ask ourselves whether the Company is just incapable of valuing and respecting people, consistently across the board.

A motion from 2009, a good year or more after the national dispute that led to the Pay & Modernisation Agreement covering such issues as flexibility, had this to say amongst other things:

a) That Royal Mail continues to bully and harass our members with its own false interpretation of flexibility.

b) That is spite of the Pay & Modernisation Agreement our members are being bullied to flex on a regular basis.

c) That our members are being bullied to do overtime under

the threat of discipline.

d) That our members are being bullied for not doing overtime on demand.[30]

The irony of course with the motion, is that in other parts of the UK people could just as easily be bullied for trying to claim overtime! If nothing else a sad backdrop to what subsequently happened with a further national strike taking place in 2009, covering in part the very same issues in the motion. It should be noted that this motion was *not* carried at the Unions' conference as it talked about withdrawing from the Agreement. The sentiments however, were fully understood.

Following this strike the 2010 Transformation Agreement was surely the time to say no more confrontation and no more bullying. It contained powerful and reassuring words to create a more positive climate for all employees to feel valued.

Sadly, bullying and harassment remains a perennial feature of many workplaces to the extent that further motions were submitted for debate. This time the outlet was a National Policy Forum in March 2013.

Commenting on the unagreed use of British Standard Institute (BSI) measurements to base changes to duties in delivery offices it was said, "That the current performance measurement of BSI is being abused by Royal Mail managers and is being used as a tool to bully and harass our members."[31]

Another motion wanted a Union policy that "eradicates the bullying and harassment culture in deliveries once and for all",[32] and another said amongst other things, "That this Policy Forum condemns Royal Mail for the unacceptable levels of bullying and harassment of CWU members in delivery offices based on unrealistic and unachievable levels of savings and productivity/efficiency levels" and that the Union should "encourage members not to suffer in silence."[33]

It is undeniably sad that such debates are taking place and it again begs the same question. Is the Company institutionally incapable of valuing its own employees? In July 2013, an unofficial walk out in Plymouth of around 100 postal workers followed claims of workers being "intolerably bullied and harassed" by management. [34]

In July 2013, Peterborough Mail Centre was brought to a stand still for four days over what was described by the National CWU as being an attempt by Royal Mail to "fit up ... the rep to get him removed from the office. Management actions leading to disputes in the South West in areas as diverse as Plymouth, Truro, Western Super Mare, Bristol and Bridgwater were seen as being caused by "provocative and intransigent" management.[35]

Perhaps as an illustration it would be helpful to note that every couple of months or so the CWU sends out a newsletter for those who work in deliveries. There is a continual stream of people contacting the Union to find out their rights. Rights to what, you may ask. Well, how's this for starters: the Union is constantly having to advise their members that overtime is not compulsory.

If this all sounds, well, a bit melodramatic, think about it a little harder. How is it possible for someone to be forced to work beyond their time? How exactly is this achieved for someone new who is on a temporary contract or for someone already in the industry who has got a few years under their belt? What could possibly be said to them to lead them to believe they have no choice in the matter?

It is only by asking such questions as this that we can begin to try and peer inside the minds of those happy to "persuade" people to do as they are told and in turn to try and empathise with those on the receiving end.

Chapter 16

Harsh Realities Part 1

We have seen how, even with the best of intentions (and sometimes not) Royal Mail seem to struggle to do anything other than take their employees for granted and perhaps it is not unreasonable to expect employees to knuckle under and accept that things aren't perfect.

There maybe some truth in that, but this perspective can only really work in reality if those working for the Company understand their place in it and by that I do not mean their place being at the bottom of the pile. I mean, their place being at the centre of what Royal Mail does with everyone recognising this.

Part of that recognition process will mean that the Company understands that every worker whilst expected to do a fair day's work for a fair day's pay, has differing abilities, different levels of health and different family backgrounds which mean they have in turn other, sometimes quite stressful situations they are coping with outside of work.

In other words, the Postcomm (and now, Ofcom) regime should have little impact on how the Company relates to its employees. If it were some how true that in 2000 there were thousands of postal workers engaging in Spanish practises and taking the management for a ride and that Postcomm was the vehicle to shake everyone out of their complacency then an argument could perhaps be constructed to suggest a little "performance management" or a "kick up the backside" might be in order. If you want to call it bullying, so be it.

But does such an argument even if true, begin to hold up as developments unfolded in the 2000s? We have read the words from some of the collective agreements reached – a litany of good intentions if nothing else and indeed, even a cursory look at

Royal Mail's annual reports and accounts will show clearly how some postal staff are rightly commended for their excellence and commitment to helping their customers with the Company additionally saying its workforce is the "life blood" of the Company.

More specifically, I would genuinely encourage the reader to check out their accounts where you will read of not only heroic work by postal workers which have been recognised by the Company, but excellent initiatives by Royal Mail themselves to support charities in the community, to encourage employees who are under represented such as women and to ensure they "reach out to people who may be experiencing disadvantage." It would be wrong to ignore this and the reality that flows from it, namely that good things are done inside Royal Mail by good people whether employees or managers.

I digress. To get back to those Spanish practises again. If there are any left, it is safe to assume no one is benefiting from them. As for the kick up the backside argument, it does seem clear that such an approach, to the extent that its proponents thought it was needed should surely have been consigned to the dustbin years ago, after all, Posties have lived under the shadow of their world collapsing at any moment due to the competition surrounding them.

It does seem appropriate then to move towards the next and final part of the jigsaw that is Royal Mail, namely the impact on individuals.

There can be few Union representatives who have not experienced the ordeal of listening to a member recount what has happened to them. Quite often the first contact can be to the Area Representative or Branch Secretary. A long, almost impenetrable scroll of an email. Everything put down. Exclamation marks and capital letters peppering the email to make a point that this DID happen to them and that it is happening quite often. "Is anyone out there who will listen to me?" Maybe they come through via a phone call. A long and rambling explanation. What shall they do next? Can the Union have a word with the manager? Maybe the Union will never hear from this person again and there is this overwhelming sense that perhaps you simply drift in and out of people's lives.

Such emails (or letters) rarely delve into the actual impact on the person, although when they do no one should really be in any doubt – can't sleep, feeling sick and anxious, feelings of anger and impotence, after all what is a red blooded Postie going to want to do when he is being bullied? Well, for starters we could safely say that a swift "smack in the face" would get the anger out. Would it solve the problem, of course not. In fact, it's not a good idea at all, but hey, we aren't in that position are we?

What can the Union do? More pointedly, what can the Union representative do to help? A meeting after hours perhaps? Somewhere neutral – a local café? A Wetherspoons? Maybe the Union has its own offices away from the workplace? Maybe you will end up at the members' home, sitting in the front room or round the kitchen table with a coffee with the members' partner there as well ready to tell you how bad it really is and that they have already told the manager by phone what they think of them. How dare they treat my husband / wife / partner in that way: It's disgusting.

Can a plan of action be sorted out? A formal complaint or maybe a suggestion to see the manager with the local rep, explain how you are feeling and ask if we can start over. Maybe the manager is aware they have over stepped the mark and will therefore have an opportunity to gracefully back down without being seen to do so. Maybe the manager will see the approach as undermining their authority in the workplace. Who is in charge after all? In fact, the informal efforts didn't work. The huge emotional effort required to front up the manager and explain how you feel hasn't worked. Maybe in the end, you just couldn't bring yourself to articulate your weakness. Do you really want to the manager to know he has got to you? Do you trust him to be discrete, to reflect on his own behaviour and to look at other ways of sorting out whatever the problem was?

Of course, you know he's picking on you because your mates have told you – they can see it for themselves. The manager's a "complete shit" they tell you. Actually, you know this and in fact you know of a few others in the office as well. There's Sandra and Jon and Marc. Newcomers who are racing around covering full time jobs on part time contracts, no overtime allowed and being told they are not good enough. Marc, well he's a mad as a hatter and claims that it's alright as he doesn't mind. No one complains, even though there is a Union to which most of them belong. Anyway, you had a word with the local rep and he had a chat with the manager, but it's not worked and you are back at square one again. What to do? How long can it go on for? You are sure that someone put in a complaint of bullying and harassment a few months ago now, but nothing seemed to happen and whoever it was went off sick for a few weeks, came back and nothing changed.

Maybe you should just "go sick" and be done with it. Yes, that's it. Give yourself some breathing space to sort "your head out." Hang on though, what about when it is time to come back to work? What if the manager starts phoning me up to see where I am and what the illness is? Will I get a warning for my sickness? I can't tell him he is the one bullying me. Anyway, he knows what he's doing to me, but he doesn't care. It'll carry on I suppose when I return. What shall I do then?

Well, if you are in the CWU you might, just might, go to them for help. The Union are very sympathetic. Yes, it is outrageous what has happened. Suddenly someone is on your side, but nevertheless can you actually bring yourself to make a formal complaint? Maybe you are just a bit happier now you have got it off your chest. Have a think about it and take things from there as the Union says they can't guarantee you will succeed in your complaint and you are told that the Company may not even accept you have a complaint of bullying and will instead claim it is just a grievance.

In fact, if this Postie goes away and completes a diary of sorts to log down what is happening, the longer it goes on the harder it can be to take that step. It is not unusual for a CWU Representative to be faced with a few months of incidents. Some of it doesn't have a date as the person forgot to do it that week, or maybe they just lost hope and gave up for a while only to restart it again after another incident? Go past three months and you could find that the manager will simply deny the allegation and say they can't even remember it anyway. Goodness me, they will even throw in to the mix the fact that only yesterday they had a chat about the footie on the telly with the very person who is making a complaint against them!

Have you ever had a situation when you felt sick and anxious and couldn't sleep? How long did it go on for – a day, a week, a month or two? Have you ever walked into work with that feeling knowing there is no way out and no one, least of all your manager is listening? What did your family think about it? Heart racing as you try and keep up a quiet dignity to show that in fact you are ok and everything's fine and dandy. Well, you managed it for a while, but in the end it's off to the "Quack" to see if they can do something for you.

In 2011 Royal Mail would report that 10% of their workforce had experienced some form of bullying and harassment. Now, even if this figure is to be trusted as not being an underestimate, 10% equates to a figure around 13,000. Thirteen thousand employees of whom a small fraction will go on to make a formal complaint. For the whole of Royal Mail Group (Royal Mail, Parcelforce, Post Office Counters and GLS Parcels) in 2011, the staff in post figure was 163,000 full time equivalent. So, a conservative estimate then of around 16,300 people.[1]

Regrettably for the Company – and certainly those on the

receiving end – that 10% increased. Royal Mail's own employee survey for 2013 showed a national figure of 14% (with a regional high in the South West of 16%).[2]

If it was that bad I hear you say, why didn't they all complain for goodness sake? You may not complain if it was a one off incident. You may not if on reflection it wasn't that bad or if it was sorted out in the office with the Union or between you and the manager or if you are scared to do so and think there might be repercussions. You may not if you are on a temporary contract or you have a duty that means you can finish at xxxx time to get home for the kids and that might get taken away – who knows? You may not if you already know that others have complained and nothing happened to the manager or because you had a run in with the boss a few weeks ago and can't face it all over again. You may not if the bully is a colleague who is friendly with the manager or the local Union rep? Maybe you just don't want to rock the boat now you've thought about it some more? So many reasons…

In fairness to Royal Mail, some of this could just as easily come from any other employer, but in the case of Royal Mail though, they have invested so much time and effort that you begin to wonder why it still goes on and then you suddenly take stock and recognise that there must be a malign sickness that cannot be cured; a junkie hooked on bullying to get things done and managers either happy or in some cases, extremely reluctant, to do what is necessary.

And what is necessary? Treating people with fairness and respect in order to get the work done or bully them into doing so. Of course, if the budget you are given is not sufficient, as a manager how on earth are you going to run your office and not get shouted at or demoted or moved sideways by your own boss? It will come as no surprise to anyone that throughout, it is often managers who are left carrying the can and find themselves going out delivering the mail day after day themselves in order to fill staffing shortfalls or to meet a budget allocation.

There are probably few people anywhere on the planet who have not met a manager at some point in their working lives who didn't enjoy imposing their authority. Royal Mail is no different. Indeed, there are many CWU representatives, never mind employees, who will know exactly who these people are. They will have a reputation and they know they do. So does Royal Mail, but if the budget is met and no one is making a complaint from that workplace, what exactly is the problem? It gets worse though. There are managers who have a reputation of saying to anyone they cross swords with that in fact they have had complaints against them but it never got the complainant anywhere. Now that scenario is admittedly very rare but those employing such conversations are known about, but as most Postie's who experience this will know, nothing happens to them. They are, to all intents and purposes, untouchable. Perhaps no different to some other employers, but surely, such people should have been weeded out years ago?

Mercifully, many find they are supported by managers who are doing the best they can and carrying out the training that they have been given.

Why then is this not embedded into each and every manager? More to the point, an inexperienced manager will presumably take advice from their boss and what about an experienced manager. Have they accidentally forgotten how to deal with the rehabilitation of an employee? Perhaps to follow the actual Rehabilitation Agreement is just too cumbersome and so a short cut might be more appropriate?

Let's look a little closer at this area. An area many Postie's do not go near as their health holds up or they are fortunate enough not to have had a serious accident at work.

A couple of weeks off on the sick then; a referral to the Company's occupational health people, Atos Healthcare. A report to the manager recommending a rehab programme and then once back at work, well perhaps this rehab programme isn't quite working...

The manager doesn't have the patience to sort it. He reckons you could do a bit more today than yesterday and that you are ok to go out on a delivery even though that knee of yours is still pretty rough. He has good reason doesn't he? Someone else is off sick, he can't cover a delivery and you with your bad knee are leaned on to help out. You do so (reluctantly) and bingo – you can't do it. You bring the mail back. The manager is not at all happy with you. The next day is the same and so off you go again on the sick. Two periods of sickness now and you are staring at a warning for your sickness.

Of course you could always claim that you were leaned on in contravention of the Atos Healthcare report (which as it happens, recommended four hours per day on indoor work for a week, increasing to five the following week and normal hours the week after that as long as you can manage it), to do more than you were capable of and so that second period of sickness ought to be ignored. Mind you, if you do will the manager hold his hands up and say "I'm sorry I goofed up. I shouldn't have asked you to do that", or will he say, "you are responsible for your own health and if you couldn't do it, you should have said so and refused." And in today's supportive Royal Mail this type of a response will be familiar to many. Get the job done by all means necessary?

Perhaps in fact, you did say to the manager you were not really ok with it but he was insistent that it had to be done as there was no one else (there was by the way and you knew it, but it would have been on overtime) and if you struggle then it's ok to bring the mail back. If you refuse, what exactly will happen to you? You insist on doing the four hours per day on indoor work as recommended by Atos Healthcare. What then? Well, experience tells Posties that on occasion you may well be sent home as the manager says he now has no indoor work for you and then you are on the sick again.

And for those who have been off for some weeks, what about them? The motions above referring to the ill health retirement process cover the way in which a manager will make a referral to Atos Healthcare. Forget about the fact that the individuals should be able to go through any referral with the manager before it goes to Atos Healthcare, the manager will claim that Fred or Susan has been off for x weeks and that Royal Mail is unable to accommodate the employee on light duties. Alternatively, an Atos Healthcare recommendation is made that the manager then claims he cannot accommodate and in these circumstances "is ill health retirement appropriate?" What then? Has he tried to accommodate the person? Has he really? You are now facing an ill health dismissal as the manager says he can't help.

Of course Atos Healthcare don't know the situation in the office. They assume the manager has pulled out all the stops but with the best will in the world, there just isn't anything available for the hapless Postie with that bad knee / back / shoulder etc.

Of course it is not always "route one". Plenty of referrals are made and people are helped back into work even if some are only back because their Union representative has intervened to help the manager see that in fact there are light duties available after all.

It would be useful to reflect a little at this juncture. Is it really the case that a manager would claim that no reasonable adjustments could be made in the full knowledge that they could be if only a bit of "spade work" was put into it? Is this manager trained in the rehabilitation procedures? Even if he isn't, surely to goodness he doesn't want to see someone lose their livelihood? Think again. Those conference motions cover a multitude of terrible circumstances some of which will have been heard by those Royal Mail observers. Quite often these situations will be known to employees in the workplace. They will know Fred or Susan and if nothing else, such news can travel quickly round a delivery office. The question is whether that news is good and the employees can see Royal Mail helping their colleagues out, or whether the view is that Royal Mail just "want them out."

Perhaps you get back to work alright after all. There is a recommendation from Atos Healthcare for you to use a trolley. Now this issue has to some extent disappeared, following the mass introduction of electric and "golf" trollies to take the weight off the shoulders of postal workers. Notwithstanding this, it was not unusual to hear that someone had been allocated a trolley upon their return to work from sick leave only to find that in fact it takes them longer to do the delivery round. Of course it does. Think about it. Taking mail in out of a trolley, securing that trolley when you are away from it and manoeuvring the curbs and inclines, etc. So, you have a trolley to help you with your back / knee / shoulder problem and now the manager is on your back because you are taking too long and are now looking to claim overtime or cut off and bring back the mail as you can't complete in the time allowed.

The manager knows it takes longer with a trolley, but no matter. Sharp practise in a workplace to get people performing so as to meet a budget allocation set by the Company in order to save money because they can't predict their future income with any great accuracy as their hands are tied by regulation? Or, a manager who has chosen to treat the individual in the manner described because they can?

Suddenly, it is again not at all clear what the answer might be. Let me make it clear again. Most staff are dealt with appropriately, so why do some managers make a positive decision not to do so? Do they not realise how they are seen by their workforce?

Of course it isn't all out in the open like this. A Postie struggling will sometimes find an apparently sympathetic manager having a quiet word with them to suggest that maybe "you just can't cope with the job anymore?" You're ok, you reply, but the seed is sown and pretty soon you are worrying yourself sick at the thought of no job and you still have that mortgage to pay off and "the wife's job" isn't looking too good either at the moment. Such conversations go on and there will be CWU representatives who will have spoken to such people who honestly believe that they really should leave, when in fact a number of alternatives exist, but which that sympathetic manager, well, let's say, he forgot to mention them in the rush to make savings.

Some perspective is in order here. Royal Mail as we have seen have been engaged as far as the CWU are concerned, in an ongoing process of "slash and burn", cuts, savings and all the rest as they have wrestled with the constraints placed upon them by Postcomm and now Ofcom. Despite this, Royal Mail and Atos Healthcare over the years have had programmes to help employees and many will attest to the help and support given. An Atos Healthcare report stated as much is 2008 when it said, "Royal Mail Group's success in cutting absence by a quarter has been achieved through robust sickness absence management, complimented by wellbeing initiatives which include" health screening, health promotion campaigns and "increased support and training for managers to improve the effectiveness of absence attendance policies."[3]

How is this backdrop experienced by Royal Mail's own employees and what exactly is "robust sick absence management?" Whatever may be said by any interested party, that question must be answered and answered honestly. Suddenly those conference motions above begin to make a little more sense.

Of course sickness absence issues need sensitivity and careful attention. Not all managers are equipped to handle such situations. To then ask, "...and why not?" would be a good place to start. Ill health can engulf the whole life of a person. A Postie in his 50s with a bad knee or bad back is in a vulnerable situation, make no mistake. His livelihood is literally in the hands of his boss. Both fear and loathing can be generated in equal measure. The reader will not be at all surprised to hear that many postal workers will carry on regardless, dosed up with pain killers to get them through the day, rather than share their health problem with their manager. Would this be happening if Postcomm hadn't got its tentacles around Royal Mail? Would the managers be more supportive so you could take advantage of that "my door is always open" philosophy and share your vulnerabilities knowing you won't be taken advantage of?

Chronic health issues thankfully do not strike all of us and Posties are no different. Some sickness is short term – a bad cold, tummy upset, pulled back or leg muscle or whatever. Such employees come under the banner of the Attendance Procedure. Agreed with the CWU it is not about sickness as such, but about attendance. Can you attend for work or not? If you don't attend due to sickness – and it really doesn't matter what the problem is – then you are facing a probable warning. Ostensibly, absences due to an industrial accident, pregnancy or a disability (as long as you are given an opinion that you may come within the terms of the Equality Act) should mean no warning is issued. Not always. The following from Roy Mayall:

Believe it or not, sometimes Posties are made to come into work even if they are sick or injured, on threat of dismissal. The Attendance Procedure is the means by which this is done…. You are only allowed a certain number of absences in any one year. If you exceed the number … you are brought before management and a so-called Stage One warning is issued. This is regardless of whether your illness is genuine or not. Every absence is considered genuine, but each one is counted towards the Attendance Procedure….

There are three stages with stage 3 being a consideration of dismissal and there is no right of appeal against a stage 1 and 2 warning and,

> although they are meant to be discretionary, discretion is
> never used. This of course, is the exact opposite of the
> meaning of the word 'discretion.' No matter how ill you are,
> if you are on stage 2 you daren't miss work. I've seen people
> hauled up before management because they were in hospital
> for a hernia operation and have exceeded the total number of
> days allowed.... And I've heard of people on the verge of a
> mental breakdown being bullied and harassed and humil-
> iated in front of the entire office and sent home crying like
> babies. This is happening more and more at Royal Mail.[4]

Mercifully, this is not the whole picture, but from Roy Mayall's
viewpoint, who has actually seen such situations, what can one
say? This Procedure has been used as a tool to make sure people
turn up for work. If Roy Mayall says the warnings are always
issued, well maybe he is right and maybe he is wrong, but the
impact on the workforce is the issue at hand. Does the issuing of
a warning due to absence caused by a hospital operation mean
that Royal Mail are valuing that person? To be more specific, if
you (yes, you!) had been off on sick leave with a cold for a couple
of days and then you had a repeat three months later and you
just couldn't stagger in and then you went into hospital for that
hernia what would you expect to happen ?

Well, it all depends on which end of the telescope you are
looking through. Your Union representative accompanies you to
the interview. They say that if it wasn't for the hernia Joe would
not have triggered this warning interview. Joe's back now and
raring to go. Give him a break? The manager says, "Well, if he
hadn't been off with a cold on a couple of occasions I might have
let him off but if I look at Joe's record it's clear he had a cold some
10 months ago. How do I know if he's not going to go off again
with a cold?" Such a decision could actually lead to a sacking if

that was a Stage 3 interview. In fact, whether he had also had a cold some 10 months previously, would in reality make little difference. For some managers the only question to ask is whether the process has been followed and the interview stages triggered correctly. Fair enough or not? Joe may have done 20 years or more for Royal Mail, be in his 40s or 50s and thinking that maybe he was thought of as a good worker. Think about that and wonder why postal workers are so supportive of their Union as being the only protection.

Of course there are any number of reasons why someone is on sick leave. Some postal workers will find to their horror that the bad back they have struggled with and which is getting worse, may not after all be classed as a disability within the terms of the Equality Act. What to do now? The accident on duty never got recorded for some reason. You thought the manager had done it, but now you find it isn't recorded and the sickness you are now incurring is not seen as being caused by an accident at work. The stuff of nightmares if your job is on the line.

What you want to hear is that the manager – your boss who you've known now for a few years and get on with quite well, or so you hope – will admit that he had forgotten to deal with that. "Yes, I remember now you did jar your back lifting that trolley up the pavement edge – leave it with me and I'll sort that, so no, you won't be given a warning after all." Now postal workers won't say that such an outcome isn't possible, but few would bet on it. In fact, far from an admin problem over the recording of an accident at work, is the issue as to whether the manager will even accept it was an accident on duty. Maybe it was just an "incident."

A whole new can of worms is now opened and many know that it can be a fine line between an accident and an incident. In fact, if the manager thinks you should have been looking where you were going you might even be blamed and potentially disciplined. As for that sick absence you incurred due to this situation, well don't expect it to be discounted now. Again, this type of scenario has been the subject of numerous representations by the CWU over the years at local and national level.

That Royal Mail have a duty to investigate accidents is obvious. That such investigations have led to such controversy on occasions, is less so. Such debates have peppered CWU conferences for some years. A reduction in accidents at work is absolutely a good thing. That some of the reduction may come about through a lack of recording it, or classifying it as an incident or looking to blame the employee for their misfortune is also a regrettable state of affairs which sours the atmosphere against a backdrop that ought to be wholly positive. If you tripped on a pavement slab that was sticking up and jarred your knee, is that your fault? Goodness me, your walked on that pavement yesterday and the day before and the day before that.

Clearly and self evidently, you could not have been looking where you were going? Fair enough? Do we really have to have a row about this? The local rep or safety rep will say, "Just log it down as an accident on duty, Mike didn't do it deliberately and anyone could have tripped up, couldn't they?" To which a manager might reply, "Well, he wasn't looking where he was going and now he's off sick and we need to cover his job which will cost money." It is this type of situation that when added to everything else that begins to make an impact. A mental note is made and an attitude formed accordingly.

A brief detour to the Unions' conference motions again. In 2012 the following motion submitted by the South East No.5 Branch stated:

This conference records its concern that in some workplaces Royal Mail has started using accident investigations and the number of accidents an individual has incurred as a device to initiate disciplinary proceedings ... the (Union) should secure the immediate cessation of this practise and ensure that future accident investigations are carried out in line with the agreed procedures to serve their intended purpose of preventing and reducing future accidents.

It is of course demoralising that such motions have to be submitted in the first place, but again the point perhaps needs to be made that such a proposition stems from a policy inside Royal Mail to secure a particular outcome. An outcome that they hope will save them money and will as a knock on, demonstrate to other employees that this is the way that things will go if the policy is not followed. That this policy might be driven by the impact of the regulatory framework, is pretty much rendered irrelevant to those affected and their colleagues who inevitably get to hear about what has transpired. So you are perhaps off sick for a day or so and on your return you might just be facing a disciplinary and who knows a stage warning for your sickness. Such is life.

Another reason for absence is of course following "words" with your boss. Mental health related absence is reckoned to cost British industry about £15 billion every year amounting to around 91 million days.[5] If you are on sick leave due to being bullied or harassed how will your sick absence be dealt with? Who will deal with it if you don't feel able to make a complaint against your manager? What if your sickness means you will trigger a consideration of dismissal interview? What if a complaint is made but doesn't find in your favour? The only rational answer is to say to yourself, "it doesn't bear thinking about ... don't even go there."

Quite rightly, Royal Mail will state that the CWU agreed this Attendance Procedure. Well, yes they did (and since 2013 a new revised agreement has been reached which hopefully will herald a new positive and supportive approach). What was not agreed however, was the manner in which it would be applied in practise.

Indeed, if the manager wanted to keep you on by cutting you some slack and discounting that hospital operation, then they could have done so as long as they had cleared this first with their own boss by explaining why they weren't going to issue a warning. No problem there then?

That the issues with this Procedure were raised by Lord Sawyer, only goes to show that if you want to dismiss someone on the cheap due to Postcomm breathing down your neck, then some unsuspecting postal worker will always come along at some point. That not all employees are sacked who end up on this Procedure is small comfort, although inevitably if you are able to get into work, you do so. The accusation will inevitably be that this is the real way that Royal Mail are able to reduce sickness absence and that the Conference motions above referring to stopping sick pay and all the rest are the tools required for any manager looking to keep their sickness absence down.

It is worth briefly quoting some of Lord Sawyer's report in respect to sickness absence. He notes that at the time Royal Mail were facing increasing levels of sickness absence and they had to do something. Lord Sawyer would note that the Attendance Procedure was "being used in cases where it would not have been applied in the past and it has almost certainly also led to it being used in some cases where it should not have been used al all." Specifically he would note that it was "tempting for a weak manager to attempt to avoid the responsibility for giving a justified warning by blaming his superiors", or alternatively a view that "the manager will get into trouble if he or she fails to give a warning." It was also suggested that "the requirement that front-line managers should explain cases where warnings are *not given* (author's emphasis) should not be interpreted as putting any pressure on front line managers."

The sad message that postal workers internalise is that if Royal Mail can engineer something against someone, they will.

That is not the whole truth by a long chalk, but for Royal Mail it is a perception that by now should surely survive only in the minds of those long service Posties who can remember the bad old days? The fact that it persists is shameful. If Royal Mail could shift this perception then who knows what they and their employees could achieve.

To go forward, you sometimes have to return. Sawyer's report could usefully be dusted down. The good intentions of Royal Mail could be re-examined and that command and control ethos used to harness the Company for good. That there are those trying very hard is beyond doubt, but the proof of the pudding is in the eating and we must again ask whether Royal Mail are, despite the best intentions of some, just not capable of valuing their own employees in a consistent manner across the UK.

The area of sickness and health is anything but simple, but even from the little written above, the litmus test for the comments made would have to be whether the average postal worker would recognise the truth of them. For many, as has been mentioned, they have received good support and how fantastic that is when it does happen. The vulnerability melts away as the individual feels supported and helped back to work.

If the backdrop to this chapter has been that the external regulatory context led to a more punitive approach by Royal Mail towards its own employees, it will be interesting to see if all those motions above are listened to and acted upon or whether the same cycle will keep on perpetuating itself. As with all change in Royal Mail, the "poor bloody infantry" will be the best judges of what happens.

Chapter 17

Harsh Realities Part 2

If it is possible for postal workers to feel devalued and unwanted when struggling with their health, the area of "performance management" is where it is really at.

I asked above how is it possible for a manager to get someone to work beyond their hours for no pay. We have read a little of the swings and roundabouts, the abuse of the flexibility provisions and the workplaces where they are short staffed and we have read the quotes above from anonymous postal workers. All, arguably a consequence of the regulatory framework that has prevailed for so long and led to disputes and the continuing use of "command and control."

In fact, if you thought that flowing from this analysis was that every postal worker agreed with the gist of the argument that collective national agreements between Royal Mail and the CWU are something to be followed to the letter, you would be wrong.

There is an unavoidable message that underlines everything Royal Mail does, namely that there is no such thing as a free lunch and people just need to get on with the job or no one will have one. There are workplaces where employees are working together, coming in early to help out, finishing later to help out, mucking in, call it what you will. The idea of "doing the job properly" is not something that occurs to these postal workers. They all pull together for the benefit of the Company in adversity. A strike or dispute is a direct threat to their livelihoods and they will not take part.

If a postal worker is being bullied to stay on or to have to come in early, then in some workplaces such an allegation would be almost impossible to make, as people are ok to do as they are asked.

If the flexibility provisions in the Pay & Modernisation Agreement concerning the possibility of managers asking people to work over for 30 minutes on a voluntary basis should only occur on exceptional occasions, then for some workplaces people are only too happy to help out at any time. If "flexibility" is asked for on most days, no problem. That such requests are the result of poor staffing is irrelevant. If people are coming in early to help out as there aren't enough employees, again no problem. Such employees will have had things explained to them so that they understand that it is tough out there and Royal Mail needs to make savings and they need people to understand this and help out. The same argument runs true for bread and butter issue like basic pay. Some postal workers see it as being irresponsible to go on strike over pay and that if Royal Mail say they can't afford a pay rise then that is the end of the matter. No look at the state of Royal Mail can take place unless this is faced.

And yet... for those who think this way, there are quite often cultural reasons. A rural town location perhaps? A workplace where things just seem to tick over and people, well, just muck in and help out. Not your inner city militants!

Ironically, such workplaces find that they can still get caught up in the ebb and flow of life in Royal Mail. If a local Union Branch says "such an such" a workplace is not supportive, a change of manager or one cut too many and things can suddenly change. It's not unknown for Union representatives to say that Royal Mail have done their job for them and wound everyone up! Roy Mayall again:

> There's a lot of resentment and an increasing amount of bullying. There's a feeling that they are trying to wind everyone up, to get rid of as many full timers as possible. It has become so persistent, so noticeable, we believe it is a deliberate policy being driven from higher up. The old Posties have to go, to be replaced by part timers and casuals.[1]

If that perception is out there, why not squash it quickly? Who wants to run a Company where your own workforce think that this is what you are doing?!

In fact it has to be said that helping out the boss at work is a good thing, isn't it? A bit of give and take. In reality this should mean not being taken advantage of. The budget means no extra resource and so "flexibility" is demanded, only to be challenged and that if workers go over their time they should be paid properly and that, "by the way, overtime is voluntary!"

Across the UK this ebb and flow goes on in Royal Mail. In fact, it would not be too much to say that some workplaces where people are pretty easy going, find that if one of their number "steps out of line" and starts to come in on time, or cut off as they have had enough of the extra work, that they may well be on their own and their colleagues will not thank them for rocking the boat.

It's a complicated world out there in Royal Mail land, driven by a survival instinct that takes many guises, as we shall see.

Picture the scene. A local meeting in a small town of the Posties Union. There are 40 people working in the delivery office and around 20 have turned up at the local pub to talk about the problems in their office. Now this scenario has increasingly been the case since the mid 2000s. As the pace of change picked up so did the discontent. We know it's not quite as simple as that though and the issue is whether the pace of change is being carried out in line with the National Agreements.

Well the 20 who did turn up are predominantly full timers. Those who have worked the longest perhaps, but in any event whoever they are, they will have their say. The backdrop is best encapsulated by the following: "I know of someone working in a delivery office in Cambridgeshire who was in tears recently. Apparently he had been given 100 extra calls to make on his daily round but couldn't fit them into his shift. His manager told him he was going to receive 'refresher training.' When he asked what this involved, the manager replied, 'how to walk faster.'"[2]

There's more from this article: "People don't realise that the average Postie is still committed to the idea of service. It is the working conditions which make this increasingly difficult. We are being grossly overworked. 'Flexible working' actually means fewer people doing more work. Staff vacancies not being filled as a matter of policy. New staff on 20 or 25 hour contracts, but they are being made to work full time."

This was in 2009. The Pay & Modernisation Agreement was in force and there was a dispute at this time that eventually led to the Transformation Agreement 2010. In other words, it might have been a ropey time, but there were agreements covering how flexibility should have been working and how people should have been treated. Why? Because in 2007 the Company signed the Pay & Modernisation agreement, that's why. The idea that there should then still be bullying of Posties is of course ridiculous. How could that possibly happen?

As for that Union meeting, well it is clear as night follows day. They can name those not here who should be. The part timers who are being exploited. Coming in early, running round, not claiming overtime etc. "Killing the job", but with little apparent choice in the matter. And why aren't these people at the meeting? A stark reality hits you as you recognise that although part of a strong Union, ultimately these part timers and anyone else being picked on, do not relish drawing attention to themselves. In fact, they really, absolutely, definitely, do not want to rock the boat.

The concerns are everything from no training, no testing of delivery walks, vacancies unfilled and a further common theme is that they feel beaten down, demoralised and bullied. Occasionally one or two at a meeting will indeed be those being bullied.

A further complication, which for the most part disappeared with the 2010 Transformation Agreement, was the practise of postal workers using their own cars. Union representatives would be pulling their hair out as across the UK many thousands of workers would be seen loading up their cars with sacks of mail. Spending their own petrol driving round delivering letters. And the reasons are... Well, if you haven't the time to get the work done, then use your car. If you want to finish early, if you have a family commitment or pick up the kids from school then use your own car.

Postal staff know that duties were planned without taking into account the use of private cars. If a postal worker is out on their round, a van will be tasked with "accelerating" mail out to that person at a particular point. Over time, if staff used their cars such provisions would fall by the wayside. If someone, heaven forbid, decided not to use their car anymore, the sky could on occasion fall down on their heads. It was not unusual for staffing issues to come to a head and workers decide they will no longer use their own cars.

Such scandalous behaviour would invariably be seen as unofficial industrial action! Yes. You read that correctly. Whole delivery offices would be threatened with discipline if unofficial action took place by way of employees deciding not to use their own vehicles. Any employee who decided not to use their car anymore would not be allowed to do so again if they subsequently changed their minds. As for many who did use their cars, it was quite often a little vague as to whether such employees had the appropriate insurance provisions.

What can be done then? What answer is there for those who have given up their evening to meet up for a pint and a chat with the Union? A list of issues to take back to the manager. In the meantime, what about everyone just coming in on time, taking a meal break before they go out and if they can't complete their delivery, cutting off and bringing the mail back. That's not industrial action. That's "doing the job properly." Well, actually not quite, because you've guessed it, Royal Mail managers would claim this was unofficial industrial action.

Hardly any postal staff will disagree with the reality that doing the job properly would pretty quickly lead to chaos in Royal Mail. In fact, with the end of "Job and Finish" in 2007, that is what should have happened. No more incentive to skip a meal break and no more incentive to get in early and rush round to finish early.

So, we have a chunk of employees being bullied into starting early and running round to get the job done and we have another group who have been in Royal Mail some time and are doing the same but for different reasons as the job and finish culture is very difficult to eradicate. Into the mix add in budget cuts, bullying and some employees having no idea what duties they would be covering the following week with some being told on the Saturday and others being moved to cover duties because they are trained to do so (no matter that this means the same people are picked week in and week out to be, as they would see it, messed about) all the myriad of other situations and you have a heady mix of discontentment.

As any postal worker knows the reality is that if you start early but finish on time, then the job can be done in the time allowed. "No, it can't." Yes it can. If you started on time and went over your time but didn't claim overtime (perhaps you have been 'persuaded' not to do so), then the job could be done in the time allowed. If you skipped a meal break but didn't claim for it (as many still do not), then again, the job can be done in the time allowed. If you went on annual leave and your job is covered by someone younger who runs around and does it in the time allowed, this meant that you should be able to do this as well.

If you started on time and tried to claim overtime, then the job could be done in the time allowed it was just that you were not quick enough. If you started early and still had to claim overtime, you'll need to try harder, or else.

If any of the above happened on a quiet day, usually a Tuesday, then it was deemed to be almost impossible to conceive that the job could not be done in the time allowed.

These scenarios are still relevant today with awful situations that some Posties find themselves in. Ill, anxious, not sleeping, feeling sick in the stomach, sweaty palms and all the rest. If you want to read about this "chapter and verse" then the reader can do no worse than check out www.royalmailchat.co.uk. A web site dedicated to expressing the experiences of postal workers in their own words. You will be truly staggered at the experiences and general chatter that postal workers engage in.

And what is the conversation exactly when a postal worker approaches his manager to say he doesn't think he can deliver all the mail. The manager will say, "Yes you can do it." No, I can't. "Yes you can. The mail's down today so you can get it done." Is the mail really down today? How does he know? Has each item been counted then? No, really, you say, I can't get it done. "Do you want to let down your customers? How will their mail get delivered today if you don't do it. Go on, get it done." Such discussions can go on for some time, but in the end you may well find yourself taking all the mail out. In fact, you may also find that there is more than one manager talking to you at the same time to "persuade" you that the circle can be squared. Do you really want that sort of confrontation every day?

Is this all an exaggeration? A quote from the CWU bullying survey again: "I knew I wouldn't be able to finish my delivery before my finishing time – I asked the manager for assistance. He said, 'take it all out and don't bring any back or you'll face a wilful delay charge.'"

Another has this to say: "My delivery regularly takes me well over my time. I've given up trying to get overtime because of the veiled threats of disciplinary action due to poor performance."

Of course there are variations on a theme. Say you are one of those Posties. You turn up to that Union meeting and you are told what your rights are. Just how easy is it to enforce your rights then? Maybe it is you? Maybe you can't walk fast enough?

In fact, although you are bloody sure you are no slower than anyone else, perhaps it's best to keep your head down.

More pertinently, if you had decided long ago not to say anything, what if you suddenly decide you have now had enough and want to claim overtime or bring the mail back. Well, for a start your manager probably won't believe you. "You did it ok last week and the week before and the one before that, so what's changed?"

Well maybe you now have to pick the kids up from school. You can't go over your time whether paid or not. Right now, there will be postal workers worried sick about such a situation because they will be scared what the response will be.

A variation on a theme was always possible if a postal worker says they can't get all the mail delivered. If the "persuasion" fails to do the trick, you'll be asked how far will you get. Deliver all up to Acacia Avenue and we'll take it from there, ok? Well, you know that Acacia Avenue is about 20 minutes past your finish time. What then? Another argument, or do you just shrug your shoulders and get on with it? Of course Acacia Avenue now becomes the reasonable point at which mail can be delivered as there was no argument about it, was there?

Another variation will involve an amount of overtime given to someone to complete the round. How long will it take? 45 minutes extra? Is that true or is the postal worker exaggerating? He's a bit of a scallywag is Colin. He'll get his 45 minutes but it only took him an extra 15 minutes! As for the poor hapless soul who does actually need 45 minutes, well they may well find they don't get paid all of that. That CWU survey again, "I worked one and a half hours overtime, but was only paid for 30 minutes. My manager said the traffic only warranted 30 minutes and my performance was the problem." As any postal worker would tell you, quite often this will happen to someone who has performed ok for years and then suddenly a change of duties and this person is apparently incapable of getting round in the time allowed.

Some readers will know of the famous book by Joseph Heller, *Catch 22*. An anti war novel which purports to show that the crazy are in fact sane and the sane, crazy. Was it an act of sanity to fake illness so you didn't have to fly a mission and possibly get killed? Yossarian, one of the pilots is seeking to be grounded by claiming to be "crazy". A rule exists to ground those who are crazy, but asking to be grounded meant you couldn't really be crazy. Surely, not wishing to be killed was the act of a sane person? Hence Catch 22. The person requesting to be grounded may indeed be crazy, but asking would show that "anyone who wants to get out of combat duty isn't really crazy."[3]

What has this to do with Royal Mail? Well, you'd have to be crazy to run round trying to get a job done that in fact couldn't be done in the time allowed. But, the calculation was (and still is) that if you did the work anyway and said nothing this was in fact the act of a sane person. Why? Because it would be an act of possible insanity to keep on at your manager that the job couldn't be done as you might find that you became a target.

Of course proving somehow that the job could be done, even when it couldn't surely meant you were crazy as you would then have to keep up the pretence that it could be done, or face the displeasure of your manager and you really would have to be crazy to face the displeasure of your manager, wouldn't you? Some people permanently keep up such a pretence. A further example from the CWU survey shows the actions of a "sane" or "crazy" person – you decide: "My manager says if I book any overtime I'll never get a permanent contract so I just keep my head down and never claim any overtime I work."

If in fact we could question the manager concerned, would they really, honestly be able to say that the duty this person was covering could be done in the time allowed? Has this Postie made up this scenario for some warped reason? How on earth can such a conversation take place in 2012? The CWU would add in response to the publication of the survey that, "Whilst we recognise there are some Units where the managers are reasonable and adhere to the national agreements and procedures, the amount of complaints we are receiving suggests this may be a major problem."[4]

Now one of the answers to the above is to ask the management that certain walks be "tested". In other words a rep and a manager would go out and physically walk the delivery round to see what the problems were. If it was in need of extra resource then this would have to go in. The solution to the problem was of course for Royal Mail not to agree to walks being tested as this could demonstrate extra hours and therefore costs, would be incurred. You are the local manager now. How do you actually deal with that situation? No budget to use to put hours in, and the job can't be done. Well, it has to be done so get out there and do it. In fact that is just what would happen. And not just the poor hapless Postie either. Managers would be out delivering mail if no one else was available, or the office was short staffed. Some managers could be out on delivery most days.

Another example involves the computer plotting of delivery walks. Information is fed in about the number of houses, the terrain, how fast should you be walking and how many delivery points on average get mail each day (shall we say 85% of addresses ?) and a duty is formulated and churned out that should be "doable." If a fair process is gone through then all things being equal there shouldn't be a problem. But of course there is. Exactly what information has been fed in? Is this information going to create delivery duties that keep within a predetermined budgetary outcome? These issues are playing out across the UK and postal staff will know, some to their cost, that if the computer says it can be done, then that is the end of the matter. Implementing change should at least result in change that works. Royal Mail spend large amounts of money employing Planners to work with managers to get changes right. With local knowledge and the expertise of Planners and computer software, what could possibly go wrong to mean we have postal workers bullied if they can't complete their deliveries?

In fact, you would be crazy to challenge the decision of the computer programme. The only possible answer is that your performance isn't up to standard and not that the work cannot be done in the time allowed because the process of inputting the information has not been done accurately. Hence thousands of Posties are working beyond their hours for no payment.

Perhaps the answer was to come in on time, have a meal break and finish on time – Do The Job Properly. Well, you would be crazy to think that. If it were that simple Royal Mail would be forking out millions and millions of pounds in extra overtime or jobs to compensate for the fact that its workforce now only works the hours for which they are paid. No, it is much more complicated. The examples above of bullying provide a clue. In the end, the good will of postal workers to getting the job done, is to all intents and purposes taken advantage of.

The Union says if you can't deliver the mail in the time allowed and you don't want the overtime, then bring the mail back to the office. Easy? Far from it. That postal worker will sometimes tell you, "what about my customers who want their mail. If I bring it back it may not get delivered until the following day." You have conscientious staff doing this and not claiming overtime. If they did, then they would draw attention to themselves and that might not be a good idea. In fact they would be crazy to do so as we have seen. It is known that regardless of where you work in the UK, some managers will threaten and remove you from your duty if necessary – the subject of many a Union meeting. The refrain would be heard that it was all well and good for the Union to tell them they didn't have to stay out but that was easier said than done and we didn't know their manager.

In this crazy world as we have seen, someone can be bullied for cutting off when they should have claimed overtime. Others will be refused the overtime and told they should be able to get the delivery done. Royal Mail know that this goes on. Those most affected can be new employees, part timers, temporary contract people and those who just can't get around as fast as they used to. In short, any meeting of Posties will uncover a myriad of reasons why nothing can be done. Some want to get away, some like coming in early, some don't want to rock the boat and some don't want to find their temporary contract ended if they are seen as a trouble maker.

Many CWU representatives will have attended such meetings where not only are there run of the mill issues but often the attitude of the managers will be commented upon. The manager is said to "talk down to them", "speaks to us as if we are dirt" and suddenly you begin to wonder what brings a management/worker relationship to that level. Well, as we saw from the Unions' survey, it's a jungle in some workplaces.

It is a culture that Royal Mail have taken advantage of. Such a culture does not exist in a mail processing centre. Postal workers there are sorting and processing mail. They will start and finish on time. There is no individual advantage in going faster as the job is never completed – mail is being processed on a rolling 24 hour basis as one shift ends, another begins. In delivery offices Royal Mail can cut the hours allowed and many Posties find themselves going faster to keep up or to try and secure that early finish. The Job and Finish culture formalised by Allan Leighton and ended in 2007 is still out there.

The thread running through collective agreements between the CWU and Royal Mail is that workloads should be fair, equal and manageable. As for the issues above, the CWU now continually advises its members that overtime is voluntary as is the flexibility provision for "flexing up" by 30 minutes. Also, that if the mail volumes are above the model week volumes, then additional resource is needed and there should be no requirement to have employees covering additional duties.

Why they should feel the need to keep on advising their members can be put down to the reality that if Royal Mail can get away with a bit of sharp practise locally, then they will invariably do so. At least that is the perception that large chunks of their own workforce have.

This perception is best demonstrated by the CWU Deputy General Secretary who said that the Business Transformation Agreement 2010 was about introducing change in the right way but that "rather than developing a culture of mutual interest, too many managers will not let go of their 'command and control' approach. Command and control must go and managers must trust the workforce if Royal Mail wants to succeed."[5] To which can be added that Royal Mail probably knows this, but anything other than the approach they have always taken to meet budgetary targets, is a risk they do not feel obligated to make and so the same pattern repeats itself.

At the time of the 2009 strike, Royal Mail were publicly having to defend themselves against the accusation that they were bullying their employees in order to meet targets. Back to the Union meeting again and you can begin to see that in was not uncommon for meetings to start at 7pm and not finish until 10pm with the visiting Area CWU representative – if he or she is honest – sometimes losing the will to live with such a multitude of problems.

It is probably true that Royal Mail would have rather not run their Company in this way, but that was not, and is not, a message that you will hear anytime soon and many in the industry would say it is still going on today. Force up everyone's productivity and this will help Royal Mail to compete. There is of course a wealth of evidence from management consultants and the like to say that valuing employees and involving them, will bring the rewards of greater productivity. Such a "soft" approach is clearly not in the game plan and certainly wasn't at the time of the national strikes we have seen. The fact that New

Labour Ministers were happy in the 2000s to go along with this nightmare approach is proof of the complete lack of empathy never mind reflection on, the impact on postal workers of the grotesque free market experiment being carried out. It would be foolish to pretend that they weren't aware of what was going on.

In fact, a letter to the Daily Mail at the time of the 2009 strikes, from a mental health professional said,

> I'm alarmed at the increase in referrals from postal workers suffering from stress and depression because of intimidation at work. These aren't malingerers or people looking for early retirement, but a body of men and women as traumatised battle weary troops.... Never in a career of almost 30 years have I heard the same story so often – a story of bullying, intimidation and threats.... An acquaintance, a semi professional athlete finds completing his postal round on time as gruelling as any marathon, such is the pressure put on him to do so in the time limits set. He tells me of younger, less fit men in tears struggling to meet their targets. It's abhorrent that a Labour Government should be allowing this to continue.[6]

What on earth is going on when a letter like this can be written? If Royal Mail are working to reduce the amount of bullying down below 10%, or around 13,000 people, what was it like in the mid to late 2000s? In fact, many CWU representatives will have similar stories to tell and incidents where male and female postal workers have been reduced to tears. And people wonder why there are strikes in Royal Mail years after the intervention of Lord Sawyer was supposed to create a better environment. No, after all these years there are clearly more than a few bad apples.

For each scenario there is a person affected and again the only real way to try and understand this is to imagine yourself in the position of the Postie who feels vulnerable. How can you even begin to articulate your distress to your manager? The last thing you want to do is expose your feelings.

If the general impression given is that Posties can stand up for themselves, then, as can be seen, this impression would be inaccurate. Why else is the culture of bullying and harassment still prevalent? A strong Union and "bolshie" Posties would surely have stamped it out long ago? Clearly not.

Bear in mind that of course not all bullying is by a manager on a worker. As has been said before and needs emphasising again, workers do bully other workers and are sacked for it when necessary, but as we saw above with one of those conference motions the perception is that managers may not find themselves dismissed for bullying and an investigation may conclude that the manager was simply managing the individual in an appropriate manner. The fact that this manager may know what they were doing, including that the particular delivery was too large, is neither here nor there. The allegation of bullying may well not succeed.

So we have seen there is a powerful mix of complexity that has created the current situation. Agreements not followed, overtime refused, people coming in early through fear, temporary contract workers spoken to "on the quiet" to make sure they get the work done or else, workers tramping the streets on medication because they can't bring themselves to discuss with the manager in case they expose their health vulnerability, people reduced to tears and others perhaps even in the same workplace happy with their lot, flexibility abused, workers not dealt with properly following sickness, pay stopped apparently arbitrarily, people working on after their hours through fear, some not knowing from week to week what job they will be on and the list could go on and on.

We can only ask, was this all inevitably going to play out in this way?

It is a deeply ingrained culture which radiates dysfunction masquerading as performance management or just as bad; the comments in their Corporate Social Responsibility report for 2010/11, when commenting on the failure to reduce bullying and harassment below 10%, stated that the reason was the Transformation Agreement which meant change people were unhappy about – the phrase used was "dissatisfaction". Not many people like change, but should that translate into missing a target for reducing bullying and harassment? Perhaps such rationale could be accepted if you decided to suspend your critical faculties first.

All in all, whilst such comment does not paint Royal Mail in a good light, it does provide for those in senior positions in the Company to work doubly hard to get the culture right. Someone, somewhere has to ask whether this ongoing issue is a symptom of the way in which they have always run the organisation. Can the Command and Control mentality be hauled into action to get the cultures right or has its time come and gone?

At the time of writing a further dispute is just breaking out following the sell-off. Perhaps this time things really will change for the better? The oil tanker can be turned around and yes there are people at the heart of Royal Mail's management who want to do just that, it's just that they will have to shout louder for anyone to hear them now the City whizz kids have moved in.

Conclusion

That Royal Mail was prepared for privatisation is beyond doubt. Huge profits don't just materialise out of nothing. From "basket-case" to stock market bonanza in one fell swoop. The Government referred to the "froth" surrounding the sell off with the implication being that reality will sink in and a more realistic valuation will emerge once the profit taking has finished. As we have seen the Government knew it was undervalued and by implication were happy for buyers to make handsome profits and, up to the end of October 2013 investors continue to do so. It is possible that over the coming months – November 2013 onwards – that MPs and the National Audit Office will go about their jobs examining how it came about that Royal Mail was under-valued. No matter, they've already taken the swag and gone to the nearest tax haven.

No, the real issue now is not that the Government turned a blind eye to the evidence in front of them, nor whether speculators and investors will get their dividends and profits in the future, but how this will be generated.

As we have seen Royal Mail shells out billions to keep the USO in place. The European Postal Directive only says a five day week delivery is required, so straight away an area presents itself. Will Saturday deliveries disappear, or shall we pick another day in the week then?

Letter volumes are declining with every 1% fall costing around £75 million. Royal Mail are expecting the decline to continue at around 4-6% per year. Do the maths.[1]

There is the reality that the competition from the likes of TNT with their zero hour workforce and no USO to fulfil, will start to make more in-roads in the large urban conurbations. At the time of writing TNT are already looking to move into the Greater Manchester area including Salford and Wigan and will undoubtedly go elsewhere as well having already stated they are seeking to grow their business by employing upwards of 20,000 people in the fullness of time.

Whilst packet and parcel deliveries thanks to the likes of e-bay and others will help to bolster revenue, how much growth is there left to grab given the competition out there? Already Amazon are looking to open regional distribution centres using non Royal Mail carriers.

Perhaps we will see the Company sell off much of its 2000 strong property portfolio to feed the shareholders insatiable appetite for dividends. Prime London sites are reckoned to be worth between £250-£500 million, for starters.[2] There are expensive costs associated with restructuring their network to account for the decline of letters and up to now, the increase in packets and parcels. Who is going to pay for this? The workforce? The public? The shareholders?

There is always the prospect of increasing stamp prices with the threat being that if not, the USO will be at risk. Is any regulator going to take that gamble? The £1 stamp is surely not far off given that Ofcom have allowed the Company the freedom to set the price of a first class stamp until 2019? Indeed, only a day or so after the sell-off Moya Greene CEO was claiming stamp prices would have to go up as they hadn't done so in the last year, never mind that the increase before that was some 30%. Perversely of course further increases will simply exacerbate the decline in letter volumes as people give up posting other than at Christmas leaving the only real customers as being the large business community. Will there be moves to try and put VAT on stamps? Legal challenges may now be made from the competition despite provisions in Europe to keep postage VAT free.

For postal workers the fear is the possibility of franchising out delivery offices or even individual rounds – Posties turned into milkmen? Another fear for the workforce is the worry that the Company will be broken up with further attacks on their pay and pensions. Big investors will not mess around. The "pay gap" of 25% with the minimum wage competition will surely be eroded if the Company can force Posties to "see the light" and the possibility of a two tier workforce may become a reality. Indeed, perhaps we are nearly there already given that Royal Mail has a wholly owned agency supplier, Angard Staffing Solutions Limited, now outsourced to Reed Specialist Recruitment with thousands of workers going through their books at any one time.

We may even see overseas sovereign wealth funds move in and as we see from the utilities already, foreign ownership is probably just round the corner. During the sell-off it was reported that sovereign wealth funds from Abu Dhabi, Kuwait, Singapore and Norway had been allowed to purchase shares.[3] However share trading does develop, it seems beyond doubt that wealth funds, private equity, hedge funds and the like will look to gradually buy up controlling stakes.

All pure speculation of course. What else can it be now the deed is done? The UK has seen how the regulators of the water, gas and electricity industries has been unable to prevent commercial imperatives dictating prices and the service given. The idea that Ofcom will succeed where others have failed is at the very least open to question. The answer of course is that in all likelihood they will be unable to protect the public interest. The service will deteriorate, jobs will be lost, the Universal Service Obligation will be redefined following some respectable period of "consultation", the Company will be restructured beyond recognition and all to ensure that the profits keep flowing until it's time to jump ship before it all comes crashing down. Mercifully, we might have a few years before that happens and of course I could be completely wrong...

The idea that Parliament will somehow step in and make sure all is well is fanciful. The Government will be presented with hard commercial reality and will vote to do whatever is demanded by the new owners of our postal service on pain of the postal service failing. There is, ironically a provision in the Postal Services Act 2011 for a USO Support Fund. Ministers can approve such a fund to keep Royal Mail going, with all the other postal carriers told to contribute. Perhaps these postal carriers will willingly cough up the hundreds of millions required? On the other hand, perhaps it will just be a lot easier for MPs to vote to redefine the USO, reduce the service accordingly and say it was always going to end this way?

As for re-nationalising it and creating that not for profit service, you would have to be "away with the fairies" to think that will happen. I hope we will again see a publicly owned postal service, not beholden to commercial interests, but somehow I doubt it very much. The Tories and Lib Dems never will of course and as for the Labour Party, they lost their way a long time ago.

In many respects, the saddest part of this whole saga is that soon we will forget Royal Mail was ever in the public sector and those vast profits now being made by the Company will be told to the public as being nothing more than the result of private sector expertise and business acumen.

If nothing else this book has tried to give the reader a glimpse into the life of delivery postal workers. I haven't mentioned those who work elsewhere in Royal Mail, trunking the mail round and working in the processing centres and neither have I mentioned those who work in Parcelforce or Post Office Limited and many of their experiences are regrettably all too familiar. If anyone in Royal Mail management has read this book, it is not my contention that managers are all bad (that should I hope, be clear enough) and many will attest to feeling ground down by the relentless stresses of the job and occasionally swamped by the enormity of the task to deal with competition, modernise and take the workforce with you and there are excellent examples across the UK where good work is being done. Good, supportive, professional managers are employed in the organisation as many postal staff will confirm. Just not nearly enough.

The litmus test must surely be that not only will relations between workers and the management improve, but that underneath this, it will not been seen as dangerous to show a vulnerability to a manager about a health issue or some other concern that might impact on your work responsibilities. That an adult to adult conversation will always take place to discuss problems and that, as the Posties' Union hopes, there is acceptance from Royal Mail that postal workers do have their best interests at heart.

For the CWU, no other trade Union has fought so hard to prevent a privatisation for so long. It continues to operate against the backdrop of threat centred management and apocalyptic scenarios if it doesn't "bend the knee." Despite this being a very personal and self-selective look at the last 13 years, it is my contention that no reasonable person could possibly conclude that the CWU has been anything other than a forward looking, progressive Union battling against the odds to protect working people and their families. At the time of writing the CWU are embroiled in negotiations to protect pay, jobs, pensions and terms and conditions. Peace in our time then or yet again, conflict deferred as investors look to dismantle hard fought agreements once a respectable period of calm has been achieved?

As for the Posties, it may be a new beginning in the private sector, but the reality is surely that all that will follow is more of the same? I hope I am wrong but I fear that given the inevitable share-holder pressure, the command and control philosophy will not be dispensed with any time soon, with budgets, bullying and propaganda to try and ensure everyone stays in line. "You don't want your shares to go down now do you? Off you go then and get that mail delivered..."

References

Introduction

1   Royal Mail Group (RMG) Accounts 2010/11 and RMG employee survey summary 2012.
2   FoI request response 23 July 2013. The reader is encouraged to check out all the results, if only to get a feel for what the Company's workforce actually think about their employer.
3   RMG Accounts 2010/11
4   Royal Mail / Communication Workers Union (CWU) joint statement on "Fairness, Dignity and Respect in Delivery", March 2013

PART 1

Chapter 1 – Beginnings

1   The UCW was the forerunner of the CWU. The CWU was formed out of a merger between the Union of Communication Workers (postal workers) and the National Communications Union (broadly speaking those working for British Telecom at the time of merger)
2   CWU "Delivering Quality", November 2005
3   www.postalheritage.org.uk/statistics
4   RMG interim accounts to 29/9/2002
5   CWU "Delivering Quality", November 2005
6   Postcomm (Postal Services Commission) Corporate Plan, 7 April 2000
7   Letter to Alan Johnson DTI Minister from Graham Corbett 19/12/2000
8   CWU briefing on the Postal Services Bill, 2 February 2000

Chapter 2 – The Genie's Out of the Bottle

1   CWU advice document to representatives, December 2001
2   The Guardian 13 December 2001

3   CWU press release 3 October 2001
4   CWU "Delivering Quality", November 2005
5   CWU press release 20 November 2001
6   CWU pay strategy document, October 2001
7   Sunday Times 24 March 2002
8   The Guardian 23 January 2002
9   CWU publication "No Logic – A guide to Postcomm" , 2002
10 CWU Letter to Branches (LTB) 49/2004
11 RMG interim accounts to 29 September 2002, Marisa Cassoni, Group Finance Director
12 RMG Accounts 2006/07
13 RMG interim accounts to 28 September 2003
14 Sir Richard Hooper "Modernise or Decline", December 2008
15 Ofcom calculations quoted in CWU LTB 996/2011

Chapter 3 – Complexity Rules
1   The Independent 9 May 2005
2   The Daily Telegraph, 2005
3   Sir Richard Hooper "Modernise or Decline", December 2008
4   The Daily Telegraph, 21 June 2006
5   CWU evidence to the DTI Select Committee, December 2006
6   RMG Accounts 2005/06
7   RMG Accounts 2005/06
8   House of Lords debate, 2009 quoted in House of Commons Parliamentary briefing paper on RMG pension scheme, 7 January 2011
9   CWU pensions policy paper, "Time to Deliver" 2009
10 House of Commons Parliamentary briefing paper on RMG pension scheme, 7 January 2011
11 Sunday Times, 27 May 2001
12 RMG Accounts 2005/06
13 RMG Accounts 2006/07
14 Mail on Sunday, 2005 ("Royal Mail 'only three years from being wiped out'")

15 The Daily Telegraph, 2005 ("Third of my managers not up to it, says Crozier")

16 Sir Richard Hooper, "Modernise or Decline", December 2008

17 CWU policy document to the Hooper review, Review of Liberalisation, March 2008

Chapter 4 – Wake Up and Smell the Coffee

1 Compass, "Modernisation by Consent", 2009

2 www.postalheritage.org.uk/statistics

3 CWU briefing paper on the Postal Services Bill, February 2000

4 Theses programme were shown respectively in April 2004, July 2005 and February 2010

5 New Statesman on-line, 23 September 2009

6 The London Review of Books, 24 September 2009

7 RMG Accounts 2005/06

8 CWU "Delivering Quality – CWU submission to Sir George Bain", November 2005

Chapter 5 – A Grotesque Experiment Comes of Age

1 CWU policy document to the Hooper review, Review of Liberalisation, March 2008

2 Extracts from Sir Richard Hooper's interim report, May 2008

3 The Daily Telegraph, 13 March 2002

4 RMG Accounts 2007/08

5 Letter from the Minister to the CWU Western Counties Branch, 15 November 2007

6 Royal Mail submission, "Royal Mail's proposed solution to the challenges facing the UK postal services sector"

7 Compass report, "Case Not Made – A response to the Hooper report on the future of Royal Mail" 2009

8 Compass report, "Case not made" page 17

9 Every survey ever done shows large majorities of the public against privatising the Royal Mail. The figure of 23% comes

from a YouGov poll between 30/9/10 and 1/10/10.

10 The Sunday Times, 27 May 2001

11 Lord Mandelson , "The Third Man – Life at the heart of New Labour" , 2010, Harper Collins

12 CWU pensions policy paper, "Time to Deliver"

13 Business and Enterprise Select Committee, April 2009 quoted in "Time to Deliver"

Chapter 6 – Rearranging Deckchairs and Moving Goalposts

1   Explanatory notes: Postal Services Act 2011, para 16

2   CWU "Keep the Post Public – Protecting postal services. Understanding the past. Working for the future." 2011

3   Ofcom, "Securing the Universal Postal Service" 20 October 2011

4   Royal Mail submission, "Royal Mail's proposed solution to the challenges facing the UK postal services sector"

5   RMG Accounts 2011/12

6   www.myroyalmail.com and via the in-house staff journal, The Courier. March 2013

7   "Secrets of your missing mail", Channel 4 Despatches 29 April 2013 and "Postal privatisation and the zero-hour workers nightmare", Guardian on-line 29 April 2013, by Paul Mills

8   Royal Mail statement, "Concerns about the potential impact of end to end delivery on the universal service", 16 April 2012

9   CWU letter to members, November 2012

10 RMG Corporate Social Responsibility report for 2010/11

11 Special edition of CWU members' journal The Voice, April 2013

12 Guardian on-line, Comment is Free, 28 October 2010

Chapter 7 – You Own It Already, Don't Buy It!

1   The Daily Telegraph, 25 March 2012
2   www.skynews.com, 8 July 2013
3   The Guardian, 30 May 2013
4   www.reuters.com, 12 May 2013
5   UNI Global Union (Posts and Logistics), "Postal Liberalisation: the issues, the impact and Union responses." October 2012
6   CWU LTB 347/2013
7   The Sunday Times, 23 June 2013
8   The Financial Times, 21 May 2013
9   The Guardian, 30 April, 16 May and 13 September 2013
10   Guardian 13 September 2013
11   From the text of a CWU motion to the Labour Party Conference, September 2013
12   YouGov poll, 8/9 July 2013
13   "Save Our Royal Mail" press release based on a survey carried out by on-line organisation www.create.net on 19 July 2013
14   The Bow Group, "Royal Mail Privatisation – Where is the debate?" 13 May 2013
15   See, www.saveourroyalmail.com
16   www.thesun.co.uk, 9 July 2013
17   Quoted in UNI Global Union (Posts and Logistics), "Postal Liberalisation: the issues, the impact and Union responses" October 2012 under the heading, "Royal Mail will be difficult to privatise" from May 2012.
18   www.skynews.com, 10 July 2013
19   Private Eye, 26 July 2013
20   CWU LTB 418/2013
21   RMG Accounts, 2012/13
22   The Courier, "Pension Special", August 2013
23   CWU letter to members, "Challenging Royal Mail on all fronts" July 2013

24 The Sunday Times, 11 August 2013
25 RMG Accounts 2011/12 and 2012/13
26 "Safeguarding your Pension: The Company's Pension Proposal", June 2013
27 Widely quoted within the CWU and in the media, the facts were that the proposals were not legally enforceable and would not protect workers in the event of a privatisation. LTB 445/2013
28 CWU LTB 445/2013
29 CWU press release, 1 August 2013
30 Sunday Times 22 September 2013
31 UNI Global Union (Posts and Logistics), "Postal liberalisation: the issues, the impact and Union responses." October 2012
32 CWU LTB 459/2013, Special Report to CWU policy Forum 31 July & 1 August 2013.
33 www.bbc.co.uk Sunday Politics 15/9/13
34 Guardian 8 October 2013
35 Sunday Times 6 October 2013
36 CWU research paper from LTB 680/13, 14 October 2013
37 Financial Times 12 October 2013
38 Guardian 11 October 2013
39 Financial Times 19 October 2013
40 Guardian 25 October 2013
41 Financial Times 19 October 2013
42 Guardian 11 October 2013
43 CWU press release 16 October 2013 & LTB 692/2013

PART 2
Chapter 8 – Reality Check

1 Lord Sawyer quoted on bbc.co.uk, 15 December 2009
2 The Times 12 September 1860. Thanks to CWU member Fran Choules for this quote.

3   The Guardian, 24 May 2001
4   The Guardian, 24 May 2001
5   The Guardian, 23 January 2002
6   The Guardian, 13 December 2001
7   The Independent, 22 January 2002
8   The Sunday Times, 16 December 2001
9   The Sunday Times 31 January 2002

Chapter 9 – Actions Speak Louder than Words: The Beginnings of Change From 2000

1   Open Royal Mail letter to employees, April 2002
2   CWU Postal Executive report, 11 December 2001
3   CWU Annual Postal report to members, 2003

Chapter 10 – The Fuse is Lit: Pay and Major Change

1   The Times, 9 July 2003
2   A Q&A sent out by the CWU to its members and a letter to members from Dave Ward, Deputy General Secretary
3   Open letter from Allan Leighton to employees, 6 August 2003
4   CWU LTB 540/2003
5   Open letter from Allan Leighton to employees, 26/8/03
6   The Guardian, 10 September 2003
7   The Guardian, 1 November 2003
8   Letter from Allan Leighton to employees, 22 October 2003
9   The Guardian, 1 November 2003
10 CWU LTB 648/2003
11 The Times, 9 July 2003

Chapter 11 – False Dawn: Shaping Our Future 2006

1   RMG Accounts 2005/06.
2   CWU letter to members, "Shaping Our Future – The First Steps", 3 August 2006

Chapter 12 – The Gloves are Off: Pay and Modernisation 2007

1   CWU paper, "Later Deliveries and the Industrial Dispute with Royal Mail", 2007

2   CWU leaflet for the public, handed out during strike days in 2007

3   CWU letter to members, 13 April 2007

4   CWU paper, "Later Deliveries and the Industrial Dispute with Royal Mail", 2007

5   Letter from Allan Leighton, Chairman and Adam Crozier, CEO to employees, 8 June 2006

6   Open letter to Allan Leighton, Chairman from Dave Ward, Deputy General Secretary, 13 June 2007
Daily Mirror, 8 June 2006

8   Europe Economics, David Stubbs, "Executive Brief: The Impact of the UK Postal Strike", 23 October 2007

9   www.personneltoday.com, 21 September 2007. These figures were also quoted extensively elsewhere

10 Open letter from Adam Crozier CEO to Dave Ward, 15 June 2007 and quoted in the press generally

11 The issue around so-called Spanish practises was also raised in the DTI Select Committee on October 2007

12 Daily Mirror, 7 July 2007

13 Daily Mirror on-line, 1 and 3 August 2007

14 CWU article in The Voice, "The Gloves are off"

15 Open letter from Adam Crozier to Dave Ward, 15 June 2007

16 CWU report to members on talks with Royal Mail and ACAS, 26 July 2007

17 Daily Mirror, 24 July 2007

18 CWU LTB 709/2007

19 The comments come from the document given to the CWU. In effect this was a draft national agreement which Royal Mail wanted the CWU to sign up to.

20 Taken from a specimen letter to employees, used when Royal Mail had decided to introduce unagreed later start

times.

21 Europe Economics, David Stubbs, "Executive Brief: The Impact of the UK Postal Strike", 23 October 2007

22 CWU letter to members on the Pay & Modernisation Agreement, "Your Questions Answered"

23 RMG Accounts 2006/07

Chapter 13 – The Gloves Stay Off: Transformation 2010

1   Open letter from Royal Mail's Mark Higson to employees, October 2009

2   The Guardian, 9 October 2009

3   www.hellmail.com, 1 September 2009

4   The Independent, 11 October 2009

5   CWU Briefing to representatives, 15 September 2009

6   CWU letter to members advising them of the industrial action ballot timetable, September 2007.

7   The Guardian, 8 October 2009

8   Guardian on-line Comment is Free, 24 October 2009

9   www.hellmail.com, 8 August 2009

10 CWU LTB 911/2009

11 The Guardian, 22 October 2009

12 Mail on Sunday on-line, 24 October 2009

13 Daily Telegraph on-line, 22 October 2009

14 The Guardian, 1 November 2009

15 CWU LTB 195/2010

16 CWU "Keeping you posted" leaflet to members, "Ten Reason why Royal Mail is planning to fail"

17 Special Postal edition of the Voice, April 2013

18 CWU newsletter to members, September 2012

19 CWU LTB 300/2013, joint statement on completing the BT2010 Transformation Agreement in Delivery.

20 CWU Voice magazine, August/September 2013

21 RMG Accounts 2009/10

PART 3

Chapter 14 – Enter Lord Sawyer

1   www.roymayall.co.uk
2   CWU Annual Postal reports to members, 2002 and 2003
3   CWU Annual Postal report 2003
4   RMG interim accounts to 30 September 2004
5   RMG interim accounts to 30 September 2004
6   CWU Annual Postal report 2003

Chapter 15 – Alarm Bells

1   CWU Voice magazine, November/December 2012
2   Leaflet produced by Belfast Trades Council during the strike
3   CWU Voice magazine, November/December 2012
4   Royal Mail / Communication Workers Union (CWU) joint statement on "Fairness, Dignity and Respect in Delivery", March 2013
5   RMG Corporate Social Responsibility Report 2010/11 and FoI request response 31 May 2012
6   FoI request response 21 May 2013
7   FoI request response 23 July 2013
8/9   Greater Manchester Branch
10/11   North Wales & North West Divisional Committee
12/13   South Central No.1 Branch
14   Eastern No.5 Branch
15   South & East Thames and Croydon & Sutton Branches
16   Portsmouth & District Branch
17   Merseyside Amalgamated Branch
18   Bristol & District Branch
19   Portsmouth & District Branch
20   Greater Manchester Branch
21   Scotland No.2 Branch
22   South East Divisional Committee
23   Merseyside Amalgamated and North Lancs &Cumbria Branches

24   London NW Counter and Clerical Branch

25   Solent Branch

26   Northern Home Counties Branch

27   South East Divisional Committee

28   Eastern No.3 Branch

29   RMG Corporate Social Responsibility Report 2010/11

30   South Central No.1 Branch

31   NE Divisional Committee and Yorkshire Branches

32   Newcastle Amalgamated Branch

33   SE London Postal & Counter Branch

34   www.bbc.co.uk, 4 July 2013 "Royal Mail staff walk in 'bullying' claims"

35   CWU Voice magazine, August/September 2013

Chapter 16 – Harsh Realities Part 1

1   RMG Corporate Social Responsibility Report 2010/11

2   FoI request response 23 July 2013

3   Atos Origin IT Services UK Limited, 2010, "Royal Mail Group Inspired Initiatives" (via website)

4   "Dear Granny Smith: A letter from your Postman" by Roy Mayall, Published by Short Books 2009

5   ACAS, "Promoting Positive Mental Health at Work", 2012

Chapter 17 – Harsh Realities Part 2

1   "Dear Granny Smith: A letter from your Postman" by Roy Mayall, Published by Short Books 2009

2   Guardian on-line, 24 October 2009, "So it goes on – innovation to the point of idiocy" by Roy Mayall

3   Joseph Heller, Catch 22, 1955

4   Bullying and harassment in Deliveries – survey letter to members from CWU, November 2012

5   The Voice, November/December 2012

6   Letter in the Daily Mail. Undated cutting given to the author

Conclusion

1   Daily Telegraph online, 1 October 2013
2   Daily Telegraph online, 1 October 2013
3   Daily Mail online, 12 October 2013

zero
books

Contemporary culture has eliminated both the concept of the public and the figure of the intellectual. Former public spaces – both physical and cultural – are now either derelict or colonized by advertising. A cretinous anti-intellectualism presides, cheerled by expensively educated hacks in the pay of multinational corporations who reassure their bored readers that there is no need to rouse themselves from their interpassive stupor. The informal censorship internalized and propagated by the cultural workers of late capitalism generates a banal conformity that the propaganda chiefs of Stalinism could only ever have dreamt of imposing. Zer0 Books knows that another kind of discourse – intellectual without being academic, popular without being populist – is not only possible: it is already flourishing, in the regions beyond the striplit malls of so-called mass media and the neurotically bureaucratic halls of the academy. Zer0 is committed to the idea of publishing as a making public of the intellectual. It is convinced that in the unthinking, blandly consensual culture in which we live, critical and engaged theoretical reflection is more important than ever before.